THE HISTORY OF THE BOOK
Edited by Bill Katz

1. *A History of Book Illustration: 29 Points of View*, edited by Bill Katz. 1994
2. *Dahl's History of the Book, Third English Edition*, by Bill Katz. 1995
3. *A Bibliographic History of the Book: An Annotated Guide to the Literature*, by Joseph Rosenblum. (Magill Bibliographies.) 1995

DAHL'S HISTORY OF THE BOOK

Third English Edition

by
BILL KATZ

The History of the Book, No. 2

The Scarecrow Press, Inc.
Metuchen, N.J., & London
1995

Previous editions of this title published by Scarecrow Press:

History of the Book, first English edition, by Svend Dahl, 1958.

History of the Book, second English edition, by Svend Dahl, 1968.

British Library Cataloguing-in-Publication data available

Library of Congress Cataloging-in-Publication Data

Katz, William A., 1924–
     Dahl's history of the book. — 3rd English ed. / by Bill Katz.
          p.   cm. — (The History of the book series ; no. 2)
     Rev. ed. of : History of the book / Svend Dahl. 2nd English ed.
1968.
     Includes bibliographical references (p.) and index.
     ISBN 0-8108-2852-9 (acid-free paper)
     1. Books—History. I. Dahl, Svend, 1887–1963.   History of
book. II. Title.   III. Title : History of the book.   IV. Series.
Z4.K37   1995
002—dc20   94-2686

For my friends, Sandy and Norman—and all other readers and ardent book collectors.

TABLE OF CONTENTS

PREFACE

The story of the book is the story of us all, from the earliest cave people to the computer hitchhiker. The overview offered here is compiled for the interested layperson and student. A wide-view lens is employed to catch patterns of how the book shaped and reflected major social, political and literary developments. This is a general guide to thousands of years of activity, not a detailed map. The technology of book production to analytical bibliographical findings are of inestimable importance, but only suggested here.

The present revision is loosely based upon the 1968, second edition of Sven Dahl's history. There are major additions and deletions which makes this a new approach rather than a limited rewritten work.

ACKNOWLEDGMENTS

My thanks to the numerous teachers and librarians who so generously gave suggestions, including outlines, bibliographies and detailed letters, about what a book of this type might include/exclude. Specifically thanks to:

Sidney E. Berger, University of California, Riverside; Ron Blazek, The Florida State University; James V. Carmichael, Jr., University of North Carolina at Greensboro; GraceAnne A. DeCandido, St. John's University; B.S. Donaghey, University of Sheffield; Hendrik Edelman, Rutgers; John Ettlinger, Dalhousie University; Janet Fyfe, The University of Western Ontario; Edward G. Holley, University of North Carolina at Chapel Hill; Estelle Jussim, Simmons College; Margaret F. Maxwell, The University of Arizona; Gordon B. Neavill, The University of Alabama; Mei-yue P'an, National Taiwan University; John R. Payne, University of Texas at Austin; Douglas Raber, University of Missouri-Columbia; Antonio Rodriguez-Buckingham, University of Southern Mississippi; Charles A. Seavey, The University of Arizona; Keith Swigger, Texas Woman's University; Szilvia E. Szmuk, St. John's University; Susan Thompson, Columbia University; Jon Tryon, University of Rhode Island; John Turner, Aberystwyth, University College of Wales Aberstwyth, W. Wiegand, University of Wisconsin-Madison; Paul A. Winkler, Professor Emeritus, Long Island University; H. Curtis Wright, Bringham Young University. I would also like to express my appreciation to Lynn Horowitz for compiling this book's index.

INTRODUCTION

The history of the book is a social, cultural and political record, embracing the basics of communication from oral to written to visual. The history of the book is the history of people communicating. It may be in large groups such as those who gathered around Homer or today attend authors reading from their latest work. It may be one to one, with the author silently talking to the equally attentive, silent reader.

Only generalizations may be made here and throughout this overview of major events and personalities for the millenniums of time leaps and jumps. If, for example, it is noted that the Sumerians and their ancestors saw the gods as masters and themselves as serving slaves, this helps to explain their astonishing art, puzzling governmental structures and efforts in mathematics and astronomy which, in turn, were linked closely to the plains and rivers they worked. Their written records only suggest the complexity and the length of the historical periods.

For the movie, "Quest for Fire," English novelist Anthony Burgess developed a code of grunts and gestures which he thought might best express Neanderthal ideas in the extended drive towards communication. The earliest signs of writing come from the Cro-Magnon people and their extraordinary and equally almost incomprehensible cave drawings in the caves at Lascaux and Altamira in southern France and in northern Spain. The animals, stick figures and markings parallel what are suspected to be lunar notations found on bone.

The lack of examples of such art in other parts of the world at this time (i.e. circa 24,000 or 22,000 B.C. to about 9000 B.C.) presents a problem, particularly in relating the art to the development of writing. Be that as it may, the Palaeolithic art in South West Europe is unique as an episode in human history. It is the first extant sign of the emergence of conceptual thought which, in turn, had to be applied to the discovery of writing. It represents the longest human tradition of comparable complexity throughout any society or group, i.e. some 15,000 to 13,000 years as compared today with no more than 5,000 to 6,000 for the history of books.

Their work, their art is impressive. Poet Zbigniew Herbert puts it "Though I had stared into the abyss of history [at Lascaux caves], I did not emerge from an alien world. Never before had I felt a stronger or more reassuring conviction; I am a citizen of the earth, an inheritor not only of the Greeks and Romans but of almost the whole of infinity."

Experts argue whether the Picasso like cave paintings truly represent writing, but that they are an amalgamation of art and communication there is no question. Nor will one debate the cave artists' discovery of the first link in any writing system— pictography. By the eighth or ninth millennium B.C. the abstract picture outline of a bird, man, ox or sheep appears in what is now the Middle East.

The Egyptians enjoyed a given amount of uniformity in culture and language, but beyond their borders there were many languages, many variations on literary, government and social themes. There were unifying elements, among them writing.

The classical and hellenistic period of Greek intellectual hegemony was brief, followed by a longer, certainly more far-reaching period of Roman dominance. The Romans brought the alphabet to most of Europe, while despite the Alexandria library the Egyptians faded into the historical pattern. Under Constantine in the fourth century A.D. the Near East became an important point of civilization again, and was to remain so well into the opening years of the Renaissance in Europe.

And then came printing, which over four hundred years helped to change everything from the way people communicated to the governments they established—and destroyed. Today, in less time than it took the printing press to find its way out of Germany, computers and automation offer new aspects of the history of the book.

As the world approaches the film "2001: A Space Odyssey," the history of the book takes another turn. "Hal" and other computers seen in the movie, and these days in almost every library and in many homes, offer writing in another format. Within a decade or so some predict the human voice, mastered or enslaved to Hal and the computer family, will eliminate both the need to write and the need to read. The computer now offers the early act of ''virtual reality,'' and a key to information through videos, sound, text and pictures combined. Learning and thinking visually, particularly from the ubiquitous television, are another communication development which many feel succeeds where books fail, e.g. the bringing home of the Vietnam War to Americans, the crack down on the Chinese students and, most dramatic, the fall of the Communists in Russia. While there is more to it than a video, it should give pause.

The book may be diminished by the rise of the visual, of the sound, of a return, in fact, to the oral tradition. But there is no particular reason why the two should not go on into the twenty-first century together. Ultimately, the value of each will be the test.

The history of the book takes the scholar into specific, important unravelling of minute problems from who read what in the early 19th century to who published books in the latter days of Rome. In the density of detailed history there are enough facts, raw data and interpretation to fill a modest-sized library. A less expansive view is suggested in the pages to come. The author hopes this introduction will encourage readers to go to more detailed, more explicit books—some of which are offered in the bibliography and in the notes.

CHAPTER ONE

THE POWER OF THE SCRIBES

Lo, no scribe is short of food
And of riches from the palace.
—The Satire of the Trades

There are numerous competing theories of the origins of the modern human, but general agreement is that about 1.6 to 1.5 million years ago Homo erectus appeared in Africa. Competing with Neanderthals (200,000 to c. 36,000 B.C.), Cro-Magnon people emerged from 40,000 to 35,000 B.C. in the image of today's individual. As early as 28,000, European Cro-Magnon sculptured Venus figures and by 14,000, in Lascaux and southern French areas, left vibrant images of animals on cave walls (Fig. 1). Around 9000 B.C. other signs of civilization and early forms of written communication appear. Until then, the citizen of the cave, of the hunting tribe, learned what had to be mastered by following the motions of others, and, later, by listening to the myths and practical advice passed on from one generation to the next.[1]

From the first grunt to the skillful artist who drew a picture to represent a word, communication became the cousin of the book. Experts argue about just when the book as we know it took form or, on a larger scale, when history began, when people settled to farm, to raise animals, to brew drink.[2] For most, though, a safe date to mark early writing is approximately 3500 B.C. Then the beginning of civilization as we now understand it took place with settlements in the Near East, and some 1,500 years later in China. Formal education developed as did limited literacy and the written record.

The collective result of urbanization, a formal religion and active trade required written communication. The groups which

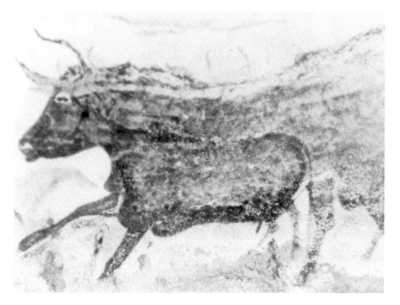

1. A Magdalenian bull from the Lascaux Caves in Southwestern France, c. 14,000 to 13,500 B.C. While the purpose of the cave drawings is really not known, they can be considered the forerunners of pictography, e.g. written communication.

rose to govern quickly understood the power in the written word. They limited literacy to a select few and were among the first to appreciate that the ideal ruler is the one with total control over communications. Only a few were taught to read and write, and these only because they were needed to help maintain a strong, central government.

Scribes became an elite, a position they would hold throughout the Near East for some 3,000 and more years. Practical education was limited to government and religious sponsored schools. Pupils, at five or six years of age, would enter and by their mid-teens move on to more advanced study as scribes, priests or government bureaucrats. Often, though, the positions were far from separate and a talented individual might perform all these roles. Drawn from the ruling classes, the students maintained continuity and conservative practices in Egypt and in much of the Near East. It seems probable that from time to time scribes came from a less than privileged class, but the primary concentration of pupils remained with the select.

No consensus exists as to whether writing began first in Egypt or Mesopotamia, although Sumerian writing dates back to 3300 B.C. and the earliest extant Egyptian writing is from about 3050 B.C. One thing all systems hold in common is the notion that the power of writing was controlled by the gods and came to people as a gift of those gods. In Egypt, Thoth, or Tehuti, is not only the god of the scribes but one who establishes order and holds down rebellion.

George Orwell's *1984* mind control was exercised for some three millennia by the rulers of Egypt and the Near East and their scribes who controlled all forms of written communication. There were some exceptions, such as the Hebrews, and from time to time groups revolted, but lacking any real way to pass messages other than by voice, the rebels were quickly subdued. A modern proximity to the situation is found, of course, in totalitarian states.

Today, there are multiple points of communication, from television and radio to films and books, but "mass communication" is a relatively new concept. The printed book, in the mid-fifteenth century, was the first introduction to the possibilities of mass communication. Full realization of the opportunity developed only in the nineteenth century with widespread literacy and printing technology.

An example of what literacy could mean to a specific people is found in the history of Israel. Both for religious and cultural reasons, reading and writing, unlike in other parts of the Near East, were stressed, often against great odds. A religious Hebrew, whether man, woman, or child, should be taught the basics of literacy. This total shift from the customs of the Near East is due to the attachment the Hebrews had (and have) for the written word, for the book. The Israelites, required to write the Torah for themselves, soon reduced the power of the scribe, but not his prestige as a teacher.

Since the time of David (c. 1004–965) and Solomon (d. 928–922) the scribe was the primary agent of religious education. Not only did he copy the Torah, he interpreted it, translated it into various languages, and explained its meaning. The community synagogue included a school with a "house of the book" and a "house of instruction," offering training from grade school through high school. Oral instruction with an emphasis on memorizing texts remained the primary educational focus. Not until the Greeks adopted an alphabet and made literacy a possibility for many, instead of the few, did the idea of individualism, no matter how limited, and the notion of freedom match that of the ancient Hebrews. This is a great simplification of two complex societies, but the parallels between literacy and freedom are a given truth throughout recorded history.

Invaded and in turn invaders, the Egyptians had long periods of relative calm, but in Mesopotamia and the Near East (i.e. what is roughly today's Israel, Jordan, Syria, Lebanon, Turkey, Iraq and Iran) it was a bloody battlefield. The Sumerians (c. 3500–2500 B.C.) came first, with the Akkadians supplanting Sumerians until c. 2000, followed by the Babylonians (c. 2000–1800 B.C.) and then the Assyrians (c. 1500–600 B.C.). These were the ancestors of the Semitic Akkadians whose language became the "lingua franca" for much of the Near East. The Hittites ruled the area from 2000 to 1200 B.C.

The idea of an average person's individual life and the world of books is lost in the 3,000 or so years before the glories of Greece, the power of Rome. The individual is not to be found in writing unless he occupies a position of power. There will continue to be a scarcity of "everyperson" until the development of printing. Almost up to the middle of the nineteenth century, the illiterate, the poor and powerless starve for attention. They come and they go, leaving little record of themselves behind. The cultural history of books is primarily the story of the few. Most of what we know now, particularly for the first 3,000 to 4,000 years of recorded history, is a matter of conjecture and inference. Archaeology and historical analysis offer a rough profile of daily life from the examination of cave paintings (c. 12,000 years ago) to early nineteenth-century tax records and letters. Artifacts are employed, but in writing little will be found of the average person until the Greeks, beginning with Hesiod's *Works and Days* (c. 700 B.C.) which gives a faint glimpse of a powerless social group.

THE BEGINNING

The first step in the history of books was writing. No one is sure when this skill was achieved but it was considerably later than spoken language, which evolved over 40,000 years or more. Signs of writing systems are found in cave art. Between the markings and paintings of early people and about 10,000 B.C., there are fragments which indicate slow developments in writing. Between 9000 and 3500 B.C., urban centers and farming developed in the Near East, and the first signs of trade and more advanced methods of communication appear. If the massive walls and towers of Jericho date back to the 9th millennium, as is now believed, Egyptian civilization began about the same time. Probably there was writing, although during this period there is nothing extant other than marks on tokens used in trade. Nearly all writing as we know it today (with the exception of Chinese and pre-Columbian scripts) originated in the Near and Middle East between 4000 and 3000 B.C. The availability of writing does not make a society, but it is hard to find a group where social, economic and political efficiency does not follow or parallel a successful method of writing. Removing the need to memorize masses of information freed the mind for more intellectual pursuits and the development of civilizations.[3]

Dating difficulties persist in almost every aspect of digging up the past. Recent records of the early use of the horse now indicate that men learned to ride some 1,000 years earlier than suspected— probably on the steppes of the Ukraine in 4,000 B.C. The evidence is wear made by an ancient bridle bit on a stallion's tooth and a 4,300-year-old clay figurine of a horse discovered in Syria in 1992. The discoveries show the horse played an earlier, more important role in the development of Middle Eastern empires. The greater mobility made differences in military tactics as well as in trade, which encouraged urban settlements which, in turn, meant an increase in the need for writing. Fixing the time and place of early horseback riding may seem distant from the history of the book, but it is only a reminder that most aspects of early human activity relate to writing.

More important than the horse, the discovery of irrigation probably did much to insure settlements in the Near East. The Egyptian Nile and the Euphrates in Mesopotamia provided means for large crops and, in turn, for urban centers and population growth. Trade, temple and palace evolved, and to link the three, fixed communication was necessary.

The complex question remains: why did it occur to some, but

not to others, to master writing, to keep records, to build on an oral
tradition. A simple, partial response is that writing developed out
of a trade-oriented society. Lacking trade, agriculture, settlements, etc., there was neither civilization nor writing.

WRITING SYSTEMS

There are four main methods of written communication: picto-
grams, ideographs (or word signs), syllabic signs (phonographs),
and the alphabet. Often two or more of the systems functioned
within a given area or civilization, although despite differences in
appearances the scripts developed in much the same way.

Writing system forms are fairly well understood and evolved in
this order: 1) *Pictographs:* literally pictures of the object. This
appears to be the first form of written communication, and is in
limited use today, e.g. a Texas company has developed a chart of
pictographs to which hospital patients can point to make their
needs known. 2) *Ideographs:* the same picture, but more sophisticated in that: a) the picture is reduced to an abstract sign which can
mean an entire word or phrase (these are often referred to as
logograms); and b) various symbols or determinatives are employed to differentiate one similar sign from another. For example, the Sumerian word for arrow and for life are pronounced the
same. The Sumerians used the arrow as a pictograph of the arrow.
Where they wanted to use the more abstract word for life, they
simply added a mark, or determinative next to the arrow. This was
the ideograph, or logograph, which takes the pictograph a step
further. Even with determinatives, the Sumerians had over 2,000
signs to learn in order to write. Similar systems, such as Chinese,
use as many as 50,000 signs for literary works and a minimum of
5,000 to 8,000 for elementary, daily writing.[4]

Ideographs remain important. As the globe becomes a path for
millions of travelers, attempting to tell a woman's bathroom from
one used by men requires these symbols. A little drawing for a
bath will mean in French ''bain,'' in German ''bad,'' and in
Spanish ''bano,'' but the ideograph of a tub or shower will solve
the problem in any language. Many times a group of ideographs
are more efficient than alphabetic notations.

In Egyptian hieroglyphics, the simple form of the logogram or pictograph would show the sun as a small circle within a larger circle. Through determinatives and/or context the same sign would signify "day." The problem is that this requires thousands of signs, and understanding them requires as well an understanding of the culture. Hence, the natural move was to phonograms with phonetic meaning.

3) *Phonographs:* Here the same pictographs/ideographs are used to express sound, and the basic unit or mark no longer represents simply an object, but a part of speech. Writing becomes independent of the culture, freed from the confines of pictures and ideas that usually only a single group can understand. As the phonographs or phonograms became more abstract, more involved with sound, one moves to the advanced stage of writing known as "phonetic." Here the signs usually have little or nothing to do with objects, but are learned to express specific sound, and fewer symbols are needed. In the phonetic the primary unit is the syllable. This consonantal, syllabic system was managed with probably no more than 500 to 800 signs in Sumeria. Much later the Babylonians probably used no more than 200 to 300 syllabic marks.

The steps from the picture of a cow to a pictograph which suggests the sound for a cow is not a straight line, and many civilizations jumped or skipped over a method or two in the process of development. It is questionable whether any individual delivered up a given system. Most evolved gradually, as much from need as from the imagination of the reader/writer.

It often is charged that one system is better than another. Marshall McLuhan and Harold Innis, for example, drew the conclusion that the lack of phonography in China, Japan and much of the Far East accounts for an early lack of technological development. There is considerably more to it than that. While Japanese is a syllabic system (with 50 phonetic characters and over 7,000 ideographs) it lacks an alphabet. This hardly seems to have held the Japanese back in terms of technology, and, in spite of lack of an alphabetic script, Japan is one of the world's most literate countries.

THE ALPHABETS

First developed by Semitic people, about 1700–1500 B.C., then carried to the West by the Greeks, the alphabet differs from the phonograph/syllabic form in that it allows one to express a single sound (i.e. phoneme) of a language. The main speech sounds (vowels and consonants) are represented individually. Thus it is available for all spoken languages. More important, the letters representing sound makes it possible for any diligent individual to learn to read and write, thus removing the necessity of the middleperson, or scribe.

The Semites developed a system which stressed the oral rather than the pictorial. Images, by both the Hebrews and later some Christian groups, were forbidden. Lacking the reliance on essentially picture-oriented early writing systems, the Semites took an oral path to writing.

Traders carried the rudiments of the alphabet to the Phoenicians, then living in what is now Lebanon and parts of Syria and Israel, about 1500 B.C. The Phoenicians, masters of dyed cloth and sailing, brought the alphabet to the Greeks around 1000 to 800 B.C. (Incidentally, along the historical path of the alphabet the mistaken notion that it was a Phoenician development arose, and is still current. Actually, as indicated, the Phoenicians simply borrowed from their southern neighbors.)

On the rough facts about the development of the alphabet the Greek and Roman historians, from Herodotus to Pliny, are agreed. They are supported by today's archaeologists and experts on writing systems, although exact dates of transmission remain uncertain. Evidence is scarce. The oldest extant example of the beginnings of the Semitic alphabet are on an ostracon (i.e. a pottery fragment) of about 1200 or 1000 B.C. The 80 hastily incised letters seem to be a student's work, and imply that the alphabet was in use many years earlier. A pictographic form, with 27 signs, indicates that the Semitic alphabet was developed in all probability in Canaan from 1700 to 1600 B.C.

By the second half of the eleventh century B.C., the Phoenician alphabet, with 22 linear letters, was in use, and by the mid eighth century the alphabet was carried throughout the Mediterranean area by both the Phoenicians and Greek traders. The archaic Greek alphabet, which appeared first from about 1100 B.C. to c. 750 B.C.—the date is far from certain—used the 22 West Semitic letters.

Only a few Greeks used the new writing. It was not until the widespread use of the alphabet that writing paralleled and then replaced reliance solely on oral communication. Homer, for example, makes only a passing reference to the art. Parenthetically, while the common explanation for the spread of writing is that it aided trade, government and religion, a few scholars believe the early Greeks adopted the alphabet in order to preserve Homer and other poets. The alphabet, they believe, was used first to codify the *Odyssey* and the *Iliad.*[5]

The Mycenaeans, who c. 1250 B.C. probably destroyed Troy, are the inspiration for Homer's epic. With the downfall of the Mycenaeans and the end of the Bronze Age, the Aegean world of Greece entered a dark period devoid of the slightest record, and for that reason more baffling than the Dark Ages of Western Europe. Greece reappeared about 800 B.C. in Homer's songs and adventures.

The Mycenaean past, as Knossos and much of Crete centuries earlier, receded into myth, into a "golden age" of gods and heroes where, at least for the Greeks, their history began. The story about the War between the Greeks and the Trojans was the West's first, and still greatest, epic poem. Its importance to the development of the book is two-fold: (1) Homer conveniently marks, as close as one may presume, the introduction of the Greek alphabet and the move from memory to record. (2) It is the beginning of an enormous admiration for Greek literature which was to extend to the Romans, throughout the Middle Ages and until the early part of the twentieth century. Greek culture remains with us today, although rapidly seeming to fade as a familiar part of education.

Unfortunately for those who believe the Greeks were at home with the alphabet by 1100 B.C., there is no direct evidence for the date. The first signs of the alphabet appear on an Athenian jug of about 725 B.C. Fittingly enough for those who claim poetic dominance of early writing, the extant line reads: "Who now of all the dancers perform most gracefully. . . . " Apparently the jug, or its contents of oil, was a coveted prize.[6]

About 575 B.C. appears the spectacular François Vase, a krater with 121 inscriptions of signatures and names. This exuberant display indicates to many that writing was still a novelty.[7] Later black figure vases have inscriptions which mean absolutely nothing, but signify that the illiterate purchaser probably thought the piece more valuable because of the writing. As guests were likely to be equally illiterate no one would be shocked by the

mumbo-jumbo inscriptions. By the fifth century, with the rise in
the educated male class, the nonsense inscriptions disappear.

In 403 B.C., Athens passed a law to make the Ionian alphabet
compulsory in official documents. The city adopted the 22 letters
in the Semitic alphabet, added four, but later dropped two. In the
seventh century the Romans adopted the alphabet, probably from
the Etruscans who had actively traded with the Greeks, and added
and dropped letters to suit Latin. By the first century B.C. the
Romans had conquered Greece and fixed the alphabet at 23 letters. The missing J, U, and W were added by medieval scribes in
the eleventh to twelfth centuries. The Latin alphabet was the base
for all western European scripts. Upper case (majuscule) and
lower case (minuscule) letters developed and by the Middle Ages
various national handwriting became common.

CUNEIFORM AND HIEROGLYPHICS

For some 3,000 years before the Greek alphabet, there were two
basic methods of writing in the Near East. The Egyptians used
hieroglyphics (literally, ''sacred carving''); and much of the
remainder of the Near East employed cuneiform (marks made by
a wedged stylus on wet clay, hence ''wedge'' or ''cuneus'') (Fig.
2).

In Sumeria and surrounding areas clay was the major writing
surface. It was plentiful and cheap. It was formed into small
tablets, and the average writing surface was oblong with convex
sides. Using a stylus, the scribe wrote on the damp, soft surface.
Once baked, the tablet would last forever. This explains why there
are so many more cuneiform tablets today than highly perishable
papyrus rolls which the Egyptians preferred.

There were problems. To avoid excessive weight, numerous
tablets might be used for a message, e.g. it took over 50 oversized
tablets to contain a bilingual dictionary. Diplomatic correspondence might, literally, weigh down the messenger. And there were
earthworms. Still, clay proved a durable and practical writing
surface.[8]

The ancestral line of cuneiform dates from Sumeria, c. 3300–
2900 B.C., where inscribed tokens were apparently used for trade,
government and religion. The logographic writing employed

2. Cuneiform tablet containing a hymn to the Babylonian king Dungi.

signs for men, stars, slaves, hills and the like which could be combined and developed into a system of sounds. The Akkadians, by about 2500 B.C., moved from logographs to the now familiar wedge-shaped cuneiform, which consisted of syllabic signs and understood vowels.

Akkadian writing dominated Mesopotamia from the third to the first millennium B.C., much as Latin did in the European Middle Ages.[9] It wasn't until the spread of the alphabet, c. 800 to 700 B.C., that cuneiform lost its popularity. Even then it continued for almost another 1,000 years in a limited way as a method of transcribing certain scientific and religious works. A modern equivalent might be the college diploma which is hand-lettered, despite the printing press and the computer.

The diffusion of a writing system from a single source in Mesopotamia is challenged by some who believe such systems developed independently in various areas. Still, evidence today seems to support the view that cuneiform spread through cultural contacts to numerous peoples throughout the Near and Middle East.

HIEROGLYPHICS

The Egyptian writing form, hieroglyphics, developed from pictographs carved into stone and various religious and political artifacts (Fig. 3). The earliest inscriptions are from the late Predynastic Period (c. 3100 B.C.). The strikingly beautiful hieroglyphs were individual works of art and often are found in combination with wall paintings. Forming the hieroglyphs took not only skill, but time. With the need for a more efficient way of writing, with the development of a brush and a writing surface other than stone, the hieroglyphs were reduced (c. 2500 B.C.) to a cursive hand known as "hieratic," i.e. priestly. The simplified signs served as the major non-monumental script for administration, business, religious, literary and scientific documents through most of Egypt's history. By the first millennium, "demotic" or popular was introduced as an even faster, easier method to master writing for trade and everyday activities of government.

By about 500 B.C. the number of hieroglyphics had increased from fewer than 1,000 to over 6,000. There were many fewer signs to remember in hieratic and demotic, but on the whole it was a system which became increasingly difficult to master. As such it had little influence outside of Egypt. By the time of Christianity few understood the scripts. The Greeks believed the hieroglyphs were magic symbols and allegories. The notion was carried on to the nineteenth century.

The recognition of the Egyptian hieroglyphics as a writing system came when the Frenchman, François Champollion (1790–1832 A.D.), used the Rosetta stone to decipher hieroglyphics. The black basalt, found by Napoleon's troops in 1799 and sent to the

3. Late hieroglyphics as seen in a fragment of an Egyptian Book of the Dead, intended for a person of rank. Above the text there is a colored pictorial frieze with artistically drawn figures.

British Museum in 1802 (where it remains today), is better known to lay persons than any of the Egyptian monarchs. The Rosetta stone was erected in 195 B.C. to honor a Greek dynasty which ruled Egypt. It bears an inscription in three forms (Greek, hieroglyphics and demotic). Champollion employed the Greek inscription as a key for decipherment. His findings were published in 1822.[10]

Extant writing in Egypt deals almost exclusively with the same matters found in other Near Eastern areas; but there is one major exception. As much preserved writing is found in tomb stone inscriptions and art, we have a peculiar Egyptian message. This is the emphasis on the care of the dead, or, more precisely, on methods of insuring the continued "life" of the dead in other worlds through such tomb inscriptions. Hieroglyphics could bring to life what they depicted. Therefore, to destroy the name of a person was to deprive the individual of identity and render him or her non-existent.[11]

CUNEIFORM DECIPHERED

Lists of names of kings of the Near East are found in many places. The Sumerians compiled their own King list as, later, did the Babylonians, Hittites and Assyrians. Rulers were determined to leave a trace of themselves and their accomplishments in tombs, statues and anywhere else where the name might be safe for eternity. Sometimes, as in the cuneiform script along the mountain wall at Behistun [left to mark the reign of Darius the Great (c.558–486 B.C.)], the name lists gave later generations a key to the writing form. The so called "Rosetta Stone of Asia," on a mountain side 150 feet high and over 100 feet long, offered a nineteenth-century East Indian Company representative, Henry Rawlinson, the data he needed to decipher cuneiform. Darius chronicled his deeds in an almost inaccessible place, not only for the glory of display, but to be sure no one removed his name—a common and well-founded fear among Near Eastern rulers. The conquests were outlined in three languages, Old Persian, Elamite and Babylonian.

Over a period of ten years Rawlinson risked his life to copy the Old Persian text. With this and work done earlier by the German

G. F. Grotefend, he produced a translation of the whole in 1846, followed in 1851 by the transliteration and translation of the Babylonian cuneiform. This was only the beginning; even today work is carried on to decipher other cuneiform texts from earlier periods.

SPREAD OF PAPYRUS

Lack of more than tomb-related writing, as well as limited catches of official business and military activities, is due in no small part to the primary writing surface employed by the Egyptians for over 3,000 years. This was papyrus (Fig. 4). The paper-like plant grew in abundance in Egypt and was used as early as 3100 B.C. (Industrial growth killed it in modern Egypt, although it is found still in the Sudan area.)

Sheets from the papyrus plant were pasted edge to edge and formed into 20- to 30-foot rolls, or ''biblion.'' Text was written on the surface, usually about 20 inches in width, in columns. The reader unrolled the work as it was read and took it up on a second spindle. It proved to be highly perishable, particularly when rolled and unrolled more than a few times. A modern microfilm user has some notion of how this worked, and it could be equally inconvenient, particularly as it had to be rolled back to the beginning.

While papyrus was used extensively in the Near East, little has survived outside of Egypt. Much of what is extant today is rather late in origin and comes from Egyptian tombs and graves. An uninscribed roll was first found in a Dynasty grave (c. 3100–2890 B.C.). It was the custom to make cheaper coffins of discarded papyrus sheets glued together and covered with a layer of plaster. Several papyrus texts have come to us in this manner. A far greater number, however, have been preserved through the general religious custom of placing various sacred texts, prayers, etc. in the grave as protection during the soul's journey into the realm of the dead.

The Greeks and the Romans prized papyrus, but it proved expensive for most daily uses. The early Europeans often turned to substitutes such as wooden tablets with wax cores. Forms are found throughout the Near East, as well. The notebooks could be

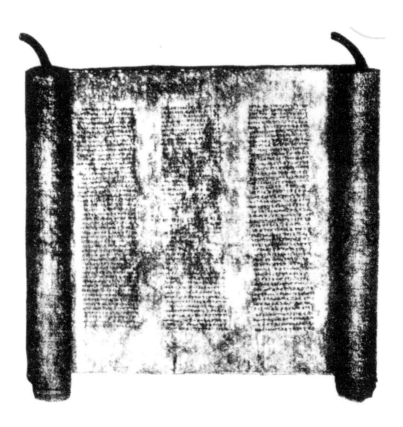

4. Papyrus roll with Greek text in columns.

used over again when the wax was melted down and simply
poured back into the hinged, hollowed-out tablets. Consequently
until almost the Renaissance, anyone learning to write or drafting
a letter or document did so on a wax tablet.[12]

The substantial substitute for papyrus was parchment, i.e. the
skins of goats and sheep, or vellum, from calf skins. This writing
surface dominated until paper, invented by the Chinese c. 105
A.D., reached Europe. Arabs began using paper as early as the
ninth century A.D., but it was not introduced to Europe much

before 1000 A.D., and was not popular until the advent of printing in the fifteenth century.

THE EDUCATION OF THE SCRIBES

Given a command of writing, the Near Eastern scribe tended to be conservative. Drawing upon high social and economic prestige, the scribal schools recruited sons of governors, senior civil servants and even candidates from among the rulers. The post was similar to a doctor or lawyer in America today, although with considerable more mystery surrounding the activities. Literacy, even among the ruling classes, was rare in the Near East. This gave the scribe more power and, not incidentally, more leisure. Toward the end of Egyptian power, knowledge of writing became somewhat more democratized in that lower classes entered the scribal ranks, but this tended to be the exception rather than the rule (Fig. 5).

The world's first known architect and physician, Imhotep (c. 2686–2660 B.C.), was a scribe. He developed the technology of pyramid building, and despite his common birth became the patron of the scribes. The Father of Egyptian science probably was the first to devise the 365-day calendar. As in any society, Imhotep was an exception. Most scribes, as most people, were hardly that imaginative or important. They toiled as bureaucratic crafts people rather than empire builders. But unlike average people, they had definite advantages.

In the *Satire of the Trades* (1320–1200 B.C.), an Egyptian scribe compared his work with other professions. He wisely concluded: "Set your heart on books." Throughout there is a familiar refrain: "No Scribe is short of food, or of wealth." And "Writing...is better than all other professions. It pleases more than bread and beer, more than clothing and ointment. It is worth more than an inheritance in Egypt, than a tomb in the west."[13]

Much effort went into educating the scribe. It seemed as difficult to become enrolled in what the Babylonians called a "tablet house" as it is today to join the student body of the Ivy League Prep schools. The youth, normally about the age of today's first or second graders, might come from a privileged family, but he had to learn the difficulties of cuneiform or hieroglyphics by copying, over and over again, lists of household objects, of rulers and gods.

5. A statue of an unknown scribe (Cairo Museum). The Egyptian is sitting in the standard position with his left hand holding the papyrus roll and the right hand ready to write. The scribe is a high official.

If the scribe was late to class, or made too many errors, he might be caned. Gradually he rose in the schoolboy ranks until he became a "big brother," somewhat the equivalent, say, of an honored member of an English boy's school. Upon graduation he was told: "You are a scribe!" and he was ready for the world. By the first millennium, at least in parts of the Near East, from Babylonia to Nippur, there were tablet houses equivalent to modern universities. Here the scribe received advanced training in everything from mastering other languages to diplomacy. With this training, which is echoed in universities from the Middle Ages to the twentieth century, the scribe rightfully considered himself among the social elite. Although warned by superiors to avoid conceit, this was difficult to achieve when it was realized that few military campaigns or business ventures could function without his presence.

Scribes are portrayed in most Near Eastern art, and usually close to the ruler. Typically, an Egyptian will be shown sitting cross-legged, with his left hand holding a papyrus scroll and his right hand ready to write. The scroll rests on his kilt, which served the dual role of clothing and desk. Assyrian and Babylonian scribes are found adding up the booty from warfare.[14]

Such was the prestige accorded being able to read and write that scribal tools often are shown with portraits and sculptured figures of everyone from gods to rulers to military commanders and traders. A scribe's implements served as a type of symbol of prestige, much as someone today would be photographed with an expensive suit, watch, car or the like.

LIBRARIES

Thanks as much to the preservative quality of baked clay as to the interest of Mesopotamia in maintaining business government and religious records, there is hardly a place in the area which does not have remnants of a store of archives. And small private libraries equally are evident.[15]

The scribes were often archivists or librarians. Their careful work in inscribing, cataloging and shelving documents offers early glimpses of recorded history. Throughout greater Mesopotamia scores of libraries, or more properly official archives, prospered from the beginning of writing to the time of Alexander the Great. In the city of Lagash, 30,000 tablets were found. In the palace at Nimrud, there was a whole wing assigned to the library. Numerous other libraries or archives of cuneiform tablets have survived, the most famous being at Nineveh, Nippur, Assur and Boghazkoy. The earliest is the Sumerian findings at Ebla (c. 2600–2500 B.C.); the latest at Ninevah (c. 700–600 B.C.). The latter is the most famous of all, and the holdings of Ashurbanipal offer a marvelous source for reconstructing the life of the period, as well as library/archive practices.

Tablets are found in numerous new archeological digs. Thousands of cuneiform tablets were discovered in the 1970s at Emar in the palace archives of a Hittite vassal kingdom (c 1400–1200 B.C.). In the late 1980s and early 1990s archaeologists found at Nippur (just south of Baghdad in Iraq) the site of 5,000-year-old Sumerian structures. Among the ruins of building and rebuilding for some 3,000 years they dug up clay tablets which indicate that the area was a site for early medical treatment.

The Royal Archives at Ebla, in northern Syria, were explored in the late 1960s. Consequent diggings revealed a rich, yet typical Mesopotamian library. By 1980 some 17,000 clay tablets and fragments were recorded from two main and several secondary rooms in the palace. The tablets were stored on wooden shelves, probably in baskets, jars or boxes. The material was filed on separate shelves, and/or in a series of rooms by subject.

Clay tablets which served as catalogs are extant from c. 2000 B.C. Identification of a tablet or tablets was by the first few words of the text—a practice followed by Europeans until the sixteenth century A.D. The "incipit" (begins) led one to the tablet, usually in a box or basket on shelves. Typical incipits of Sumerian hymns read "Honored and noble warrior" or "Where are the wild oxen" or "In former days." The method appears rough, yet it worked as long as no more than one or two tablets began with the same words. Where there were similar words the incipit was lengthened to include what was unique for each tablet, or series.

Another "cataloging" device was to add a colophon; i.e., a title and summary of contents as well as the number of tablets in a series. For example, in the Epic of Gilgamesh one version is on 12 tablets, with the story of the flood on the eleventh. The colophon identifies the flood epic by its first line: "He who saw everything, eleventh tablet."

EGYPTIAN LIBRARIES

While discovery of numerous libraries has helped to trace the history of Mesopotamia, the archaeologist in Egypt must rely on tomb and coffin inscriptions for information. As of the end of the century, no extant Egyptian libraries have been discovered. (The Alexandrian Library, to be considered later, is more a Greek or international library than Egyptian.) At the same time, there are tantalizing references to archives and libraries throughout Egyptian records and literature. Reference is made as early as 2400 B.C. to a "house or writing," and there is a scattering of both papyrus and cuneiform tablets from various periods, but no one place which can be identified as a library.

The famous correspondence between two kings (c. 1350 B.C.) was found at El-Amarna in a pit. This probably was discarded from a nearby, lost library.[16] Bits of private libraries and records indicate there were some limited collections of papyrus in homes. This evidence is so rare as not to allow generalizations either about individual reading habits or literacy.

The shadow of libraries is found in numerous wall paintings. Here one finds pictures of papyrus rolls unrolled by a reader or stored in what appear to be wooden chests or jars. Individual rolls are identified by pasting on the roll a small piece of papyrus which carries its description.

THE USE OF WRITING

Writing was used primarily by government, trade and religion. Along the way it served to celebrate the individual monarch, and often the scribe and other bureaucrats.

One of the earliest personalities to survive is the Sumerian ruler Gudea (c. 2141–2122 B.C.). His idealized likeness is captured in small, square black statues. The pensive figures often are inscribed with cuneiform. For example, one bit of writing explains why Gudea erected a particular temple: he saw a woman "holding in her hand a stylus of flaming metal." This is the familiar stylus of the scribes, but here it has magical power to engrave "the tablets of good writing of heaven." Apparently the woman is an early representation of science.

By the 1770s B.C. the most famous king of Babylon appears. Hammurabi is remembered today for his laws, which set legal patterns for hundreds of years to come. He had the sense to post the laws throughout the Near East, not on perishable wood or metal, but engraved in hard, black stone pillars or stela which can be seen and studied in museums today. Hammurabi's words are reflected in the Old Testament. The rules prevent the strong from oppressing the weak and they "give justice to the orphan and the widow." Justice is swift and merciless. "If a man has committed a robbery . . . [he] shall be put to death." A woman who brings about the death of her husband will be "impaled on stakes." And a son who strikes his father will have a hand cut off.[17]

The Assyrian king Ashurbanipal appears between 629 and 627 B.C. While Ashurbanipal was an enlightened monarch, and one of the first intellectual rulers after the Egyptian ruler Akhenaton (d. 1362 B.C.), he quite lived up to the unsavory reputation of Assyrians in Byron's famous poem, "The destruction of Sennacherib," which begins: "The Assyrians came down like wolf on the fold."

As the first recorded bibliophile, it is he who seems responsible for the library and archives in his great city of Nineveh. He frantically gathered books, and was matched only by the Alexandrian Library several hundred years later. A form letter went from the King to his military commanders: "When you receive this letter, take three men and find all of the tablets in [the particular conquered city or area]. Hunt for those in homes and in temples. Those which do not exist in Assyria, send them back to me." The scribes attached to the military carried out most of the searches and proved successful. So much so that one can say Nineveh was the first national library.

Ashurbanipal's impressive library lay buried in the sands until discovered by pioneer British archaeologist Henry Layer in the mid-nineteenth century. The bas reliefs from the Assyrian's palace (many of which are now in the British Museum) are an early effort at a type of massive book illustration. The running story is explained not only in marvelous art, but in cuneiform as well. The pictures of battles, hunts, and palace life suggest the other side, the Byron side of the ruler: "600 of their warriors," Ashurbanipal boasts, "I put to the sword. Hulaid, their governor I flayed, and his skin I spread upon the wall of the city." In more poetic terms he sings: "I mounted my steed, I rode joyfully, I held the bow, I shot the arrow." And later: "sickness of soul, distress of body, have bowed my form. I spend my days sighing and lamenting. Death is making an end of me."

The impressive prose style may or may not be that of Ashurbanipal. Perhaps some unnamed scribe, some later cousin of Homer, wrote the words. The ruler is aware of the problem. He is quick to explain his abilities in prose and verse: ''Nabu, the universal scribe, gave me a grasp of wisdom. . . . I have solved the problems of division and multiplication . . . I have read the script of Sumer and the obscure Akkadian.''[18] Luckier than most, Ashurbanipal left evidence of, at a minimum, his interest in culture and philosophy. One can't help but wonder how much more was lost over the preceding 2,500 years. How many other versions of the Assyrian king in Egypt and throughout the Near East wrote equally well but are now little more than names on a list?

EGYPTIAN LITERATURE

The fragility of papyrus and the dominance of inscription on tombs conspire to give a less than balanced notion of Egyptian writing. One is left with scribes remembered primarily for a literature of the dead. What was saved outside of the tombs comes to us primarily second-hand through Greek or Latin authors who transcribed quotes, themes and myths. Unlike the Assyrian-Babylonian remainders, the poetry, romances, letters and moral precepts are considerably more personal. One at least has a sense of what the otherwise illiterate population might have sung and recited.

The Egyptian fragment, ''The Tale of The Shipwrecked Sailor,'' shows the wild imagination at work.[19] Advice given by fathers to their sons is a recurrent reminder of the timelessness of sometimes tiresome maxims. There is little originality in the prose. Similar patterns, even similar phrases, are found in the literature for almost 3,000 years.

As in other parts of the Near East, the individual Egyptian is lost. There are marvelous fragments of what might have been unusual, exceptional prose and poetry. King Akhenaton is one of the few names one can associate with prose—in this case the ''Hymn to Aten,'' which often is compared to the 104th psalm.[20] Then there is the much earlier ''Song of the Harper'' (c. 2700 B.C.), which is similar in tone, if not in style. There is always the reminder: "A man is not permitted to carry his property with him to death. Beyond, no one having departed is able to come home again."[21]

Some five small collections of love poems survive from c. 1600–1500 B.C. and a few were broadly translated by Ezra Pound. Many resemble the "Song of Songs": "If I kiss her and her lips are open, I am happy without drink." "The dawn breaks through her beauty. Mephis is a dish of love apples set in front of the fair."[22]

THE BOOK OF THE DEAD

The Egyptians fought mortality. If death could not be defeated in life, it could be conquered beyond the grave. First the king and then almost anyone with money and position could escape death and acquire happiness enjoyed by the gods. In order to achieve this, virtue was important, but of even more importance was preservation of the body. From the pyramids to simple tombs, a whole industry developed in Egypt to build tombs which would insure body protection. Beyond that, the dead relied on the living to make needed offerings and libations to insure continued life in the tomb. And this, in turn, explains The Book of the Dead (Fig. 6).

The Book of the Dead (better translated as "Chapters of coming forth by day") is by far the most famous extant Egyptian work, and can claim to be the first fully illustrated book. It takes numerous forms from about 3000 B.C. to near 1000 B.C., but whether a text engraved on a pyramid or a mummy coffin or a papyrus roll, it served the purpose of assuring the dead a safe passage which, through magic spells, gave them eternal life, even to the point of being at times able to return to earth. The best versions are from the 18th and 19th dynasties (c. 1560–1320 B.C.) with superb hieroglyphics and fine illustrations of gods and demons. Then mass production set in, and as more and more of the guides were copied, one from the other, errors crept into the text and the pictures became increasingly crude. Cheaper editions, and these became numerous, had few if any illustrations.

The book trade virtually was nonexistent in the Near East, where the wandering bard or the official equivalent of a town crier passed prose and promulgations to persons on streets and farms. It

6. Book of the Dead. A typical illustration where the priests are performing the standard rites to insure speech of the dead in the next world.

is true that Books of the Dead were sold to what would be equivalent to upper-middle-class Egyptians, but a single, religious work hardly consists of a trade.

The Book offers a complex version of the path of the dead and the afterlife. An important judge is the ibis-headed god of the scribes, Thoth, who records the life of the deceased and presents the evidence to Osiris and 42 judges. With modesty, Thoth often says in Books of the Dead, ''I am Thoth the perfect scribe, whose hands are pure, who opposed every evil deed, who writes down justice and who hates wrong.'' Suffice to say, the Book of the Dead never records someone who did not pass the tests . . . particularly as that individual, whose stereotypical portrait often appears at the opening, paid a considerable sum for the work. There are numerous familiar figures, from the ''ferryman'' who takes the dead across a body of water separating sky and earth, to formulations of one's goodness such as: ''I gave bread to the hungry, clothes to the naked. . . . I respect my father, I pleased my mother.''

The illustrations were presumably drawn by an artist before the scribe wrote the text. In most instances the pictures formed a border that ran the entire length of the roll above the text. Their artistic value varied greatly, but all exhibited the stylistic features so well known in Egyptian relief carvings. A few Books of the Dead had colored illustrations or other special treatments. These were presumably intended for persons who had been very prominent or very wealthy. The ordinary man had to be content with smaller and more modest productions.[23]

Earlier Egyptian wall paintings, coffin texts and similar efforts to spin the same protection as offered by The Book of the Dead give the earliest examples of illustration. Even here, illustration is reductive of complex, cultural ideas. Contemporary explanations, for example, of the illustrations in The Book of the Dead fail to capture the emotional overtones the drawing had for both the literate and the illiterate. The bas reliefs on Ashurbanipal's palace seems clear enough, but, again, a modern viewer has no real idea of their impressions on Assyrians.

Drawings, too, help to support arguments, if not always resolve them. For example, a drawing on an incense burner dated about 3100 B.C., or possibly earlier, in Nubia (what is now about a thousand-mile-long area from Aswan, Egypt along the Nile to Khartoum in the Sudan), shows Egyptian motifs. Combined with other evidence, it is clear that Nubia had its own civilization and was not simply an upriver land used by Rameses II in the thirteenth century B.C. to gather slaves. Whether or not Egypt was a black society with Nubian roots is a matter of current debate, particularly as numerous African and African-American scholars support this Afrocentrist view; e.g., see Martin Bernal's projected four-volume work, *Black Athena*.[24]

TRANSMISSION OF TEXTS[25]

A never ending problem, with few specific solutions is suggested by the question: "How reliable are ancient manuscripts?" Some preserved archival cuneiform and Egyptian work is original, although almost all of the limited literature represents a copy of a copy of a copy, etc. The Hebrews often buried original texts, but much of the glory of Greek literature is second-hand, from quotations and commentaries by Romans and early Christians. Only fragments of most original Greek works are available, the earliest being c. 460–400 B.C.

Most ancient literature is far removed, often by a millennium or more, from the original written or oral transmission. As the process of copying went on, from the Egyptians to the Greeks to the Romans to the scriptoria of medieval monasteries to the sixteenth century publisher, corruptions were introduced at every stage. The problems are fearful. Between scholarly research, great guesses and brilliant discoveries, an accepted notion of the true text has been confirmed or dismissed or modified. Today we have at least a nearly correct version of many landmarks in the history of the book.

THE BIBLE/THE OLD TESTAMENT

The Bible is a good example of transmission of text. It is uncertain who recorded from the oral tradition the early versions of the Old Testament or Scripture. From the first stage of manuscript transmission of the Old Testament text, the material available indicated a wide variety of traditions which had to be resolved in the final codification. Beyond that, there is the recurrent problem of translating from the Hebrew to the Greek to Latin to the vernacular. The 1611 A.D. King James Version is a standard text for Protestants, but in 1952 there was a Revised Standard Version, and in 1990 a New Revised Standard Version which drew on recent research into the Dead Sea Scrolls. There was, though, some tampering with the masculine idiom, and masculine renderings not referring to the deity have been eliminated, especially where translators felt the intent of the original Hebrew or Greek was more inclusive. For example, ''Man does not live by bread alone'' (Matthew 4:4) becomes ''One does not live by bread alone.''

The Torah, or first five Old Testament books, known in Greek as Pentateuch (meaning five scrolls), are traditionally the work of Moses and became established canon with the prophet Ezra in 450 B.C. Historical research gives other explanations, usually a combination of sources, from circa 1200 B.C. or about the time of the Exodus from Egypt.[26]

Some Biblical stories draw on the oral culture of the Israelites as well as the Sumerians and other Near Eastern neighbors. The story of the flood was adopted by an Old Testament scribe in the eight to sixth century B.C. from the first great Sumerian epic poem, *Gilgamesh.* Sir Leonard Woolley, among others, believes the tale may go back even before 3000 B.C. Extant cuneiform tablets of the epic are copies from about 650 B.C. The exuberant figure of Gilgamesh is found on cylinder seals as early as 2400 B.C.[27]

Piecing together the flood story entails setting the approximate first oral recitals of Gilgamesh. Prior to writing, prior to scribes and well into the twentieth century, the oral tradition functioned as a bridge between literature, religion and myth. Instead of referring to cuneiform tablets, hieroglyphs or, later, books, people turned to bards or reciters of historical tradition. From Gilgamesh to Homer to the sages of Iceland, groups of people relied on oral communication. Narrators with enormous repertoires still are found in Scotland, Ireland and many other parts of the world, including Yugoslavia.[28]

Part divine and part human, Gilgamesh goes through a series of adventures culminating in an effort to find a method of escaping death. Rilke, as many others, consider it the supreme literary contribution of the ancient world before Homer. Henry Moore once described it as having simplicity and bigness without decoration. The Old Babylonian version tells the epic with simple, direct phrases which grip the modern person as it must have the early settlers of Mesopotamia. The message is that life is harsh and there is no way to escape death, but at least one may live with dignity and courage. Gilgamesh is told to ''fill your belly, day and night be merry, and let every day be full of joy.''[29]

Other Bible sections are reflected in even earlier Near Eastern works of literature. The Book of Job, for example, is a version of ''The poem of the righteous sufferer,'' which probably was recited as early as 3500 B.C. The Babylonians, too, had their own version of Ecclesiastes. Nevertheless, the Old Testament is a unique document and primarily the history of the Israelites—the first history which moves forward rather than in cycles. From Abraham, the first Hebrew patriarch to leave Sumeria (c. 2100 B.C.), to Canann and the Exodus (c. 1300–1200 B.C.), it is a record of movement towards a goal. The Sumerians, to the Greeks, tended to hold cyclical views concerning time and history. Aristotle believed arts and science had been discovered many times and then lost. A world in decline might turn again to a world of prosperity. The Jews, conversely, believed the linear concept based on a teleological idea of history as the revelation of God's purpose.

The by now famous Dead Sea Scrolls (c. 299–99 B.C.), discovered in 1947, offer evidence to support the present version of the Bible.[30] Comparing the Essenes' version of scriptures, which were hidden in c. 68 A.D. to protect them from the Romans, one finds they have not radically changed in 2,000 years. Written in Aramaic script, all books of earlier Hebrew scripture are present [except Esther] and are not significantly different than the Septuagint version.

Legend is that from 285 to 246 B.C., 70 or 72 translators (hence Septuagint) at the Library in Alexandria translated the first five books of the Old Testament into Greek directly from Hebrew original manuscripts. There is no extant copy of this version of the Old Testament, and there is continuing debate as to which Hebrew version may have been used.

By 230 A.D. the early Christian Father, Origen, compiled his Hexapla (six-fold [text] Bible based on the Septuagint). Here he offered Hebrew and, in parallel columns, the Hebrew in Greek letters, the Greek translation of an earlier Biblical version, and the Septuagint. Only fragments of the resulting hand-written book exist today. Drawing upon this work, Saint Jerome translated into Latin the Old Testament of the Septuagint in the last decade of the fourth-century.

The earliest extant Old Testament is the fourth century A.D. Vaticanus copy. The oldest fragment of the New Testament is a few lines from the book of John, dated c. 120–130 A.D., or written about 50 years after the production of the Gospel. The fourth century Codex Sinaiticus, discovered in 1859 at a monastery at the foot of Mt. Sinai, is the earliest, complete version of the New Testament.[31]

While there is no reliable history of how the Bible received its formal, official status, the earliest extant Hebrew Bible Codex was not established until 895 A.D., or some 400 years after St. Jerome (d. 419–420 A.D.) completed the Vulgate Latin translations of the Bible based on the Septuagint and the early Church Fathers. Over the centuries, some 8,000 surviving manuscripts of the Bible show its changes and modifications. The printed authoritative Catholic version of the New Testament was published in 1516 by Aldus after an edition edited by Erasmus. This, in turn, became the basis of the King James or Authorized Version of the Bible in England, published in 1611.[32]

BEYOND THE NEAR EAST

Until the Greek alphabet made its way into Europe, there was no written language, although pictographs are evident throughout the area. Rock paintings with pictographs are found throughout the world, and this first stage of writing was found in Brazil 11,000 to as much as 30,000 years ago. There is a scholarly debate over the origin of the Indo-European languages themselves. One group believes the Proto-Indo-Europeans originated in the region north of the Black Sea about the fourth or fifth millennium. Another theory is that the origin was in the fifth millennium in what is now Turkey, or Anatolia. Linguistic and archaeological evidence is so thin and scattered that arguments based on both or one may be made for all theories of origin.

At the time of writing in the Near East, Western Europe was a cultural wilderness. If one may look to the scribe as typical of Near Eastern interest in writing, a more typical figure in Europe would be the nomadic hunter. One member of this Indo-European group had an accident about 2000 B.C. His body was found in 1991 in the ice of the Tirolean Alps. He wore weatherproof clothing of leather and fur, lined with hay. On his back was wood packboard, and a leather pouch with a fire flint, a knife and an axe with a bronze head attached to a cleft shaft.[33]

It is difficult to make any comparison between this hunter and the dim portrait we have of the average Near Eastern scribe. They literally and figuratively were in two different worlds—one matching wits with the environment, the other with the ruling classes. Just as the Alps put an end to one European's life, so did the alphabet in a much less dramatic form, and over a considerably longer period, end the power, if not the life, of the scribe. A broader set of intellectuals now were literate. Again, though, the ubiquitous, illiterate "everyperson" is generally lost to history.

It makes no sense to try to rank who gave the most to the

development of writing and literature before the Greeks. Historians lack the scales of comparison, particularly if China and Asia are considered along with the remainder of the world. There were advances and declines within each culture. Progress in writing seemed to span divergent and sometimes foreign traditions to culminate, at least in the West, with the alphabet.

NOTES

[1]Richard Leakey and Roger Lewin. *Origins Reconsidered* (New York: Doubleday, 1992). There are massive arguments about the time frame of the origin of people, and here one has an excellent, if biased overview of evolution in terms of new discoveries.

[2]A charming idea among a few archaeologists is that the first settlements were to grow grain in order to brew beer, circa 9000 to 8000 B.C. Some think people may have begun to make beer as soon as, or even before, they domesticated barley in the early transition to agriculture in Mesopotamia. Sumerians were brewers by 3500 B.C. See: "Jar in Iranian Ruins . . . ," *The New York Times,* November 5, 1992, p. A16.

[3]Denise Schmandt-Besserat. *Before Writing.* 2 vols. (Austin: University of Texas, 1992). [For a summary see the author's article, "Reckoning Before Writing," in *Archaeology,* May/June, 1979.] An examination of some 7,000 small baked clay tokens, ranging in date from 15,000 to 3000 B.C. indicates the beginnings of writing considerably before the earliest records on solid tablets of clay around 3000 B.C. Mesopotamian stamp seals, often with images of wild animals, go back to the sixth millennium. See Holly Pittman, *Ancient Art in Miniature* (New York: Metropolitan Museum of Art, 1987). See also: Alexander Marshack, *The Roots of Civilization* (New York: Macmillan, 1972). This is now by way of a classic and shows how cave people may have used writing much earlier than suspected.

[4]Rick Weiss, "Dragon Bones to Data Bases," *Whole Earth Review,* Winter, 1987, pp. 10–13. The number of characters in Chinese accounts for the drive to simplify. "There is no possible way to work quickly on a [computer] keyboard that requires a minimum of 5,000 keys." *The Economist* (August 19, 1989, p. 54) noted that Japanese are slow to use computers because executives have a tradition of hand-written communication instead of typing "because (Japanese) requires 7,000 ideographs plus two sets of more than 50 phonetic characters."

[5]Homer. *The Iliad.* Loeb Classical Library, Vol. 1, p. 275 (i.e. 6/168–9): ". . . he sent him a Lycia, and gave him baneful tokens,

graving in a folded tablet many signs and deadly.'' (This probably was a tablet. See footnote No. 12). This is the only passage in Homer which suggests knowledge of writing. See: G.S. Kirk, *The Songs of Homer* Cambridge: Cambridge University Press, 1962).

[6]The scratched-on inscription is on the shoulder Dipylon prize jug (Athens, National Museum). The writing may have been made later than 730 or 725, but appears to be contemporary with the decoration. The relationship between Greek art, and particularly Greek vases, and writing is an important interaction. The iconography demonstrates, as well, what well may have been the interest of now lost illustrated papyrus rolls of the period. Martin Bernal. *Cadmean Letters: The Transmission of the Alphabet to the Aegean and Further West Before 1400 B.C.* (New York: Eisenbrauns, 1991). There is debate as to when the Greek alphabet took form and where it originated. Bernal argues that the alphabet was invented in the early Bronze Age, as early as 1800 B.C., or about 1,000 years before, most believe. Bernal's book is one of many on the subject. See, too, the tangential, yet important aspect of the same argument in Homer and the tradition of oral composition. A summary of the various points of view will be found in an excellent overview article by Hugh Lloyd-Jones, "Becoming Homer," in *The New York Review of Books,* March 6, 1992. There are numerous books on the history of writing. Some of the more basic include: David Diringer, *Writing* (New York: Praeger, 1962); Robert K. Logan, *The Alphabet Effect* (New York: William Morrow, 1986)—subtitle: "The impact of the phonetic alphabet on the development of western civilization"; Wayne Senner, ed., *The Origins of Writing* (Lincoln: University of Nebraska Press, 1989); I.J. Gelb, *A Study of Writing* (Chicago: University of Chicago Press, 1952); Stanley Morison, *Politics and Script* (Oxford, Clarendon Press, 1972)— This covers the subject from the development of Graeco-Latin Script until the twentieth century; Oscar Ogg, *The 26 Letters* (New York: Crowell, 1961); Jan Best and Fred Woudhuizen, *Ancient Scripts from Crete and Cyprus* (Leiden: Brill, 1988. Edward Chiera, *They Wrote on Clay,* George G. Cameron, ed., rev. 1938 ed. (Chicago: University of Chicago Press, 1969); Donald Jackson, *Story of Writing* (New York: Taplinger, 1981).

[7]The narrative subject matter of the François vase (Florence, Archaeological Museum), by the painter Kleitias, is a mythical encyclopedia and/or the illustration of an oral work by the early sixth-century lyric poet Stesichoros. See Andrew Stewart, "Stesichoros and the François Vase," *in* Warren G. Moon, ed., *Ancient Greek Art and Iconography* (Madison: University of Wisconsin Press, 1983).

[8]Monumental and legal and dedicatory inscriptions were written on stone, metal, glass and ivory. See, for example, the numerous stone

statutes of Gudea, ruler of Lagash (2141–2122), which frequently are inscribed; and the law code of Hammurabi of Babylon (c. 1792–50 B.C.) or (c. 1728–1686 B.C.). Dates uncertain.

[9]Samuel Kramer. *In the World of Sumer* (Detroit: Wayne State University Press, 1986), the autobiography of the outstanding scholar of Sumer and Mesopotamia and cuneiform. Along the way he describes much of his work, past and present, and adds new details to his basic contributions, e.g. *The Sumerians,* 1963; *Sumerian Mythology,* 1944. Written in the cuneiform script, Akkadian contained about 600 word and syllable signs. Except for sacred literature, which continued to be written in Sumerian, Akkadian was the lingua franca of the Near East, although by the ninth century B.C. it gradually gave way to Babylonian and then Aramaic, the probable root of the Greek/Roman alphabet as well as the ancestor of modern Hebrew. Note, too, Akkadian is a sub-branch of the Semitic family.

[10]Decipherment took place over a much longer period by many people, and the total story of "cracking" hieroglyphics rivals any spy code yarn. See, for example, Maurice Pope, *The Story of Decipherment* (London, 1975). Another little discussed aspect of this concerns fakes of cuneiform and hieroglyphics for Western collectors. See "Fakes," in J.T. Hooker, ed. *Reading the Past* (London: British Museum, 1990).

[11]The cartouches (i.e. name rings of dead rulers) often were obliterated to insure loss of power and life—or, for more mundane purposes, to appropriate a grave for the use of another. The old name was removed, the new added. Particularly dangerous animals and creatures are not found in Egyptian tombs for fear of their magical efficacy. The Old Testament helps to make the point about the importance of names. It begins with God giving the name "day" to light and with Adam giving "names to all cattle, and to the fowl of the air, and to every beast of the field."

[12]Among common Latin words, exarare (to plow) is one of many metaphors to write in, as, e.g., Cicero in his letters notes, "I have plowed out these letters." In the Vulgate, St. Jerome frequently uses metaphors for wax tablets; e.g., "And I will write on the tables . . . " (Deuteronomy 10/2). However, the tablet here probably was of wood or metal. Jerome simply considered all tablets as wax. See R.H. Rouse and M.A. Rouse, "The Vocabulary of Wax Tablets," *Harvard Library Bulletin,* Fall, 1990.

[13]Miriam Lichtheim, ed. *Ancient Egyptian Literature* (Berkeley: University of California Press, 1975). Pap. ed., vol. 1, pp. 185–191. For information on the education of scribes, see R.J. Williams, "Scribal Training in Ancient Egypt," *Journal of The American Oriental Society,* 1972, pp. 214–21. See, too, M.A. Hussein, *Origins of the Book* (Greenwich, CT: Graphic Society, 1972), subtitled: "Egypt's contribu-

tion to the development of the book from papyrus to codex.'' See, too, Budge; and Jaroslav Czerny, *Paper and Books in Ancient Egypt* (London, 1947).

[14]While there are many images of Egyptian scribes, there only are a few surviving of Mesopotamian scribes, and most of these from a late date. The wall paintings at Til Barsip (c. 700–600 B.C.) show standing scribes writing—apparently in the act of recording booty. Similar scribes are shown on other reliefs, particularly from Nineveh (c. 600 B.C.).

[15]Recent excavations at Tell ed-Der by Belgians revealed an early bibliographer, or more precisely a priest, with over 3,000 tablets in his private library. Correspondence indicates he was to receive several probably looted libraries from Babylonia.

[16]The international correspondence at El-Amarna in Egypt was discovered in 1887 and includes texts on cuneiform tablets from Amenophis III (1417–1389 B.C.) to rulers of Hurrian in the area of the upper Euphrates. The records give an excellent profile of life in both urban and rural areas of the Near East. A local ruler, for example, writes about ill-treatment afforded his envoys. After the usual formalities, which center around property (''May it be well with you and your chariots, soldiers, country, and whatever is yours''), the complaint is fired: Why are the envoys held, ''are my messengers not birds, that fly and come back? Let my brother release my messenger.'' James Pritchard, ed., *The Ancient Near East* (Princeton University Press, 1958). Vol. 1, pp. 262–277.

[17]*Ibid.,* ''The Code of Hammurabi,'' pp. 138–167.

[18]Quotes of Ashurbanipal from D.D. Luckenbill, *Ancient Records of Assyrian and Babylonia* (University of Chicago Press, 1926–7). Vol. 2, p. 986; Pritchard, *op. cit;* Brian M. Fagan, *A Return to Babylon* (Boston: Little Brown, 1979); and Albert Champdor, *Babylon* (New York: G.P. Putnam's Sons, 1958). For the most part, the Assyrian documents are primarily court records, along with notations about astrology, medicine and religion. The selection of hymns and prayers, while important, is minimal. The armies of Assurbanipal, as Byron suggests, decimated the Near East, and the prisoners, such as were not killed, suffered cruelty which is dutifully recorded. Assurbanipal carried Assyria to the edge of its eventual collapse.

[19]Lichtheim, *op. cit.* vol. 1, pp. 211–215. One of the few surviving prose tales from the Middle Kingdom period (c. 2040–1050 B.C.)—the sailor's experiences are as fresh today as they were three or four thousand years ago—this is a reminder of the Sinbad yarns.

[20]*Ibid.,* vol. 2, pp. 90–94.

[21]*Ibid.,* vol. 1, pp. 193–198.

[22]*Ibid.*, vol. 2, pp. 181–193. For a free translation, which may be as much Pound or his fellow translator as Egyptian, see: Ezra Pound and Noel Stock, *Love Poems of Ancient Egypt* (New York: New Directions, 1962). (This is a 33 page pamphlet).
[23]E.A.W. Budge, ed. *The Egyptian Book of the Dead* (New York: Dover, 1967). A reprint of the 1895 edition published by the British Museum, of a decipherment of the hieroglyphics in a 1500 to 1400 B.C. Book of the Dead. The hieroglyphics are printed with the deciphered lines directly beneath. There is a useful 150-page explanatory introduction, the text and then a 152-page free translation of the text. Anyone who wishes to understand both the significance of the world's first illustrated book and the use of hieroglyphics would do well to begin here. See, too, A.J. Spenser, *Death in Ancient Egypt* (London: Penguin Books, 1982), which sets The Book of the Dead in context with funeral customs, including the process of mummification.
[24]For a brief overview, see: "Nubian Treasures Reflect Black Influence on Egypt," *The New York Times,* February 11, 1992, p. C1+.
[25]The problems of text transmission are covered in numerous works. See L.D. Reynolds and N.G. Wilson, *Scribes & Scholars.* 2nd ed. (New York: Oxford University Press, 1974); and R.R. Bolgar, *The Classical Heritage* (Cambridge: Cambridge University Press, 1954).
[26]Ancient Palestine, what is now Israel and surrounding territory, had settlements as early as 3100 B.C., although people were in the area 9000 to 8000 B.C. The Old Testament time of Abraham and the Patriarchs (c. 2000–1200 B.C.) was under the dominance of the Egyptians, although by the end of the period the Israelites, under Moses, had arrived and by 1000 B.C. had established a unified monarchy, which by about 922 B.C., with the death of Solomon, divided into the kingdoms of Israel (in the north) and Judah (in the south). During this time (c. 925–520 B.C.) the Old Testament came into being, and was more or less completed from c. 198–150 B.C. No one really knows who composed or edited the first five books of the Bible—this side of divine voice—and much is written on the subject. One of the more imaginative, and debatable, efforts: Harold Bloom and David Rosenberg, *The Book of J* (New York: Grove, 1991).
[27]Sir Leonard Woolley. *Ur of the Chaldees,* rev. ed. (Ithaca, N.Y.: Cornell University Press, 1982). This and earlier works are an invaluable and fascinating guide to early Sumerian civilization.
[28](I.e., what was Yugoslavia). The classic work in this area of oral transmission is, of course, Milman Parry's. See *The Making of Homeric Verse,* edited by his son, Adam (New York: Oxford University Press, 1971) as well as Albert Lord, *The Singer of Tales* (Cambridge: Harvard University Press, 1960), and Kirk, *op. cit.*

[29]There are several translations of Gilgamesh. See, for example, John Gardiner and John Maier's work (New York: Knopf, 1984) as well as Pritchard, *op. cit.,* vol. 1, pp. 40–75.

[30]The legend is that no Jew in Alexandria could read Hebrew, and Ptolemy II had to send to the 12 tribes for translators, each of whom worked in a separate section of the library and came up with identical translations. The septuagint may mean the 72 translators, the 72 days it took them to translate—or what myth you read. See, too: Robert Eisenman and Michael Wise. *The Dead Sea Scrolls Uncovered* (Shaftesbury (England): Element, 1992). This goes over the controversy of the Scrolls, their wide publication in 1992 and various interpretations. It is one of scores of books on the subject.

An equivalent find for the New Testament is the thirteen Nag Hammadi codices. Dated between the middle of the third and end of the first half of the fourth century A.D., the Gnostic NT version can be compared with the Codex Vaticanus (dating from the fourth century A.D.). The latter was completed by an ortho scribe(s); the former by Gnostics with different ideas about the true NT. For an overview see "The Gnostic Library of Chenoboskion," *Biblical Archaeologist,* March, 1978.

[31]Until the end of the second century the New Testament primarily was memorized and transmitted orally. The question of a canon, of course, was closely related to defining Christianity, and this was more or less settled by the Hexapla. The Sinaiticus contains the Old Testament, but parts are missing. There are no illustrations. The earliest illustrated Biblical manuscript is a fragment from a fifth- to sixth-century Book of Genesis, known as the Cotton Genesis after the name of the owner, and in the British Museum. The succession of different aspects of the Flood story and Noah gave a notion of the style of early, but now lost Christian illustration.

[32]Actually, the King James version is very widely based on William Tyndale's translation of 1525. In 1992 long overdue acknowledgment to Tyndale was given in the publication of his Old Testament, edited by David Daniel (New Haven, CT: Yale University Press). This brief discussion only hints at the thousands of volumes available on the subject as well as various interpretations of origin, literary and/or divine narrative, analyses of historical import, etc. A relatively current work covering much of this is by Robin Lane Fox, *The Unauthorized Version: Truth and Fiction in the Bible* (New York: Viking, 1992). A suggestion of the amount of comment can be found in Mark Powell, *The Bible and Modern Library Criticism* (Westport, CT: Greenwood Press, 1992). Over 1,700 items are listed and annotated.

[33]Much has been written about the discovery and at least one television documentary on it was produced by PBS in 1992. For a quick summary, see: "Man in Glacier . . . ," *The New York Times,* July 21, 1992, p. C1+.

CHAPTER TWO

GREECE: THE CLASSICAL HERITAGE

> I [Prometheus] invented for them the combining of letters,
> creative mother of the Muses' arts, wherewith to hold all
> things in memory.
> —Aeschylus, *Prometheus Bound* (460–461)

Classical antiquity, from the fifth century B.C. to the first century A.D., introduced the world to the full implications of an alphabet, writing, recorded literature, and the concept of scholarly libraries. At the Alexandria library the poet Callimachus compiled the first catalog (his Pinakes), and here the world's books were gathered for study. As Callimachus' most celebrated Pinakes indicated, the library of the Museum of Alexandria included everything from Homeric manuscripts to cookbooks, and, yes, probably the poet's elegiac poem, the *Aetia,* where he pays a tribute to writing: "on your bark may you bear so many carved letters as will say that Cydippe is beautiful."

Inextricably bound up with what we know as modern civilization, Greek literary and philosophical writing is a central principle of our humanity and views of government and individuals. Blended into Jewish and Christian ideas, Greek thought, from Homer to Hellenism, is a way of life. The alphabet and writing were active in bringing Greek thought down through the ages. Writing assumed a marked role in forming Greek society and later Western democracy.

The rapid diffusion of the alphabet is a major explanation why literacy in Greece was never limited to a minority group of scribes. Writing spread too quickly to afford any narrow specialists a monopoly. The variety of early writing subject matter (from laws and lists to owners' names on vases), among other evidence, presupposes that a number of people were able to write and to read. With the spread of writing, several social changes came about. Traditional notions of the group gave way to the idea of the individual who could express thoughts in writing and, most important, over time modify and change the ideas. The Greeks effectively destroyed the joint hammerlock the scribes and the ruling class had on culture and government by making it theoretically possible for every male (if not woman) to read, and to come to considered conclusions. Once it was possible to record other than official thought, language could be used to question, to challenge, and indeed, to introduce not only the idea and importance of the individual but the parallel political framework of democracy.[1] Writing became not only what it had been before, i.e. a symbol of permanence, but a tool for independent, abstract exploration of self and society. Literacy was the first and most effective blow against absolute governments, which dominated the Middle East for over 3,000 years.

Analysis of recorded views became possible, as did the concept of history and philosophy which depend on a cumulation of preserved observations. No longer a slave to memory, Herodotus (c. 484–425 B.C.) spun out a lengthy narrative in his fifth century *Histories* which not only listed, but explained. He apparently soon captured a relatively wide audience—a nucleus of people who earlier might have gathered to hear and participate in the recitation of the *Iliad*. The inability to read cut off a majority who had enjoyed the recitation. Actually, to be sure, story tellers and oral communication continued well into the nineteenth century A.D., but at least writing for more than scribes guaranteed a major way of preserving the past. The literate could appreciate a historian who told stories and in so doing combined the oral with the written. Thucydides (c. 470–400 B.C.) would write his history with a full knowledge that it would be read. His *History of the Peloponnesian War* (c. 411 B.C.) was the first Greek work to show the full influence of writing.

LITERACY AMONG GREEKS[2]

Arguments are waged by scholars about the number of people who were able to read and write at any period in history. There is little disagreement that mass literacy is a phenomenon of the modern world alone. Elementary education, cheap reading matter and free libraries must be present. With all of that, the United States in the early 1990s had from one to 25 per cent of the population deemed illiterate—depending on who gave the figures and the definition of literacy. There is a consensus about Greek literacy: (1) When the oral tradition dominated, when the alphabet had not spread widely, a small group of scribes (as in Near Eastern countries) were in command of writing and reading. (2) With the spread of the alphabet and an easy writing/reading method, literacy developed among the male population, at least by the fourth or fifth centuries. (3) Literacy was limited to males, rarely shared by women. (4) Literacy was used for a great range of activities, from government to poetry to voting. (5) Widespread education, again of males, was common from the fifth century B.C. (6) Despite the significant rate of literacy, the majority continued to rely on the oral culture.

An increasing amount of mundane correspondence and letters during the Hellenic Greek period indicates the scope of literacy. The literate might include educated slaves. No one thought it strange that by 300 B.C. an Athenian merchant was exchanging correspondence with a slave about trade.

One illustration of the problems which arise when one attempts to establish the number of literate people in Greece can be found in the often cited case of ostracism. The term is derived from bits of pottery, or ostrakon, upon which many voted. The shards were used as we might use note paper or scraps of stationery. Instituted in early 508 B.C., ostracism was a peculiar Athenian practice. If 6,000 of probably about 100,000 residents of Attica voted in the affirmative—indicating their vote on the ostraca—any politician could be checked by exile for a given number of years. Ostracism often is used to validate the assumption that many Athenians were literate.[3]

The complex relationship of literacy, writing and the development of Greek, or more properly Athenian, democracy may be said to have begun when Solon (c. 640–559 B.C.) posted the new Athenian constitution and laws of large wooden tablets for all to read. At the same time the sixth-century lawmaker relied on recitation to back up and explain the written laws. The idea of posting laws and legislative decisions continued, and while it was understood that not everyone could read the inscriptions, at least the public postings were an invitation to all to become literate.

The theory that society was open to anyone who could read and write would have been unimaginable in Middle Eastern cultures, where writing was controlled by scribes and their masters. Literacy and writing in Greece became symbols of democracy, of freedom. They would remain so into our time, and most likely well into the future.

WRITING VS. MEMORY[4]

Neither Homer (c. Ninth century B.C.) nor Hesiod (c. Eighth century B.C.) considered writing important, and before the general introduction of the alphabet and the easy mastery of reading and writing, the Greeks had developed an impressive oral literature. Texts were passed from generation to generation by sophisticated methods which insured accurate recital from memory. While the verbal authority of the speaker was a major factor, it must be remembered that the audience equally knew much of the verse and were similarly involved in memorization. A banal example in our time is the movie, ''The Rocky Horror Picture Show.'' By the 1970s it was a cult film which students, otherwise unable to memorize lessons, knew word for word, and they could accompany the actors in the script from beginning to end with raucous shouts of the actors' words.

Plato (427–347 B.C.) who looked to writing and publishing to preserve his ideas, took a skeptical view of the delights of writing. He thought it would destroy memory, the same memory that kept alive Homeric verse. In *Phaedrus* (c. 360) the philosopher observes that writing ''will produce forgetfulness in the minds of those who learn it, by causing them to neglect their memory. . . . Acquiring [by writing] much information unaided by instruction, they will appear to possess much knowledge, while, in fact, they will, for the most part, know nothing at all.''[5] The argument is too easy. Modern research indicates that memory does not suffer, at least in the short run, from being literate; and in non-literate cultures the memory of the usual individual may be no better or worse than in a literate society. Memory feats tend to be obscured by exaggeration and specific cases. There is no empirical evidence that literacy necessarily destroys memory. From the Greeks onward, the better educated, the elite continued to have a strong oral component, based on memory, as well as a command of reading and writing.

The notion that the spread of literacy might have a negative effect seems limited to a few—and ironically, to the few who could read. Many Greeks felt the problem with writing was that it opened the door for duplicity. Aeschylus thought a written message might be obscure, and both Herodotus and Thucydides gave examples of the deceptive possibilities of writing.

The hostility towards writing, or certain types of writing, was shared by the leading Greek intellectuals of the fourth century. Perhaps this was due to the notion of a past golden age, without writing. Christians would overcome the academic argument against writing by claiming that the book was not an invention of man, but part of the natural law given man by God. As the Hebrews, the Christians considered the book revealed divine wisdom.

Actually, the oral and the written are interdependent. Today this can easily be demonstrated by the pragmatic use of radio and television by advertisers who also use written newspaper and magazine copy. Less mundane, the sophisticated Athenian plays of the fifth century made the same point. They were usually performed only once from the playwright's written script, and the audience had no opportunity to read the play before or after. Nevertheless they grasped the subtle meanings, particularly the association between morality, rhetoric and politics which might be considered in the play. Plato challenged the results, pointing out that reason gave way before emotion when someone saw a well-acted, well-scripted play and was moved by the actors. It is supposed, although never decisively proven, that many of the plays did find their way into papyrus rolls for sale and for reading by the better-off middle class and aristocracy.

Most extant evidence powerfully demonstrated that the oral tradition dominated during most of Greek history. For example, the symposium was a favorite method of passing time for men. Reclining on couches at banquets, the men had elaborate poetic and verbal contests. This continuation of the oral tradition is captured in both black figure and red figure kraters (mixing bowls) from which the talkers were served wine. The picture of mythical figures and aristocratic Greeks reclining in couches around the rooms are as common as bits of Greek verse and phrases on the vases. When archaic aristocrats wished to recall the joys of life in death, they had themselves shown at a symposium, often with verse explaining the funeral bier of a dead hero: "Then he will lie in the deep rooted dark and share no more in the banquet, the lyre or the sweet cry of flutes."[6]

By the end of the sixth century writing had broadened to cover many literary, religious and political functions. Still, the written word hardly involved most Greeks who depended on the oral tradition for communication. Then, as later, it was only among the highly educated that the written word was important. The elite, ruling culture, although broader than in the Near East, was still a minority removed from the grueling year-round work of labor. Here and there one finds the lot of the unsung majority as in Hesiod's *Works and Days,* which is not only a history of the Greeks before c. 700 B.C., but says much about the peasants who "strip down to sow, and strip for plowing".

THE BEGINNINGS OF GREEK LITERATURE

From the seventh century B.C., the development of the relatively democratic city-state was paralleled by a better educated public and an attempt at literacy for at least the middle-class males. The center of the activity was Athens, where, by the fifth century B.C., the foundation of modern physics, chemistry, politics, literature and government was established.

Greek literature opens in a recorded form with Homer, but actually goes back to the first millennium B.C., if not earlier, and evidence of this is found in the deciphered Linear B writing from Crete and mainland Greece, i.e., Mycenae.[7] Homer and Hesiod mixed myth, religion, and imagination in oral accounts of pre-classical battles, Gods and work. Intermingling the present with the myths of the Mycenaen age, Homer gave the pre-classical epic its form, as did Hesiod more didactic work, about 100 years later.

From Archilochus of Paros in the seventh century to Alcaeus and Sappho a century later, the themes and style of Greek poetry were established (Fig. 7). Their successors in the fifth and fourth centuries' classical period gave the world not only poetry, but

7. This is possibly Sappho reading her own poems from a papyrus roll. The muse is off to the right. (From an Athenian vase of c. fifth century B.C.)

drama and philosophy. The greatest dramatists of all time (from Aeschylus and Sophocles to Euripedes and Aristophanes) flourished then, as did Plato and Aristotle, who introduced Alexander the Great to the Greek tradition and who, in turn, heralded in the Hellenistic period from the fourth to the end of the first century B.C.

THE EDUCATED GREEK

There is no record of the earliest Greek educational methods, but by the time of the Persian Wars (c. 492–449 B.C.) there were schools in Athens. From early youth, the typical Athenian male entered a school of gymnastics which combined both sport and poetry, sung or recited, as a method of teaching the wise and the good life, as well as literacy. One has to turn only to Solon and his sixth-century elegies to find the moral and ethical foundation of the collective Athenian educational system. He urged strongly that to be free, people had to be literate, and he urged fathers to teach sons (if not daughters) reading and writing. Homer, if only by implication, insisted that the superior warrior had to have a command both of arms and of words which shaped the formal, moving speeches of the fighting men.

By the time of Socrates (c. 470–399 B.C.) schools had developed and become normal for the upper classes. The earliest extant Greek text which addresses education is found in Plato.[8] The ideal city will have, according to Plato, schools for both boys and for girls. He explains and justifies the need for universal literacy of the free population. Aristotle (384–322 B.C.) also recommended compulsory education.

Schools were open to anyone who qualified—that is, who had the necessary funds and leisure to attend. This meant primarily men, but some girls and women were included in the educational process, which was much as today, i.e. from six through about 20 years of age. More often than not a slave was the master of the grades (ages 7 to 14) and here the student learned the alphabet, and then words of one and more syllables. Apparently individual words were taught before the student learned to read a complete text. The same plan was employed to teach writing. Pragmatic advancement in society seemed to be the central concern, and the

Sophists or professional teachers stressed the importance of rhetoric which, in turn, depended upon a thorough understanding of dialectic and humanism. Aristotle focused on practical matters in the lower grades. There was a shift to the theoretical in higher education. His Lyceum was the model followed by other cultures that came under the Hellenistic influence before and after Alexander the Great's conquests between 334 and 323 B.C. The Hellenistic ideas of education governed much of Europe and the Near East until well into the Byzantine period (c. 300–1300 A.D.).

THE BOOK TRADE[9]

Education was expensive, made more so by the cost of books, i.e. papyrus rolls. Actually, little is known either about how books were employed in Greek schools and homes or how they were published and distributed. Most is conjecture based on occasional references in extant literature. Plato, in the *Apology* (14:26), has Socrates purchasing a book in the Agora, the Athenian market-place. The title likely resembled the damaged rolls and fragments we have from c. 450 B.C., or the more complete books primarily from the third and second centuries B.C.

There is indirect reference to the existence of publishers in Athens as early as the fifth century B.C., and there was trade in books with the Greek colonies. With the rise of the Alexandrian library (c. 290+ B.C.) the opportunities of the book trade were expanded, partly because the library itself became a large-scale customer and partly because the library made available an outstanding collection of manuscripts from which copies could be made for sale.

While major books were on papyrus—and later on parchment - the cost of the material was so high that most writing, particularly of an ephemeral nature, was confined to wax tablets, ostraca, wooden boards and other inexpensive surfaces. Extant correspondence, poems, plays, etc. often refer to the use of writing tablets, and rarely to papyrus. Some ideas as to the cost of papyrus can be found in the fact that in the year 407 two papyrus rolls were worth seven times as much as a day laborer's wages.

Greek publishers hired scribes (or used slaves) to copy books for publication. This practice was common right up until the fifteenth century and the advent of printing. The all-powerful Near Eastern scribe of centuries past was reduced to a paid employee, if paid at all. Still, the majority of scribes who wrote the literary manuscripts constituted a sizeable professional class with considerable education. They were paid partly by number of lines, presumably of standard length, and partly according to the nature of the text. When the scribe had finished his work the manuscript was proofread either by himself or by an editor, who corrected the errors and might also make critical notations in the margin to clarify the text (the so-called ''scholia'') or insert signs (asterisks, etc.) to call attention to linguistic peculiarities.

Mass production of books to the Greeks, and all the way up to the invention of printing, was a simple matter of a scribe or group of scribes scrupulously copying a previously written text. Until the Greeks, other than the Egyptian production of copies of Book of the Dead, there seemed to be little or no effort to produce multiple copies—understandable in view of the limited literacy. The scribe might follow the text with his eyes, or someone might dictate what was to be copied. The eye or the ear depended on the time, the place and the need. If only one copy was required, it was more economical to copy by eye; but if many were required it was faster for someone to read and have a dozen or more scribes transcribe. In most situations visual copying and copying from dictation were done simultaneously. Generalizations are impossible for lack of any real evidence. Individual manuscripts must be studied individually, and even then one can't be sure of the method. The room for error is evident regardless of what method of copying was employed. Booksellers apparently proofread the material, but, as today, they could be quite indifferent to major and minor errors.

WRITING PRACTICES

The instrument for writing literary works was a thick hollow reed stalk, cut to form a pointed pen. Only capital letters were used (the small Greek letters did not evolve until the Middle Ages). The script was a formal type of calligraphy which the scribes were taught, but each scribe developed individual characteristics in his writing. For ordinary daily use there was a more rapid cursive script with less definite lines and with combined letters. About four-fifths of the papyri that we have [mainly public and private documents and letters] are in cursive script.

Following the Phoenicians, from whom they borrowed the alphabet, the Greeks at first wrote from right to left (a practice employed today in Hebrew and Arabic). Vase painters often wrote in either direction on the same vase. This writing of alternate lines in opposite directions became known as *boustrophedon.* The scribe writing, say, from right to left reached the edge of the document or inscription and simply, as a farmer plowing with an ox, went in another direction, i.e. left to right—and then right to left, etc. Furthermore, there was no punctuation. The Romans did write in one direction, but they ran words together. The joined-up writing (scriptio continua) required the judgment of readers to understand. The context of the words in a given type of communication—from literature and law to poetry and business—gave important clues which, with practice, made it relatively easy. Remember, too, that in Greece and in Rome (where the practice of no punctuation continued) the readers were mostly a social elite or trained scribes.

The lack of punctuation explains, in part, why reading aloud continued into the Middle Ages and beyond. There was no need for minimal punctuation in that the reader was, literally, conversing with the listeners and/or him or herself. The text alone was meaningful and neither the author nor the editor-publisher, via punctuation, could control how it was to be read, where emphasis was to be placed, etc.[10]

The papyrus book roll, by 350 B.C., followed a more or less standard format. Briefly: (1) Writing was from left to right; the text was in tall, narrow columns (sometimes with no more than eight to twelve letters per line). The back of the roll tended to be blank, although in some cases where space was precious (e.g. the 160 rolls of Pliny's notebooks) the back would also be used. (2) There was no punctuation and words ran into one another. When punctuation was introduced there was some separation between sentences and sections, indicated by a mark. Lacking proper punctuation, texts were written without word division and without accents. Changes of speakers in dramatic texts were not indicated; and lyric verse often was written as if it were prose. (3) Usually no more than 70 of what would today be printed pages could fit on a cumbersome 20- to 22-foot long papyrus roll.

Location of papyrus rolls was assisted by tags, usually affixed to the rolls to identify their contents. Rolls might be stored, when several were needed for one book, vertically in boxes (capsas). The scribes, in transferring the material from roll to codex, copied what was found in individual capsas, then moved on to another box. The format made it nearly impossible to insure cross references, proper indexing and the like, with the result that many scholars relied primarily on the beginning of a roll for quotes.

No complete Greek roll has been preserved. The amount of papyrus used by the Greek publishers and later by the Romans must have been considerable. A number of varieties, or brands, came on the market, some named for Roman emperors (charta Augusta, Claudia, etc.). In the later Roman Empire factories were established in Rome to make papyrus sheets from material imported from Egypt.

It appears likely that the Ptolemies imposed a tax on the exportation of papyrus, and the papyrus trade later became a government monopoly. The top sheet in a bale was called *protocol* and received a sort of official stamp. This monopoly continued even after the Arabs conquered Egypt. Among the oldest Roman papyrus are those from excavations of Herculaneum. About 1800 carbonized rolls were found in this town, which had been destroyed by the eruption of Vesuvius in 79 A.D.

LIBRARIES

The Greeks were the first to cherish written texts other than records of government, trade and religion.[11] By the fourth century B.C. the transcription of plays, poetry and history was seen as a way of gaining not only living fame, but a type of immortality. All of this attitudinal change took from decades to centuries, but it explains in part the Greek interest and involvement with libraries at Alexandria and Pergamum. Until this historical point, archives were important primarily to government, trade and religion; but in no apparent sense as a record *per se* of the past which could be consulted impartially by scholars. The Greek library offered the early idea of scholarship as important in itself as a way to communal and self-knowledge.

Unquestionably archives, if not libraries, existed before classical Greece. Few hints survive of either the extent or the content of the early Greek archives. At Pylos business records were found stored in baskets and in what had been wooden boxes. The Linear B, from about 1550–1200 B.C., is repeated again at Knossos in Crete, along with Linear A; but again, the archives are suggested by all too few remains. During the Greek Dark Ages there are no signs of writing or libraries; but by c. 400 B.C. one finds evidence of extensive archives on the Acropolis. Again, these tend to be laws, minutes of meetings and records. Probably official copies of plays existed for what we consider early copyright.

Libraries were common in all major cities and courts throughout the area conquered by Alexandria, but most were small, personal and of limited interest. The followers of Aristotle had settled in Alexandria and were encouraged to do so by the Ptolemies, who equated culture with the glory of Greece. The supposition is that among these scholars there were some who struck on the idea of a Museum and a library.

THE LIBRARY AT ALEXANDRIA[12]

The Alexandria of the 1990s is a rundown Egyptian port, but the city founded by Alexander the Great in 332 B.C. became the Paris of the Mediterranean, due in part to the presence of the Alexandria Library. Although in an Egyptian community, the library was a Hellenistic institution. The combination university, think tank, foundation and library contained most of the world's books (primarily papyrus scrolls). Little was missing, and the majority of Near Eastern works had been translated into Greek. The largest library in the world (until the eighteenth- to nineteenth-century national libraries) was founded by Ptolemy Soter, one of Alexander's best generals and king from 305 to 285 B.C.

Famous scholars such as Euclid (c. 330–275 B.C.) and Aristophanes (c. 257–180 B.C.) studied and taught there. Working from numerous copies, in many languages, Aristophanes of Byzantium, for example, edited Hesiod and revised and continued the first catalog (the Pinakes of Callimachus). As well, he established the standard texts for many of the Greek classics. Unfortunately, almost all the originals were destroyed, but the influence of the library was such that through quotations, examples and a combination of memory and second-hand copies, the classical tradition came down to us.

The lure of Alexandria was such that it became celebrated in prose and poetry. The Mimes of the Hellenistic poet Herondas (c. third century B.C.) include the story of a young Greek woman who broods over the loss of her lover to the delights of Alexandria. Sitting at home in a Greek city, the young woman imagines that her man in Alexandria has "everything that exists or is made anywhere in the wide world." This includes everything from gold to "the Museum, wine, and in short everything he might desire."[13] Today a young woman or man would list similar temptations, but would they include a library as well?

As sources about the library are scattered, fragmentary and often contradictory it is difficult to suggest an accurate historical account. It is known that the library was located in a Museum (where the muses were worshipped and celebrated by poets, musicians and scholars). The Greek philosopher Timon (d. c. 230 B.C.) described the center succinctly, if not with a touch of envy: "In the populous land of Egypt they breed a race of bookish scribblers who spend their whole lives pecking away in the cage of the Muses."

Enough is known about the early scholar-librarians to make several generalizations. The goal of the librarians was to collect all of the then-known texts, in all languages and from all cultures. This effort at universal bibliography was supported by the rulers, and by both cash and a confiscation program. No ship which entered the port of Alexander, carrying books, was safe from having those titles not already in the library removed.

There is no certainty as to how many books were in the library, but medieval scholars set the number at close to 500,000 papyrus rolls, of which about one-fifth were individual works. In terms of today's book format, the actual texts would consist of from 70,000 to 80,000 specific complete titles.

Distinguished men of letters joined with the first librarian, Eratosthenes (c. 245–214 B.C.), who was equally the father of scientific geography. Dear to the heart of modern librarians, Callimachus (a major third-century B.C. poet) organized a guide and catalog to all branches of Greek literature. His Pinakes (tablets) was a series of 120 books which dutifully listed and arranged ''persons eminent in every branch of learning together with a list of their writings.'' Lost, the Pinakes is known today only by tantalizing fragments.

Homer is a single example of how scholars and librarians at the Alexandria Library saved a text. In most respects Homer's is a remembered world, but the epics as credible history remain in question. The Mycenaean world of the end of the Bronze Age is the one familiar to Agamemnon, if only in broad outline. How accurate it is depends on the now fitful, the now faithful rendition by the poet of a time 400 to 600 years prior to his songs, i.e. c. 1250 B.C. and the time of the Trojan war.

In the early Hellenistic period, the scholar and head of the Alexandria library, Aristarchus of Samothrace (c. 217–145 B.C.), codified the *Iliad* and the *Odyssey* as we know them today.[14]

Under Aristarchus, in the middle of the second century B.C., the definitive version was established by drawing upon the chaotic texts of Homeric manuscripts. The few surviving fragments of Homer from the third and second century B.C. confirm the numerous textual divergences that the library considered.

Aristarchus not only determined the text, but established the number of verses and eliminated spurious repetitions or additions. Passages he considered suspicious, but was uncertain about, he left in the text and dutifully marked. The problem remains how much of the deletion, how much of the change was based on examination of earlier manuscripts and how much came from Aristarchus's judgment. The common idea that at Alexandria the epics were divided into standard units is probably not true. The divisions for oral purposes go back well before written versions.

The library was destroyed partially by the eighth Ptolemy (better known as Potbelly). He expelled the Jews, who made up a majority of scholars, from Alexandria. At the same time he withdrew financial support from the library. The real blow to the institution came with Caesar, Mark Anthony and the harbor fire of 48 B.C. which seems to have destroyed many books, if not the library itself. Those who know G. B. Shaw's play, *Caesar and Cleopatra,* not to mention the later movie, will recall the role of the great fire in moving ahead the play's action.

Gibbon argued that the true end came in 391 A.D. when zealous

Christians emptied the library of what was left of the collection. Others turn to 641 A.D. and Caliph Omar, who allegedly finished the job by using the remaining books to heat the water for 4,000 public baths. Arab or Christian or Egyptian—take your choice, but most is myth and little is likely ever to be known about the ultimate destruction of the library.

Short on cash and long on hope, the Egyptian government has described plans for a new Library of Alexandria. At a gathering in 1990, celebrities signed a plea calling on the world to contribute money to build the library on a site donated by the government. A note of pessimism was sounded by some Egyptians—global warming and other factors may raise the level of the Mediterranean to drown Alexandria in another 50 to 100 years.

OTHER LIBRARIES

Next to the library at Alexandria, the second most famous was at Pergamum (founded c. 175 B.C.) on what is now the Turkish coast. There are several references to the library; e.g. by Strabo the geographer (c. 63 B.C.–21 A.D.) and Pliny the Elder (c. 23–79 A.D.). Pliny notes that Pergamum was among the first places to use parchment for books because Alexandria had cut off the export of papyrus to its rival. Parchment was a writing surface, if only in a limited way, in Egypt and Palestine years before the founding of Pergamum. Another famous story is that Mark Anthony seized 200,000 papyrus rolls from the library when it was overrun by the Romans. Pergamum and its library probably never attained as illustrious a position in the scholarly world of the time as that held by Alexandria and the library there, and it is possible that the Pergamum library was actually incorporated into the Alexandria library by Anthony's gift to Cleopatra. Shipped to Alexandria, the rolls were destroyed in the harbor fire of 48 B.C. The remnants of the library seem to have been disbanded with the Muslim conquest of the area in the seventh century (Fig. 8).

The Pergamum library very likely used the Alexandrian library as a model in matters of organization and cataloging. We have some idea of the library's quarters through excavations. The temple of Athena in Pergamum had four rooms, the innermost of which contained a colossal statue of Athena and was presumably

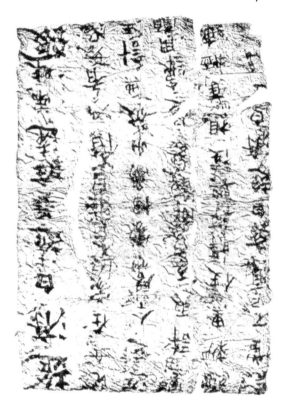

8. Uncial manuscript typical of the fourth century A.D. and of the type found in the ruins of the Alexandria and the Pergamum library. Often the ancient parchment was used for later texts by monks.

a sort of meeting or reception room, while the three adjoining smaller rooms may have been used for books. All four rooms opened into a colonnaded archway—an arrangement that we find in many other library installations of ancient times.

A second century A.D. Latin author, Aulus Gellius, mentions that Pisistraius (600–527 B.C.) established a library in Athens with books in the liberal arts, but the library was carried off to Persia by Xerxes (c. 480 B.C.). Chronicled 600 years after the fact, this is so questionable as to be discounted by historians. There is much conjecture that Plato, Euripides and Aristotle had private libraries. Possibly, the latter's collection—estimated between 700 and 1,000 papyrus rolls—was the heart of the new library at the University at Athens, c. 200 B.C.+. But by the time of the Romans the remnants of Aristotle's library was as much myth as reality. Be that as it may, Aristotle was the first extant writer who made it plain that he consulted other books, i.e. used a library for itself. There are other off-hand references to public and private libraries, but none is reliable.

TRANSMISSION OF GREEK TEXTS

The Western debt to Greece is enormous but the haunting question is how much was lost through the destruction of the library at Alexandria. The casual attitude displayed by later Greeks, Romans and Christians towards the Greek classics equally was harmful. There are no originals of complete classical Greek works. Fragments hint at what was available. The earliest extant papyri include prose commentary and a religious poem c.460–400 B.C. More pieces are found during the Hellenistic period, but it is not until Rome and the Early Christians (c. 50–350 A.D.) that complete books and documents were salvaged. The survivors primarily come from tombs and dumps, particularly in Egypt where the sands and climate preserved the fragile papyrus.

In the transmission of Plato's ideas there is a gap of some 1,000 years between his death, c. 347 B.C., and the first extant copy of his writing in 895 A.D. How much of his writing was lost, and, more important, just how accurate is the work we now have? Is it really his, or the guesses (and the errors) of countless scribes who copied the original work? Another example of what happened to these early manuscripts can be found in Sappho's poetry (c. 600 B.C.). Thanks to the popularity of the first lyric poet, several of her seven books survived into the Byzantine period. Later Christian intolerance, coupled with lack of interest, destroyed most of the seven books. Thus the first Greek poet to elevate love as a value was among the first to disappear in a society dedicated to love.

From time to time there are occasional finds, such as the fragments of about 800 leather book rolls known as the Dead Sea Scrolls, as well as papyri, parchment and even wooden writing tablets from the Euphrates to Roman Britain. Matching and combining these later finds with the earlier known fragments [and the references to classical literature throughout the medieval period] makes it possible partially to reconstruct numerous ancient texts.

Aristarchus' codification of Homer was lost with the dispersion of the library at Alexandria, but in true text transmission form it reappeared. Bits, pieces, whole books were carried in various manuscripts until c. 900 A.D. when the earliest complete written copy surfaced in the Venetus Marcianus.[15] Prior to that there were numerous fragments, and to this day some continue to be found. Among the earliest is the famous *Ambrosianus Iliad* (c. third to fifth century A.D.) which offers tantalizing illustrations and only about 800 lines of Homer.

The *Iliad* and the *Odyssey* generally were not available in Europe until the fourteenth century. To be sure, both works were liberally quoted, and there were copies, but these were few and not well known. A convenient date for the general resurrection and rediscovery of Homer is 1354, when Petrarch (1304–1374 A.D.) acquired a manuscript of the two epics. Unfortunately, Petrarch could not read Greek, and Boccaccio (1313–1375) persuaded another Italian to provide a rough Latin translation which, legend has it, Petrarch was annotating the day he died in 1374. The first printed version was in 1488, but it was years before readers who did not understand Greek or Latin could read Homer in their native languages. The first English version was George Chapman's translation, 1611.

ILLUSTRATIONS[16]

Illustrations probably were usual in papyrus rolls, even though few, and those mainly of a mathematical or similar nature, have been found. In a number of instances a portrait of the author was reproduced, and the suggestion has been made that the columns of Trajan and Marcus Aurelius in Rome are to be interpreted as large-scale reproductions of picture-rolls.

Lacking extant copies of complete or even partial Greek books, a notion of both content and illustration will be found in brief inscriptions on Greek vases (Fig. 9). Combined with painting and

9. A scene from the François Vase (Florence). Made about 570 B.C., the volute-krater shows the type of Attic Black Figure illustrations and the inscriptions identifying figures and explaining the action.

portraits, the few words on vases are often poignant and historically of value. For example, a seventh-century B.C. Corinthian perfume pot neck bears the owner's portrait within an ornamental border of the lovers' names. Vases and other pottery are a constant reminder of what is lost in Greek art and book illustrations.

Although little enough of illustration is extant before the fourth century A.D., hints of what might have been found in papyrus codexes are also found in Roman wall paintings, inscriptions, etc. The problem of time is evident. While today anyone may understand why Noah is found in a boat and Daniel flanked by lions, the rich connotation of extant Roman art, drawn from a lengthy Greek tradition, can't be recaptured unless one turns to parallel writings of the period, and even then the various meanings of the figures, beyond an obvious symbol, are lost.

Only a few rolls with illustrations are known. Among the earliest extant papyrus rolls, a fragment from a first-century B.C. mathematics work shows simple diagrams. The oldest illustrated Greek papyrus known is a second-century B.C. astronomical text. Crudely drawn signs of the zodiac are evident in the text itself. There are a number of codices from the first centuries A.D. with pictorial embellishment, including illustrations which represent the contents of the text or serve as purely decorative designs. The pictures are colored but have practically no shading. The figures and faces are reminiscent of those on monuments, coins or wall paintings. As early as the fourth century A.D. there were Greek and Coptic manuscripts in which the first letter of each section was enlarged and decorated with various flourishes in color, usually red, thus introducing the initial (*initium* = beginning).

NOTES

[1]The Jews and the Greeks are the first to leave us information about individuals other than mythological personalities or those in power. Still, it is an error to equate Greek individuality with the present concepts of individual personalities. From the Jews to Plato and Christianity, as well as up through the Enlightenment, harmony and preservation of the group comes much before individual members. For a summary of this attitude, see Isaiah Berlin, "Giambattista Vico and Cultural History," in his collection of essays, *The Crooked Timber of Humanity* (New York: Knopf, 1991).

The alphabet, or at least the ability of people to write with ease, opened up the road to theoretical thought, offered a framework for conceptual analysis; e.g. Anaximander (611–647) helped in the development of science, and the notion of the cosmos as a geometric structure—an idea spread by writing in centuries to come, and one which could be debated from generation to generation as it was not dependent on oral transmission. For a thorough (and sometimes debatable) discussion of this aspect of the alphabet, see R.K. Logan, *The Alphabet Effect* (New York: Morrow, 1986).

[2]Arguments persist as to the number of Greeks, although by the fifth century B.C. the ability of numerous male citizens to read and to write seems a given. How well they could do either is debatable. By now most in a general way would agree with Oswyn Murray that "in a city like Athens well over half the [free] male population could read and write, and that levels of literacy . . . were higher than in any period in western culture" before the twentieth century (*The Oxford History of the Classical World.* New York: Oxford University Press, 1968, p. 228). At the same time, any assumption that Greek literature reached a popular audience of readers probably is not true. The readership for literature, then as now, was small. While some upper-class women did read, the question remains: in a society which valued liberty, why apparently were

women treated as slaves? Others suggest (see, for example Orlando Patterson, *Freedom*. New York: Basic Books, 1991) they had great power in the family and sufficient rights that they could exercise influence over males. Be that as it may, they remained illiterate.

[3]An indication of problems associated with such "proof" is that a handful of scribes could have written on the ostra for the vast majority of citizens who voted. In one case, an archaeologist noted that 191 ostraca written against Themistocles were inscribed by only 14 hands.

The uses of literacy in government, administration trade and armed forces is a related matter. But here it was used to support well-defined needs, and documents might be written and read by trained slaves as well as literate freemen. This is an important consideration, but, at best, literacy in these circumstances was limited to a few in official or business positions, and hardly included the public at large.

[4]Rosland Thomas. *Oral Tradition and Written Record in Classical Athens* (Cambridge: Cambridge University Press, 1990). She has an extensive bibliography. For an extension into later times: John Foley, *Traditional Oral Epic* (Berkeley: University of California Press, 1991). See, too, Tony M. Lentz, *Orality and Literacy in Hellenic Greece* (Carbondale, IL: Southern Illinois University Press, 1989). The author shows the slow process from communications based primarily upon memory and speech to wide use of the alphabet and the development of literacy. Also: Frederick G. Kenyon, *Books and Readers in Ancient Greece and Rome*. 2nd ed. (Oxford: Clarendon Press, 1951).

[5]Irwin Edman, ed. *The Works of Plato* (New York: Random House [The Modern Library], 1928), p. 323. (274): The words are put in the mouth of Socrates by Plato. (The translation used here is slightly different from the Edman treatment).

[6]Examples, among other places, of symposia on Greek vases will be found in J.D. Beazley, *Greek Vases* (Oxford: Oxford University Press, 1989), pp. 80–81.

[7]J.T. Hooker, ed. *Reading the Past* (London: British Museum, 1990). See "Linear B" by John Chadwick for a discussion of the Mycenaean script as well as background on the whole area before Classical antiquity, including the mystery of "Linear A" of Minoan Crete, which has yet to be deciphered. Incidentally, Chadwick worked with Michael Ventris to decipher "Linear B". There are numerous books on the Mycenaean and Minoan worlds, but one of the best is Emily Vermeule, *Greece in the Bronze Age*. 5th ed. (University of Chicago Press, 1972).

[8]For a brief discussion of Plato's and Aristotle's theories of education, see Michael Grant, ed. *Civilization of Ancient Mediterranean* (New York: Charles Scribner's Sons, 1988), Vol. 2, pp. 1088–1089. In Platon Protagoras (325) he explains that education begins when the boy learns

the letters ''and is beginning to understand what is written, as before he understood only what was spoken.'' He is then taught poetry and music as well as physical education, so that he may not ''be compelled through bodily weakness to play the coward in war or on any other occasion.'' Aristotle divided education into the same branches, but added drawing.

[9]E.G. Turner. *Athenian Books in the Fifth and Fourth Centuries B.C.* (Oxford University Press, 1952). The growth of the book trade in classical Athens, as far as it is known, is given here in detail. See, too, Turner's *Greek Papyri* (Oxford University Press, 1968) and the related *Greek Manuscripts of the Ancient World* (Oxford: Oxford University Press, 1971). The exhaustive, more current work in this field is Robert Pfeiffer, *History of Classical Scholarship,* 2 vols., 1968–1976. The first volume covers material to the end of the Hellenistic Age; the second from about the mid-twelfth century to the mid-nineteenth century.

[10]M.B. Parkes. *Pause and Effect: An Introduction to the History of Punctuation in the West* (London: Scolar, 1992). Scholars in the Alexandria library [and particularly Aristophanes of Byzantium] were among the first to introduce limited punctuation, particularly in editing ancient texts, but it was quite limited. Parkes points out that the early Christians introduced punctuation because a religion of the book was required to firmly establish basic syntax to firm up meaning. For when God is the author, His text must be stable. Punctuation, division of words and sentences followed slowly the Christian lead on the Bible, but most punctuation came only after the advent of printing in the fifteenth century.

[11]Precisely why there should be this universal interest in literature by a people at a given time in history is the subject of countless monographs. Also, there is always the possibility that in past centuries Near Eastern literature existed, flourished and disappeared. Gilgamesh may have been but a single survivor of many in the heroic world before Homer. It is a slippery argument to move from the survival or lack of survival of written documents to the real beliefs and habits of a society. For a discussion of this and numerous other questions see: Charles Beye, *Ancient Greek Literature and Society.* 2nd ed. (Ithaca: Cornell University Press, 1987).

[12]Luciano Canfora. *The Vanished Library* (Berkeley, CA: University of California Press, 1989). An Italian scholar gives a dramatic, discursive history of the ancient library of Alexandria. High points of the story are in the first part, covering from its foundation in the third century B.C. to its destruction c. 640 A.D. The second half considers the reliability of the sources upon which the history is based. Canfora's work was criticized for lack of documentation and a bit too breezy an approach; but it is an ideal introduction for students and lay persons. The facts are offered in

an entertaining and even suspenseful manner. The Library and its scholars represented the great age of scholarship—from about the latter third century to the late second century B.C. For a lively discussion of personalities, academic infighting and the realities of library life (much of which is reflected in today's universities) see Robin Fox, "Hellenistic Culture and Literature," in *The Oxford History of the Classical World* (Oxford: Oxford University Press, 1986). For those who wish more scholarly apparatus, see El-Abbadi, Mostafa, *The Life of the Ancient Library of Alexandria* (Paris: UNESCO, 1990). A case history of the transmission of a text, i.e. Homer, can be found in G.S. Kirk's *The Songs of Homer* (Cambridge: Cambridge University Press, 1962), p. 301+.

[13]Herondas or Herodas offers the only glimpse we have of the life of the average person at Alexandria. The mimes are supposed to be in the language of the people, although wildly exaggerated.

[14]Others, to be sure, contributed to Homeric studies; e.g. Aristophanes of Byzantium (c. 257–180 B.C.) earlier produced a text of Homer as did, later in the first century B.C., Didymus and Aristonicus.

[15]This is known as Iliad A and was discovered in the Marican library at Venice in the eighteenth century. It possibly is a copy of a manuscript from the library of Arethas of Patrae (c. 862–932 A.D.). At any rate the manuscript is not from an Alexandrian copy, but from a near contemporary copy. Comparison of today's Iliad and Odyssey with fragments, quotations, etc., shows little variation from Medieval copies, which seems to indicate that the transmission is relatively accurate. In listings of fragments of Greek literary works, Homer's are by far the most numerous.

For additional information on Greek texts and the transmission of Greek texts, see H.L. Pinner, *The World of Books in Classical Antiquity* (Leiden: A.W. Sijthoff, 1948).

[16]Kurt Weitzmann. *Ancient Book Illumination* (Cambridge: Harvard University Press, 1959). This presents what was known up to 1960 about the use and type of illustrations in classical antiquity. Little evidence has changed the basic findings. See, too, articles and other works by Weitzmann on this subject.

CHAPTER THREE

THE ROMANS TO EARLY CHRISTIANS

> All Rome loves my book:
> It's praised, shops have it;
> And it's in every hand.
> —Martial (*Epigrams,* 60)

Long before the 48 B.C. fire, which may have destroyed many books ready for the Alexandria library, the political glory of Greece was over. Alexander the Great (356–323 B.C.) had conquered the world in the name of Greece, but shortly after his death his empire fell apart. Rome emerged as the great power. By the end of the third century B.C., Rome, one of the earliest of the strong Italian city-states, had gradually expanded over Italy and surrounding regions. Following the third Punic War (140 B.C.), Rome gained mastery of the Mediterranean, including the Middle East, and by 147 B.C. had annexed most of Greece.

Rome would rule the western world for another four hundred or so years. The gradual descent from a popular Republican form of government to the reign of Julius Caesar and his assassination (44 B.C.), to the final ascent of Augustus (27 B.C.), came four centuries before its fall in 410 A.D. The Byzantine empire—established in Constantinople by Constantine in 330 A.D.—divided the empire into East and West. Latin dominated in the West, Greek in the East.

Even with the barbarian invasions, Europe maintained Latin as the written and spoken language of the government, the Church and the learned. Only gradually did the various vernaculars command any attention. Conversely, Greek continued as the official language through the Middle and Near East, culminating in the Cyrillic alphabet in what are now the Russian states.

Every educated Roman was familiar with Greek art and philosophy, and probably had attended a school influenced by Greek ideas of education. This sometimes grudging admiration for Greek culture infiltrated and influenced early Christianity and, of course, political and philosophical thought from the Renaissance until well into the present century.[1]

As the empire expanded, the use of literacy for government, administration, trade, the armed forces, etc. became increasingly important; but, as with the Greeks and earlier Near Eastern governments this was limited to a few. Actually, trained literate slaves might function in many of the capacities necessary for trade and government; and, of course, oral communication was used to spread the necessary rules and regulations among the people at large. A trained bureaucracy was a far cry from a literate nation and equally a thing apart from book-reading, book-owning individuals, who were apparently fewer in Rome than in classic Greece.

The early Greek-Roman syndrome was similar to the perhaps better understood relationship of the early Americans looking to Europe for books and for cultural leadership. What was to become the United States, after all, was primarily a frontier with little interest in publishing, although deeply involved with education. Americans went to England for basic machinery and ideas about publishing and printing.

ROMAN EDUCATION AND LITERACY[2]

The literacy/education level in Rome differed little from that of Greece. The written culture was limited to a privileged minority and existed side by side with oral culture.

Reading, writing, and the sale and collection of books, private and public, was extremely limited. Literacy required education and this was the exclusive province of upper class Roman men and, as such, quite expensive. Women may have been educated at home, but to a large extent they fared no better than slaves. They had the domestic power to persuade and to urge, but lacked most legal rights.

Education required books, and they were relatively even more costly. The evidence of libraries, books, literacy and the like is confined almost entirely to the extant literature of the period, which was generated, of course, by literate males, most of whom were upper class. The division between the educated and literate and the uneducated was as in thousands of years past—vast. And for that reason one can only guess at what went on among the majority who were illiterate. Most of them received poetry or laws from oral recitation, and storytellers were as common as in Greece.

Writing, as in Greece, was common in much of the Roman Empire. Some argue that therefore literacy must have been high. Not necessarily so. America, for example, is flooded with printed matter, yet there is a high illiteracy rate. One could always have a slave or better educated person do the accounts, write letters and the like. Proclamations usually were oral as well as in writing, and many other transactions seem to have been carried on without writing.

Yes, but what of the well-known series of women in Pompeiian paintings holding stylus and writing tablets (Fig. 10). The significance may be that the paintings are no more than decoration. One can hardly draw conclusions about literacy, at any period in history, particularly from examples drawn exclusively from the homes and effects of the aristocracy. One may grant the women were literate, but, again, it must be recalled they are upper-class images found only in rich homes.

Prosperous families sent their male children to schools, organized much on the order of the Greek schools. The masses were not educated. This tightly closed order carried over into government and the military. It assured the stability of the Roman Empire, where, as in many societies since, the educated few dominated the mass of uneducated. Illiteracy was a formula for a long-lived, successful totalitarian state.[3]

Drawing upon an agrarian, conservative tradition, the early upper-class Romans stressed the importance of family and community in education. Particularly in the early Roman years, the teachers tended to be educated Greek slaves; and for most of the Empire slaves dominated the teaching profession.[4] By the second century B.C., Cato (234–149 B.C.)[5] reportedly taught his son to read, feeling that it was better for a father to assume this role than to have an educated slave serve as teacher. The family education continued until the boy was 16, and he then passed on to an older

10. Portrait of a young woman (Pompey, c. 70 A.D.) holding her stylus to her lips and with the other hand gripping writing tablets.

man who taught him rhetoric and the cultural necessities of the time. From there it was the army and political life, or more study. Some, usually the ruling class members, went on to what would be universities today. The best ones were in Athens and Rhodes. Alexandria, equally superior, generally was ruled out as being too wild a place for youths.

ROMAN LITERATURE

Primarily known for their laws and for their government, the Romans did have an impressive literature. Able to read and write, the educated young man then moved on to the literature which would make him cultured and, as such, welcome in upper-class circles. This became more necessary with the triumviral period (c. 43 B.C.), which led to the Augustan age of poetry.

Most of the great writers worked before the rise of Imperial Rome, and many claim, with some evidence, that creative writing died with the death of Augustus (63 B.C.–14 A.D.) and the rise of the Emperors.

Roman literature begins with heavy borrowing from the Greeks (c. 250 B.C.) and virtually ends with the death of the Republic (c. 14 A.D.). Terence (c. 185–159 B.C.) and Plautus (d. 184 B.C.) dominated the early period from 250 to 150 B.C. The Augustan Age, with Virgil (70–19 B.C.), expanded upon the ideas and the forms inherited in large part from the Greeks. Virgil's *Aeneid* follows the Trojan Aeneas who, in the ancient town of Lavininum, lay the foundation for what would be the Roman empire. Cicero (106–43 B.C.) took the oral tradition beyond the Greeks and brought Latin rhetoric to its high mark. Others of the Augustan Age—from Lucretius (99–55 B.C.) and Catullus (84–54 B.C.) to Ovid (43 B.C.–17 A.D.) and Seneca (4 B.C.–65 A.D.)—developed a Latin literature which influenced all of then civilized world.

With the death of Augustus and the overthrow of even limited democracy, Roman culture drastically deteriorated. As literature faded, government and legal documents dominated the ever-growing Roman empire. If all of the Roman literature disappeared, there would remain countless examples of writing in legal and government archives.

Tacitus (55–117 A.D.) helps to explain the Roman fascination with law. His *The Annals of Imperial Rome,* along with the earlier surviving books of Livy's *History of Rome* (c. 59 B.C.–17 A.D.), offer an unparalleled view of Roman culture. The danger, in sweeping generalities is to overlook Martial (c. 40–104), Marcus Aurelius (121–180) and many others whose work illuminated another side of the pragmatic lawyers, military men and government officials.

By the third century A.D., political disasters were matched by the careless transmission of texts and the decline of publishing, such as it had become. It was a period of how-to-do-it handbooks, often less than reliable. Still, it was the period, too, of one of the most widely read authors of the Dark and Middles Ages—the grammarian Donatus (c. 300). His two grammars were the basic textbooks of the period, and found everywhere. Donatus, as well as other grammarians, served the double purpose of offering instruction and preserving, through quotations, much of the literature of the classical period.[6]

PUBLISHING

Thanks to the necessity of promulgating laws and regulations throughout Europe, after Augustine a large government-sponsored publishing program existed. Beyond that little is known of the ever-changing establishment of publishers, either public or private.

Authors such as Seneca mentioned publication of their works. They were neither copyrighted nor the source of profit. Also, once the original left the author, it may or may not have been copied time after time, correctly or otherwise. Cicero complained of poor editing and transcribing by the copyists. Not without reason did Horace (65–8 B.C.) boast that his verses would be read on the shores of the Black Sea and on the banks of the Rhone and the Ebro. Horace occasionally mentions books in his odes and epistles, and in one letter indicates the book trade is much the same today as it was some 2,000 years ago; e.g. ''Book, you're staring wistful at the gods of buying and selling . . . of the marketplace . . . open for sale.'' He suggests, too, that books which did not sell in Rome eventually were shipped ''down to

Africa, or off to Spain,'' to be used as scrap papyrus.[7] And as today, they often did not sell because of literary critics and a poor reception, or as Martial puts it: ''Frail book, although there's room for you to stay snug on my shelves, you'd rather fly away to the bookshops and be published.'' He then warns the book about ''our know-all crowd'' which is ''hard to please.'' ''Nobody sneers as loud as a Roman.'' And in another epigram he implies that his worst critics are fellow poets who find his verses ''crude.''[8]

While Rome was the primary book center, there are indications that books were sold, if only in a limited fashion, throughout the Empire; e.g. Pliny the Younger in a letter to Geminus (IX/II) is pleased that his books are being sold in Lugdunum (Lyons), ''for it is gratifying to find that they retain in foreign parts the popularity they have won at Rome.'' The extant literature indicates that books were to be found throughout the Empire, but it must be remembered these are authors talking about their own books.

The primary method of distributing books, particularly literature, was for the author himself to make a copy or two for a friend rather than rely on a publisher. Another method was for one book owner to have a copy made and then trade it with a fellow for a title he wanted. As a consequence of this: (1) One should be careful about exaggerating the number of publishers; and more or less (2) the number and extent of bookdealers in Rome and throughout Europe and the Near East. They both existed, but seem to have been less than widespread.

Atticus put his staff of trained copyists to work for Cicero and other friends. The famous series of letters between Cicero and Atticus gives a picture of book publishing in the last days of the Republic. Informal, and likely to result in numerous variations from copy to copy, publication of books seemed to be more among friends helping one another than a centralized, organized business. With the spread of more common secondary education and Virgil's entry into the curriculum, as well as that of other Roman poets and prose writers, the need for books for the educated became pressing by the first century A.D. Various writers, and more particularly Aulus Gellius (130–180 A.D.) in his *Attic Nights* (a forerunner of the factual oddities in compilations such as Brewer's *Dictionary of Phrase and Fable,* or Benet's *Reader's Encylopedia*) gave hints about Roman communication and publishing. Public readings were common and at one, Gellius reports an argument arose whether the poet whose work was being read had said *equus* (horse) or *eques* (rider). Today one would simply consult the printed work. But then one had to consult with book dealers, probably in Rome's Shoemaker's Street, for a handwritten copy contemporaneous with the life of the poet. Gellius reports this was done at great time and expense, and in the copy located *eques,* not *equus,* was written. As any lover of facts, Gellius "was interested in old books for their own sake. He talks of old copies of Cato (and others) which dealers had let him consult."[9]

The book dealer, called bibliopola, used specially trained slaves (servi literati and librarii) for copying texts; they were paid by the number of lines, the standard line consisting of 34 to 38 letters. With the coming of the Empire the book trade began to flourish in Rome as in other cities; book stores were located on the busiest streets and were often meeting places for writers and scholars. Lists of new books were posted on the walls or on door columns. As a rule, booksellers were also publishers.

ROLL TO CODEX[10]

Although Roman publishers left little evidence of their work, their contribution to the form of the book was revolutionary. Papyrus rolls continued to be the primary format for books, but gradually, from as early as the second century, the rolls were replaced by the familiar book as we know it today, i.e. the codex, the Latin for a plurality of tablets or for multi-leaved tablets.

A few codex sheets have been preserved from about the end of the first or the beginning of the second century A.D. Vellum codices were certainly in use at that time, although they were probably considered less respectable than papyrus rolls.[11] They were employed for small and less expensive editions because vellum could be used on both sides and a text that would require a large roll or several rolls could be contained in a relatively small codex.

The codex replaced the papyrus book roll for numerous reasons, from convenience to lower cost. The by-now accepted fact is that Christians adopted the format to differentiate their writing from the Greek and Roman. The Christians hardly invented the codex, but they made it popular among themselves; e.g., by the second century, 158 of 172 Christian texts are in the next codex form, as contrasted, for the same period, only 1.5 per cent of some 871 Greek texts.

PARCHMENT REPLACES PAPYRUS

For several hundred years it was considered less than fashionable to use anything but papyrus. The poor or those jotting an ephemeral note apparently used wood or wax, and sometimes linen was favored. Wax tablets, wood, ostracon—these were the materials of daily writing. Parchment and papyrus were used only infrequently for purposes for which today we routinely would use paper with pencil, pen or computer printout. Seneca (4 B.C.–65 A.D.) advises a friend to not always be bent "over writing tablets."[12] Over a century later Pliny the Younger remarks in a letter to Fuscus (IX/36) that when he goes hunting he is never "without my tablets," which he uses for writing in case he finds no game. The advent of the codex and the high cost of papyrus, among other things, explains the gradual changeover from papyrus to parchment.

Leather had undoubtedly been used for writing at various places in the ancient world, even in very early times. Among the Egyptians and the Jews as well as the Assyrians and Persians and the Greeks, animal skins were so used. The Greeks called them diphthera, a name that was later applied to other writing materials as well. It was not until the third century B.C., however, that leather was subjected to a special treatment to make it better suited for writing, and the development of this process is usually associated with Pergamum. The processing of leather for writing purposes was done on a large scale there, and the word parchment, charta pergamena, is presumably derived from the name of the city.

As a rule, sheep, calf or goat skins were used. The hair was removed, the skin scraped, then soaked in lime water to remove fatty substances, dried, and then, without any other tanning, it was rubbed with finely ground chalk and was polished smooth with pumice stone or a similar material. The final product of this process was excellent for writing; it presented a smooth and flat surface and it was usable on both sides. Its durability exceeded that of papyrus, though it was by no means resistant to all types of destructive action. One factor that contributed greatly to its extended use was that, in contrast to papyrus, it permitted erasures to be made easily. This is the reason that among vellum manuscripts—especially from the Middle Ages and other periods when the material was expensive—we find palimpsests, that is, sheets on which the original writing had been rubbed out and new text written over it. Palimpsest means ''re-smoothed.''

The manufacture of parchment was not restricted to a single country and for this reason it was not as expensive as papyrus. It was only gradually that parchment was raised to the status of a book material, but from the fourth century A.D. papyrus gradually went out of use.

In its general features the codex was basically similar to the roll in design. Even the practice of placing the title at the end of the text was transferred from the roll to the codex, even though it was of no practical significance in the latter. It was not until the fifth century that it became the regular practice to place the title at the beginning of the work as well. One new feature that was introduced along with the codex was pagination. This device was unnecessary in the roll, where the columns were necessarily maintained in their proper order, but in the codex it became of practical importance. In the beginning, however, it was often used only on certain pages or on the front side of each sheet.

Roman papyrus rolls and later codices probably were illustrated, but none is extant. As with Greek illustrated books, scholars point to vases, mosaics, wall paintings, etc., as the source of likely subjects for book illustration. In fact, now-lost book illustration may have served as standard copy for painters to follow. But regardless of which came first, the odds are that illustrated books were not that unusual, particularly for purposes of diagramming engineering and scientific how-to-do-it manuals. By the late fourth or early fifth century, the first true miniature illustrations, which become the glory of later medieval books, begin to appear. A well-defined set of symbols, an iconographic tradition, began in monastic communities by the beginning of the fifth century.

LATIN SCRIPT[13]

The script used in the earliest codices was a special form of calligraphy, just as in the rolls, and it gradually became more and more fixed. There is a series of Greek and Coptic manuscripts[14] from the fourth and fifth centuries, of quite different content but all written in an almost identical, beautiful hand with broad, rounded lines, indicating a growing tendency toward uniformity in style of writing.

The Romans' Latin script became the written hand for the various Romance languages which developed, as well as for all of Europe and much of the western world. The basic Roman scripts explain our present handwriting form, and dictated the shape of type from Gutenberg to the computer printout.

Possibly the most famous source of information about early Roman script is found on the column of Trajan, raised in the Roman Forum in 114 A.D. to celebrate, in winding scroll figures, the conquests of the Roman emperor (Fig. 11). As a work of art, as a frozen picture of Roman life, the column is fascinating.[15] The base, however, with its square capital letter inscriptions is of ultimate value to the student of script. Here is the model for capital letters. Since the advent of printing in the fifteenth century, typographers have studied the inscription to help them shape their own alphabets. More has been written about the flawless letters than any other work of its type. The clarity, balance and easy readability of the letters astonishes even modern experts; and in one way or another the column and later copies of the letters strongly influenced monastic and later printed script forms.

By the third century the uncial (i.e. inch-high rounded letters) capital was found in numerous scripts. Incidentally, few letters were an inch high. Most were about half an inch, as found in some 400 Roman extant manuscripts.

There are numerous variations on the early capital letters (sometimes called majuscules). A few fine manuscripts—in addition to numerous inscriptions—are in Roman or Rustic capitals.

By the sixth century the capital forms were no longer used. (They would be revived in monastic scriptoriums three hundred years later.) Capitals were replaced by the familiar cursive hand used in handwriting. The half uncial or minuscule letter appeared

11. Trajan column. Erected between 106 and 114 A.D., it celebrated the Emperor Trajan's conquests. The base of the 125-foot tribute has the famous inscriptions from which the roman letter was modelled.

in the latter half of the fourth and early fifth centuries. While still not a complete cursive hand, the smaller letters gradually were to take that form. Here individual words, rather than individual letters (as capitals), stand out.[16] Romans and later church scribes found it easier and more economical to use the cursive.

Europe, by the monastic period, split off into so-called national or regional hands. If under the Romans there was a universally accepted method of letter form, this was no longer true. By the ninth century, Irish monks, for example, were using such hand as half uncials and semi-uncials. Variations, from the Carolingian minuscule in the eighth century to the familiar Gothic script of the twelfth century, arose (Fig. 12).

Christians made other changes, such as the use of large initial letters to set off a line or a section. This was as unknown to papyri scribes as was the use of red ink to emphasize certain letters. By the fourth century a special hand had been developed—the biblical majuscule—to write the scriptures.

LIBRARIES[17]

More than a fire destroyed the library at Alexandria, for by the last days of the Roman Republic many scholars deserted Egypt for Rome. Along with them came personal libraries, such as they were, and Greek poets and librarians.

Judging from the words of Roman philosophers, authors and historians, it seemed fashionable, even required, to possess a personal library. Libraries primarily were confined to the rich, and were often found in country villas as an important part of leisurely living. Excavations at Rome, Herculaneum and other areas of Italy reveal rooms for libraries, archives and art work.

Cicero speaks of "the excellent arrangement in my library" (*Letters to Atticus,* IV, 4a) and Pliny the Younger notes that a friend is looking for paintings "to adorn his library" (Pliny, *Letters,* IV, 39). Martial observes in an epigram that it is pleasant to have a library (*Epigrams,* XIV, 190). There are tantalizing fragments, notes and mentions throughout much of extant Latin literature, which indicate the general acceptance, indeed the need, of private libraries among the educated, and certainly among the aristocrats and upper-classes.[18]

West Gothic script of the 10th century.

Merovingian script of the 7th century.

Beneventan script of the 11th century.

Irish script of the 7th century.

12. National forms of Latin minuscule script of the 6th century. (After Franz Steffens.)

Cicero is a measure of how the upper-class literate men cherished their personal libraries. At the same time he indicates how the role of the librarian may have fallen from scholar to slave. ''I wish you would send me a couple of your library slaves,'' he writes Atticus, ''to employ as gluers (of separate leaves of papyrus to make a roll) and other subordinate work'' (Atticus, IV, 4b).

Until well into the Empire, it was common for Roman generals and even some enlisted men to bring home books from various conquests. Sulla (138–78 B.C.), the self-proclaimed Roman dictator, sacked a library in Athens that had many of Aristotle's books and brought them to Italy; but they later disappeared.

Juvenal (c. 60–127 A.D.) hints that books and personal libraries were considered as much decoration and a mark of wealth as a tool for scholarship. In a satire he lists how a house, destroyed, should be rebuilt and furnished with ''a gift of marble or of building materials.'' Friends offer ''nude and glistening statues . . . Others will offer books and bookcases, or a bust of Minerva, or a hundredweight of silver plate.''[19]

The number of private Roman collectors increased and gradually the bibliophile came into fashion. A sizable book collection was an essential part of a prominent Roman's house, preferably arranged in an elaborate setting that would add to the owner's prestige. They were usually divided into a Greek and a Latin section.

The Roman luxury libraries can be visualized as follows: In a room of green marble tiles the book rolls were arranged on shelves, in niches or in open cabinets along the walls; the rolls either lay enclosed in purple leather cases or stood upright in elaborately decorated containers. Busts or relief portraits of famous authors were everywhere—a custom that Pliny the Elder (123–79 A.D.) says was introduced by Asinius Pollio when he founded the first public library in Rome.

The eruption of Mt. Vesuvius (79 A.D.) buried Pompeii and the nearby community of Herculaneum. The time capsule gives up remnants of libraries, wall paintings, sculpture, and everyday working tools. Without the volcano most of this view of the past would have been lost.

One of the largest, and still to be entirely excavated private Roman libraries is near Herculaneum. Known as the ''villa of papyri'' the library includes thousands of carbonized papyrus rolls. Unfortunately most have proven to be of minor importance celebrating the work of a lesser philosopher. Some scholars believe that with further excavation more meaningful titles will appear. Buried by mud, the Herculaneum library complements what was found in the excavations at Pompeii. About the same size, the library in the House of Nenander was frozen in time by the eruption. Both libraries seem to be modeled after ideas from Greece, and variations on their relatively small size and architectural details are found in descriptions of similar retreats by Plutarch and others.

The codex occasionally was used, but the majority of extant documents are on papyrus rolls and indicate a varied approach to filing and preservation. Most documents were stored in archive rooms, and collections were dutifully labeled and often pasted together to form a coherent file, much as one today would file papers in a cabinet under a given subject or name.

PUBLIC LIBRARIES

The concept of public libraries developed with democracy and mass education, more particularly in nineteenth century America and England. With that, there is some evidence that a public prescribed as much by sex (male) as ability to read and write did have limited access to state-supported libraries, or public libraries, as early as the Greeks. But the evidence is sketchy, particularly in comparison with what we know of the scholarly libraries and archival centers. Limited literacy and a rigid class system for who was or was not educated indicates that the libraries were for the few. At any rate they had no major effect on the diffusion of books or spreading the knowledge of authors. The latter was done more effectively through public readings. Aulus Gellius (c. 130 A.D.), the Latin author, studied in Athens, and fragments of his history of Greece include references to Athenian public libraries some 600 years earlier. Others from Strabo to Pliny the Elder make brief passing references to libraries.

Later the evidence is somewhat more creditable, although sketchy. Caesar, around 49 B.C., planned Rome's first public library but was slain before the plan could be carried out. More likely it was not until Augustus that a library was actually opened. Probably the public libraries were limited to those who applied for entrance. It is questionable that one could wander into a library in Rome unannounced. Numerous writers speak of at least two Augustan libraries from about 30 to 25 B.C. Both libraries were destroyed by fire around 190 A.D. By the time of Constantine, c. 300 A.D., there apparently were as many as 14 public libraries in Rome and a few scattered in other countries and parts of Italy. The general conclusion is that by the fifth century the libraries had disappeared, although some challenge this notion.

SCHOLARLY AND ARCHIVAL LIBRARIES

As in Alexandria, the early Roman librarians first and foremost were scholars, and as familiar with organizing books as verse. The most outstanding of the group was M. Terentius Varro (116–27 B.C.), the Republic's greatest scholar and a Renaissance person fifteen centuries before Leonardo daVinci (1452–1519 A.D.), was named librarian of the never to be built public library by Julius Caesar.[20] It is he more than any other Roman who marshalled facts and stressed the importance of evidence in historical writing. Varro wrote about 74 complete works. Astonishingly witty and poetic, he could write on the nature of etymology and the next moment ask the reader to consider that ''Neither treasure nor gold can set free the heart, nor can the golden mountains of Persia or hall of rich Crassus cure worry or fear.'' Only one text survives completely, and this is on *Farm Topics* (written when he was 80). There are books and fragments from several other titles. His ideas had a strong influence on European authors to come, and particularly publishers who met the Roman love for facts with numerous guides and textbooks to almost everything from gastronomy to Latin and agriculture. Similar wide interests were shared by a second librarian, Julius Hyginus (c. 65 B.C.–c. 17 A.D.), who took charge of the Augustus, later the Ulpian library. Unlike Varro he actually operated a library, but like his master he was a proficient author and expert on many subjects, including astrology.[21]

While the Julius Caesar public library was literally cut short,

Augustus accepted the concept and opened a library in the Temple of Apollo, c. 28 B.C. This was the core of the library extended by Tiberius. Augustus or Octavia (69 B.C.–11 B.C.), sister of the Emperor, probably was the founder of the second major Roman library, which seems to have been operating well into the second century. As noted, while these beginnings are often termed "public" libraries, they were scholarly centers and probably housed official documents as well as other materials. They were financed by the state, and hence "public," but were not open to any Roman who happened to wander in off the Forum.

As Alexandria had its library and museum for scholars, so did Rome. This was the famous Ulpian library.[22] It was constructed in The Trajan Forum, about 112 A.D., by the Emperor Trajan (52–117). It housed the best in Latin and Greek literature and was the major library in the Western World after the destruction of the one at Alexandria. It seems to have been functioning as late as 455 A.D. Many of its Latin and Greek works turned up again in monasteries throughout what had been the Roman empire. Numerous copies of copies were employed by printers from the fifteenth century on to bring readers what might well have been lost had it not been for the Ulpian library.

The Ulpian library, too, was used as a public record office for Rome, but there were other libraries for archives. Build in 78 B.C., and still surviving as a ruin, the Tabularium was used to house state archives, and, in this respect was much like the earlier libraries of the Near East. The architecture of the structure was copied over and over again, particularly the cloister vaults which appear in monasteries and, often, as an introduction to the library. Another library, The Library of Celsus at Ephesus, served as an architectural guide both for other libraries and for public buildings (Fig. 13). Here the exterior entrance wall is decorated with a columnar screen, of at least two stories. The columns held up nothing, but were greatly favored by the second century A.D.

With the division of the empire, Constantine established an imperial library in Constantinople. While it became a center for early Christian literature, it also served to house the best of Greek and Latin. The Christian fathers who formed the intellectual pillars of the church unquestionably must have used the imperial library until its eventual destruction with the fall of the noble city in the thirteenth century.

13. Ruins of a Roman provincial library (the Celsus Library at Ephesus) founded 110 A.D. At the back of the large hall is an apse for a statue; along the walls are two rows of niches for book cases. The outer walls are double as protection against moisture.

TEXT TRANSMISSION

The Romans won a place in history for their laws and bureaucratic sophistication which, behind the military, brought 400 years of peace to Europe. Much of the spectacular success of the Romans was wiped from the pages of history with the destruction of their documents. A notable exception is the recovery of bureaucratic and legal materials from Dura-Europus (a Roman outpost on the Euphrates), and from other dry areas in the Middle East where the papyrus rolls were inadvertently saved.

The amount of work on papyrus was astonishing. There is the record of a regional Egyptian administrator who seems to have used regularly over 400 rolls in a month.

Latin literature, particularly in the first two centuries, seemed of little real importance. Its preservation was of limited interest to Romans. The chances of transmission from decade to decade, century to century, were slim. Cato's *De Agri Cultura* is the one work transmitted directly to us, but it is much mangled by copying and recopying. The evidence of publishing and libraries indicates there were enough books about, but no one seemed interested enough to protect the originals.

NOTES

[1]The Greek influence on Rome can be overestimated. The vast majority of Romans, as early Americans, considered themselves quite superior. Intellectuals, professionals and politicians looked to Greece for various reasons, although by the time of the Empire they felt Greece to be of minor importance. A similar superior attitude was evident about Western Europe. Few Romans bothered to learn western languages or cultural biases. For a brief study of the influence of Greece on Rome, the Near East and Europe see Gordon Williams *Change and Decline* (Berkeley: University of California Press, 1978), pp. 102–152, "The dominance of Greek culture."

[2]Stanley Bonner. *Education in Ancient Rome* (Berkeley: University of California Press, 1977). This offers a good introduction, although limited primarily to the Republican period. For a brief overall approach, see Cecil Wooten, "Roman Education and Rhetoric," in *Civilizations of the Ancient Mediterranean* (New York: Scribners), Vol. 2.

[3]At the same time, literacy in both Greece and Rome did help for many centuries to define individualism, and to insure liberty and written laws.

[4]The Roman general Lucius Aemilius Paullus (c. 229–160 B.C.) was typical in that he provided his son with a group of Greek teachers. They were familiar with all of the arts from literature and rhetoric to philosophy and politics. The handful of teachers was, in effect, a small personal academy, which was not unusual for the period. Of more interest is that Paullus, who had defeated the Greeks, sacked the royal library of Macedon and brought its contents to Rome. This was the base of numerous collections, both private and governmental, and set the pattern for the Romans importing Greek books, although they were more often bought than raided.

[5]Cato the elder is important in the history of the book, too, because his *On Agriculture* (c. 160 B.C.) is one of the earliest full extant Latin literary works we have. Also, "censor" was a title given him in 184. He, in this role, was a judge, census taker and only incidentally a supervisor of conduct and Roman morals. But, of course, this latter segment of his duties assumed the major definition for "censor" as used later by

Roman Emperors. There was no censorship, as we know it today, during the Republic. This changed with the rise of Imperial Rome. Authors became more dependent upon the state for financial help, and in so doing accepted checks on what they could or could not say. Beginning with Augustus, works and writers were banned regularly. Augustus supposedly even instructed his librarian to remove some works more for aesthetics than for politics. Tiberius prosecuted, and even had killed or exiled, authors who he claimed committed treason by being critical of his reign. For the next centuries censorship, much as in modern parts of the Western world, was employed or avoided, depending upon who governed Rome.

[6]By the Middle Ages, Donatus' name came to be synonymous with grammar, and no lay work was so often cited, or so often copied.

[7]*The Essential Horace* (San Francisco: North Point Press, 1983), p. 230. Or possibly the books were remaindered in these far distant parts of the Empire, but more likely they were more valuable for their papyrus.

[8]Martial. *The Epigrams,* tr. by James Michie (New York: Penguin Books, 1978). (1/3), p. 21; (9/81), p. 133.

[9]William V. Harris. *Ancient Literacy* (Cambridge: Harvard University Press, 1989). For documentation about publishing, or lack of it, see his chapter, ''Literacy and Illiteracy in the Roman World.'' Too much evidence for so-called widespread publishing is predicated on Roman authors and their sometimes exaggerated notions of how widely their works were distributed.

[10]Colin Roberts and T.C. Skeat. *The Birth of the Codex* (London: Oxford University Press, 1983). This is an update of Roberts' famous article (British Academy. *Proceedings,* 1954, pp. 169–204) which documented the process by which the codex replaced the papyrus roll. The excitement of discovery is matched only by the scholarship and the detailed overview. An excellent beginning for anyone interested in the Roman book and its subsequent influence.

[11]An example of a form of a codex was found in a well at Nimrud and has been dated to about 700 B.C. It seems to have been a government document and was hinged to unfold, although technically was more like a Japanese screen in its action than a modern codex. A later Babylonian inscription includes the phrase ''close the book,'' which may or may not refer to a codex. At any rate it seems likely the form, if only scattered, was in use well before the Christians.

[12]Seneca. *Letters from a Stoic* (New York: Penguin Books, 1969), (XV/1) p. 61.

[13]Leila Avrin. *Scribes, Script and Books* (Chicago: American Library Association, 1991). See Chapter 8, ''Latin Script'' for a detailed

explanation of the development of the Latin Script from Rome through the Middle Ages and into modern times.

[14]Coptic, which literally means Egyptian but is now the descriptor of Egyptian Christians, was a modified form of the Greek alphabet. Christian communities in the Near East and Egypt used the Coptic script until the thirteenth century. In the history of the book the Copts are famous because of a theological conflict with the church at Constantinople which resulted in the development of literature and another interpretation of the New Testament. Almost entirely religious, the Coptic literature throws light on early Gnosticism. Many early documents were found in codex form from the third century. See James Robinson, ed. *The Nag Hammadi Library* (New York: Harper & Row, 1977).

[15]Trajan was entombed under the marble column, which is some 125 feet high together with the inscribed base. Originally the column was surrounded by galleries and people could climb gradually (much as one views art in the Guggenheim Museum in New York) and view the scenes of the column. The low relief sculpture served as a type of early movie, although the people rather than the battle scenes did the moving.

[16]The familiar printed italic is a rough example of how much of the early cursive hand looked.

[17]Clarence Boyd. *Public Libraries and Literary Culture in Ancient Rome* (Chicago: University of Chicago Press, 1916). Dated, although useful as an overview.

[18]Cicero. *Letters to Atticus.* Books I-VI. (Loeb Classics, IV, 4a); Pliny. *Letters.* (Loeb Classics, IV, 39); Martial. *Epigrams* (Loeb Classics, XIV, 190).

[19]*Juvenal and Persius* (Cambridge: Harvard University Press, 1965). (Loeb Classics—Satire III), p. 49. Books do decorate a room, and the practice has continued down to our day. On the other hand, intellectuals, teachers and writers genuinely collected and loved books; e.g. Martial (*Epigrams* 5/20): "O could both thou and I, my friend/From care and trouble freed . . . We'd seek the book, the cheerful talk, at noonday in the shade . . . " Gordon Jennings, ed. *Masterpiece of Latin Literature* (New York: Houghton Mifflin, 1903), p. 397. Another writer and intellectual, Pliny the Younger (c. 61–113 A.D.), observes in his letter to Fuscus (IX, 36) that part of any "good day" consists of dining with his wife and a few friends during which "a book is read to us." And throughout his letters he occasionally mentions "reading aloud" to himself.

[20]Pliny the Elder followed in Varro's scholarly footsteps. He compiled the first encyclopedia, i.e. *The Natural History,* of which 31 books survive. Before literally being killed by curiosity as he examined the eruption of Vesuvius he wrote almost as many books as Varro, including

texts on javelin throwing and curiosities from the dress of Claudius' wife to an Egyptian obelisk in Rome.

[21]Anyone familiar with the Library of Congress realizes that the head of the library is appointed because of his/her reputation as a scholar, not as a trained librarian. The tradition goes back to Alexandria and to Rome. The Ulpian library had a series of authors as heads. In addition to those cited, Suetonius (69–135 A.D.) was in charge of the imperial library when not writing his *Lives of the Caesars* or serving as Hadrian's private secretary.

[22]The library was located in the great basilican law court, named Ulpia after the Trajan family. The Greek and Latin libraries were separate and celebrated Trajan's patronage of education and learning. Sections of the west library have been restored. Suitably enough, the libraries, as part of the Forum of Trajan, are near his column and the shopping arcade.

CHAPTER FOUR

THE DARK AGES

> With gliding pen the heavenly words are copied so that the
> devil's craft...may be destroyed.
> —Cassiodorus

Edward Gibbon's classic *The Decline and Fall of the Roman Empire* opens in the second century of the Christian era when "the Empire of Rome comprehended the fairest part of the earth." What follows is an imaginative analysis of the gradual decline of Rome and the rise and spread of Christianity. The early Christian communities set the stage for the transmission of texts throughout what was come to be known as the Dark Ages (c 400–800),[1] or in Gibbon's words, that period after "the most civilized portion of mankind" was conquered by the barbarians. The sack of Rome in 410 is a historical landmark, but the actual decline of Rome, like the development of the book, had taken centuries, not moments.

The Roman empire held together in part until 565 when Justinian, the Roman/Byzantine emperor, failed in his re-conquest of Italy. Today he is remembered as much for St. Sophia as the legal code which established civil law. Scholars recall his less than charitable closure of the long-lived university or academy at Athens.

The eastern branch of the Roman empire, with its capital in Constantinople (later Istanbul), constituted the Byzantine empire. As a remnant of Roman glory, the empire lasted until the Crusaders sacked Constantinople in 1204, and was officially dead in 1453 when conquered by the Ottoman Turks. As the center of civilization, and for decades the fortress of Christianity, the Greek-speaking Byzantines are important in the history of the book. They preserved and transmitted major Greek texts as well as mastering fundamentals of illumination of manuscripts.

In the West and Europe, from the fourth century and earlier, the Church provided an alternative to the barbarian rule. The Church offered career possibilities to those who had served in the Roman army and offices and courts. The ambitious in the community turned to the Church, as did those who might otherwise be more involved with their own rise to power and position. As the barbarians established kingdoms in the West, the Roman intellectuals, now often Christians, erected forts of faith in monastic communities.

In the confusion after the fall of Rome, from about the close of the fifth century until the reign of Charlemagne, c. 800, there were 350 to 400 years of considerable anarchy. Cities were in ruins, and life was conducted, sometimes at a mean level, in small communities, including Christian conclaves, throughout Europe. With the Holy Roman Empire in 800, Charlemagne brought order and feudalism, which became the normal social system until the thirteenth century.

The concept of the Roman government took a long time to die. A master of the Roman legal heritage and the classical literature tradition, Augustine, in his *City of God* (426), described the ideal in terms of the Roman city-state.[2] As late as the seventh-century invasion of Spain by Arabs, many living in the Mediterranean world felt themselves still a part of the Roman way of doing things.

RISE OF MONASTIC COMMUNITIES

The Dark and early Middle Ages are known in the history of the book for the gradual growth of monastic communities where laborious copying of texts continued until slightly beyond the discovery of printing in the mid-fifteenth century. The monasteries were a center of learning and saved many classical and antique works from destruction. Each religious order, from the Benedictines to the Carthusian monks, had a different approach to religious training, but all were comparatively hospitable to education and libraries.

The monastic principle was given life by St. Anthony (d. 356) in Egypt, although he and others took the word quite literally; i.e. the Greek roots refer to ''dwelling alone.'' Monasteries as communities, with a common chapel and group of work places, overcame the individual life style, and by the late sixth century monasticism had spread from Egypt to Italy, France and Ireland.

Cassiodorus (d. 583) was the first to define and prescribe the duties of a monk in a scriptorium. These included translation, transcription and the copying of manuscripts. His community at Vivarium (c 551–562) appears to have had a central library, which may have been an extension of his own private collection.[3]

St. Benedict's (d. c. 547) Monte Cassino was the first to provide for regular copying of books. The Benedictine order of the early sixth century established the monastic model followed throughout Europe.[4] Not all had scriptoriums or libraries, but they all welcomed books which might be produced in a nearby monastery. (Scriptorium is a self-descriptive word for the room(s) where the scribes copied manuscripts.)

Claiming to be the antechambers of heaven, the monasteries, as ordered and governed by the Rule of St. Benedict, followed a definite architectural design. The plans of Saint-Gall (c. 820), preserved on five pieces of parchment, are the most famous. The library is a relatively small space between the church and the cloister. Similar plans were employed in construction throughout Europe. Many might house from 150 to 200 monks, although only a few monks would be involved with the scriptorium. Lay person staff, unable to find a place in the monastery, became citizens of the town which grew up outside of the walls.

DEVELOPMENT OF SCRIPTORIUMS

The scriptorium was the place in the monastery where the manuscripts were written and copied. Except for private copies, books were produced primarily in monastic scriptoria from the late seventh century until about the middle of the thirteenth century, when the monastic scriptoria shifted primarily to university publishers. As each scriptorium had a distinctive style of writing, illumination, binding, etc., manuscripts or manuscript styles may be identified by the name of the scriptorium or the center where the scriptorium was located. Just as today there are certain publishing houses associated with fine book work and editing, such was the case throughout most of the Dark and Middle Ages. Given superior scribes and illuminators, monastic communities gained attention for their particular types of schools of book production. Abbeys from Reichenau to Echternach to Tours and Winchester were known for their fine manuscripts. The development of the university had similar results. Scriptoria associated with universities from Oxford to Paris and Bologna became well known for their distinctive publishing efforts.

The titles copied varied from monastery to monastery, although the overwhelming majority consisted, in order of likely numbers copied: the Psalter, the Gospels, the letters of Paul, other books of the Bible, commentary and related liturgical works, among which the most important was the sacramentary which contained the prayers of mass and celebration instructions. Other religious works of importance were: the lectionary, a book of biblical readings; and antiphonary (later the antiphonal and gradual, two separate works), liturgical chants and responses. The latter established the tradition of the Gregorian chant, named after Gregory the Great. Actually, evidence suggests that chants were used well before Gregory. The long Gregorian tradition dates back to the eighth century, a good 100 to 150 years after the Pope's death.

With the emphasis on copying scripture and commentaries the scope of the library narrowed. True, St. Augustine had approved the copying and maintenance of classics, but only those which could be used to support Christianity. By the sixth century almost all work was exclusively dedicated to scripture. The classics found in Roman libraries simply disappeared, more for lack of interest than as a result of active persecution or censorship.

At no time in the history of the West did literacy come closer to the Egyptian-Mesopotamian model than from the fall of Rome to the rise of monastery and abbey schools in the Middle Ages. Only a few, as the ancient scribes, could read or write. Only a few, as in the ancient past, literally controlled the production of books and other forms of written communication. And those few were limited almost exclusively to the Church. Manuscript production, too, was limited primarily to men until the spread of nunneries in the late eight and ninth centuries as a part of the Carolingian renaissance.

By the eighth century the only really literate people in Europe were connected with religion. The literate upper classes had disappeared or been taken into the religious communities. Estimates vary, but probably no more than two per cent of the population could be termed literate—a condition which remained much the same until the twelfth-century scholastic age, the Renaissance and the dawn of printing.

The barbarian leaders soon learned the benefits of government based on bureaucracy and law. With this understanding came an appreciation of the language that binds—Latin. In the West Latin again assumed the role of principal medium of both written and spoken communication, particularly with Charlemagne and the ninth century. It remained so among educated people until the end of the medieval period. At the same time, the vernacular exercised a strong modifying influence, and colloquialisms and verbal forms asserted themselves. By the ninth century a council of bishops at Tours ruled that it was suitable to deliver sermons in the language of the people.

Culture became almost entirely bilingual, with Latin spoken and read in the churches, and the vulgate spoken, although rarely read, by the masses. In order to educate people removed from the Roman tradition and Latin, there developed Latin glossaries. Students came to literacy through these manuals, dictionaries and the older grammatic texts. They might speak the local vulgate among themselves, and certainly among those they were trying to reach outside of the monastery, but read and spoke Latin for religious and official events. A full command of Latin was absolutely necessary to advance in the Church and government, and this knowledge set off the Carolingian and medieval elite from the simply literate.

PREPARATION AND PUBLICATION OF MANUSCRIPTS

When one speaks of medieval manuscripts, reference is to form (a handwritten codex, sometimes illustrated, on parchment or later paper) and to time (from the wide use of the codex in the fifth century to the beginning of printing in the mid-fifteenth century). The production of the manuscripts was limited to monastic communities from the seventh century until about the twelfth century. It then became widespread in universities, courts, and trade.

Manuscript study is vast and there are thousands of books and articles covering book production by time, country, type, etc. All that can be done here is to suggest an outline of the possibilities for further reading.

Preparation of the manuscript for writing and possibly for pictures followed certain definite steps. As indicated, the work took place in the monastic scriptorium. The same space might be employed as well for a library with a few precious books. Work was divided by ability and skills, although often enough one monk might act as scribe, proof reader and illuminator, as well as binder and librarian. Too little is known to generalize, although by the end of the Dark Ages and certainly by the fifteenth century specialization became apparent, particularly where a gifted illuminator labored. Then, too, the individual might wish a personal copy of the manuscript and do all of the work for himself. The number of owner produced books was few in the early Christian era, but by the time of universities and the rise of the bureaucrats, the proportion increased dramatically.

The primary book material was parchment. This was the properly treated animal skin—usually a cow, sheep or goat. Parchment replaced papyrus, which was both costly and fragile. (Vellum, often used as a synonym for parchment, can either mean the skin of a young animal, or, more precisely, a calf skin.) The precise type of skin used depended on the book and, more often, the kind of animals about the monastic community. The skins were prepared in various ways, although usually they were soaked in running water for several days, immersed in lime and then after two or three weeks removed and the hair scraped off. After another water bath, they were stretched, rubbed with pumice to produce a smooth surface, cut, and folded to size.

The gathered 24 to 25 sheets made up a quire, and it was the usual practice for a scribe to work on one quire at a time. There were standard formats: (1) Folio—a parchment sheet folded in half to make four pages about 10 to 12 inches high and 16 to 18 inches wide. (2) Folded again, there were eight sheets, or a quarto. (3) Repeated foldings resulted in smaller and smaller books such as one of the smallest, where the sheet was folded 16 times.

Preparation of parchment was time consuming, and many monasteries took a disastrous shortcut. They simply erased (via a knife) the pagan, Greek and Latin texts from parchment leaves to make way for copying Scripture. Some of the original writing was inadvertently saved and can be read under the overlay of the scribes. (These are called palimpsests, i.e. writing material used once or more times after earlier writing has been erased.) The tragedy is that many texts which escaped destruction in the crumbling Roman empire perished within the walls of the monastic scriptoria. The writing was done by a monk with a goose quill, using various inks. Each page was ruled, and today one can often make out the guidelines in manuscripts.

From the sixth to the twelfth century, there was little individual writing. The emphasis was on copying older texts. To copy a book was to take part in a devotional act. To compose one's own text was to disregard the laws of God and man. Lacking imaginative new works, monks became less rather than more literate. To copy did not necessarily mean one had to be able to read, and some of the scribes were semi-illiterate.

The combination of semi-literacy as well as lack of proper proof reading resulted in countless errors of transcription from the exemplar (i.e. the approved and correct master of the book) to the copy made by the diligent or otherwise less than enthusiastic monk. A near-sighted or careless scribe might copy a phrase or word and then look back at the original only to pick up the next word from the wrong line. Abbreviations were another problem as they varied from place to place and might be transcribed, i.e. ''corrected'' from the exemplar, but in the wrong way. The abbreviation ''mr'' for example can stand for ''mater'' or ''martyr.'' The chance of a perfect copy from the exemplar is estimated at over one hundred to one.

The scribes developed some customs found in almost all manuscripts. Usually each text began with an incipit, often a single letter. ''Here begins'' was the incipit. ''Finit'' for finish was used, and by the fourteenth to fifteenth century this became ''Finis.''

In his ''On scribes and the remembering of correct spelling,'' Cassiodorus pleads for scribes to pay close attention to what they copy and to follow spelling rules he lays down in his *On Orthography.* He addresses the need for bindings and sundials (for bright days) and water clocks (for dim days) "to point out the hour continually." When it is dark, "we have prepared cleverly constructed lamps" for the copyist[5] (Fig. 14).

Although based on the Roman, the form of handwriting or script tended to vary from place to place. Today an expert on early writing can date and place a manuscript within ten to one hundred

14. A portrait of Ezra, the patron saint of scribes, from the *Codex Amiatinus,* but probably taken from an earlier work. He writes with the manuscript on his knee, and behind him is the traditional bookcupboard.

years by identifying the peculiar aspects of a given script. Subfields of paleography include what is known as codicology, i.e. the study of writing materials and tools and external characteristics such as binding and ruling.[6]

Once the writer had completed the text, there might be one to two incomplete parts. One would be left blank for text in another color of ink. Another blank space might be where an illustration (letter, decoration, etc.) was to be placed, and art work could be no more than adding a letter in red. An elaborate manuscript might call for paragraph marks in different colors as well as line-by-line decoration. A costly work, from Gospels to complete Bibles, usually provided spaces where quarter-page to full page illuminated illustrations would be placed—usually by another scribe who, by today's standards, would be a top-rank artist.

Binding methods varied, but basically the quires were sewn together (or to several strips) with cords passed through the stitchwork (or the strips) and fastened to the book boards. The Christian book encouraged elaborate decoration from metal studs or bosses to jeweled accents and portraits. Leather covers were primarily decorated with various stamps used by the binder.

It was not until the thirteenth-fourteenth centuries, and even then sparingly, that individual scribes and illuminators signed their work. For the most part, the majority are shadows. Only their books remain. Compared to other labor in the monastic community, the scribes had relatively appealing work. Most of the copying was done during the daylight hours, which meant more was accomplished in the spring and summer. The essential problems seemed to be cold in the winter and silence in all seasons. This prompted comments, curses and general expressions of discontent in many manuscript margins or colophons, i.e. an inscription at the end of the manuscript which gives information now found usually on title pages.

As silence was standard in scriptoriums, monks apparently made their needs known by sign language. The sign of the cross would be a request for a missal, and one hand on the stomach and another on his mouth indicated need for a book for relaxation. Whether all of this is true or not, the human quality of the otherwise faceless monks is testified to in the various inscriptions and marginal notes. Among the more famous: "As the sailor longs for a safe harbor at the end of his voyage, so does the writer for the last word.'' ''Here ends the second part of the Summa of Thomas Aquinas, the longest, most verbose, and most tedious to write; thank God, thank God, and again thank God.''[7]

In a heartfelt complaint one medieval scribe summarized the grief, pride and care necessary to copy a manuscript: ''A man who can write may believe this is no great accomplishment. But only try to do it yourself and you will learn how difficult it is to be a writer. It ruins your eyes, gives you a backache and ties your chest and belly in knots. Gentle reader, turn these pages carefully. Keep your fingers far from the text. For just as hail plays havoc with the fruits of spring, so a careless reader is destructive to books and writing.''[8] (Fig. 15)

Unfortunately, few later readers gave this much attention and most of the extant medieval manuscripts are incomplete or damaged because readers cut out leaves for the miniatures, often framed separately in art museums and libraries, or for such mundane reasons as to clean boots. John Ruskin (1819–1900), who carefully destroyed ''pornographic'' work of Turner, also reports in his 1854 diary that he ''Cut missal up in evening-hard work.'' In addition, the destruction of monastic libraries during the Reformation accounted for the total loss or mutilation of thousands of individual books.

IRISH/ENGLISH CONTRIBUTIONS

Located throughout Europe and the Middle East, the monastic communities, under as many different orders, individually contributed to the development of the manuscript. The Irish had an early start with St. Patrick (368–461) and Columba (531–97), who encouraged monasteries in Scotland and northern England. Subject to myth and legend, Columba, by the mid sixth century, was credited with copying over 300 books. A St. Finnian manuscript had to be copied in one night, and the myth has it that the glow from St. Columba's fingernails illuminated the scriptorium as he worked. While on Iona, the good Saint supposedly said, ''Delightful to be in the bosom of an isle, on the peak of a rock.''[9] Actually, the words are from an unknown twelfth-century author, but they summarize the spirit which took the civilizing Irish from the bleak Island to York and Durham and Jarrow, the centers of well-known

15. This picture of St. Matthew from the Ebo Gospels, c. 816, shows the evangelist in the position of the usual scribe, although with a given amount of liberty taken by the imaginative artist.

monastic schools by the seventh century. From York and the tradition of the early English historian, Venerable Bede (c. 673–735), came Alcuin (735–804), invited by Charlemagne to instruct the unruly peoples he governed.

The world owes the Irish for three brilliant illuminated manuscripts: the *Book of Durrow* (c. 650),[10] followed by the *Lindisfarne Gospels* (c. 700) and the *Book of Kells* (c. 750–830) (Fig. 16). While each is distinctive, the insular love of pure decoration, with interlacing patterns, animal forms and intricate geometric-carpet pages, is found in all three. Intricate patterns and color are so thick as to resemble an oriental carpet, and the anti-naturalistic figures are precursors of twentieth-century abstracts.

MONASTIC LIBRARIES

Ammianus Marcellinus in 378 proclaimed ''all libraries, like tombs, were closed forever,''[11] and with that the concept of private and public libraries familiar to the Romans died. By then the Christian concept of a library, with codices instead of scrolls, had become common. Despite Marcellinus' grim prophesy, monastic libraries were found from Jerusalem to Rome to Lyons. Fashioned after the Roman archives, they were places to preserve the Bible and commentaries. They were not for active use by lay persons or, for that matter, common monks. Few books circulated and the small collection was kept in one place; later, books were even chained to desks. One of the largest, the Papal library, founded in Rome in the latter part of the fourth century, contained both Christian and classic works, although it suffered a reduction in size and scope under Gregory I (590–604).

The largest non-monastic library before the Carolingian revival was the palace library at Constantinople. The library was enlarged numerous times. It served both government and scholars. It ceased growing with the iconoclastic movement, and particularly under Leo III (717–741). The ninth-century revival of learning focused again on the library, which then increased in size and importance. Special collections developed, including areas devoted entirely to reference. The books were divided by language (i.e. Greek and Latin). The library was dismantled with the sack of the city by the crusaders in 1204, and although various efforts were made to

16. Page from the *Book of Kells,* the book of the Gospels made at the Irish monastery of Kells about 800, in Irish script with Celtic features in the decoration.

reinstate its old glory, they failed. The palace and Byzantine monastery libraries became veritable mines for the book collectors of the Renaissance.[12]

The most famous of the monastic libraries was at Monte Cassino, where St. Benedict first established his order in 529. The library was both a place to copy books and a source of individual titles for monks to read. It remained in various states of repair and use until World War II when it was destroyed, along with the monastery, by Allied bombers. Benedict's rules called for every monk to have at least one book to read during the year. ''All shall receive a book from the library which they shall read from beginning to end.'' Books were distributed in the Benedictine monasteries, with specific titles and prescribed reading established at given times in the choir, the individual cell, the refectory and the infirmary.

Subject matter was fairly uniform, moving from several copies of the Bible to works of the Church Fathers. In addition there were the standard medieval exegetical, theological and canon law texts. Collections of sermons and the lives of the saints generally were available. These might be rounded out by a few historical works, such as the *Anglo Saxon Chronicle,* and grammatical guides. In fact, Donatus was found almost everywhere. Few libraries contained translations from the Greek.

Once type of favored collection (or encyclopedia) was put together by individuals who might begin with a booklet or two, and consolidate with poetry and his own words as well as material copied from miscellaneous sources. There could be from a dozen to several dozen different items in such a work, by as many different scribes. Material would be collected over a period of years, or even a lifetime, and entered by amateur scribes, wandering professionals or the compiler himself. The medievalist encyclopedists, from Isidore of Seville (c. 560–636) to Hrabanus Maurus-abbot of Fulda in the 840s, to Bartholomaeus Anglicus in the thirteenth century, initially drew upon one another and often from Pliny's *Natural History* (77 A.D.). Cassiodorus in the sixth century and Isidore in the seventh century summed up the world's Christian learning, both following Pliny's broad design.[13] By far the most widely read and copied, Isidore's *Etymologies* (c. 636–640) was strongly influenced by the liberal arts. It contained entries from divinity to ships and games. Drawing upon Aristotle and other Greek thinkers, Bartholomaeus Anglicus (c. 1240) published an encyclopedia which explained in twenty books the properties of things and the origins of ideas. Its popularity was due to many things, but it afforded the reader information ''about all that ought to be known.''[14]

Catalogs of early monastic libraries were little more than a listing of the few titles (from a dozen to under 100) held in the library. The listing method continued until the fifteenth century when an effort at bibliographic control became more wide-spread. Books usually were arranged by broad subject, such as law, theology, medicine and the like. From the beginning lack of standardized titles as well as little understanding of the description of individual books caused problems.

The librarian usually filled a part-time position with well-defined duties. He would select books for given holidays, censor certain titles, and, most important, regulate the flow of the few books in the monastery. He knew where each title was to be found at any given time, including the few which might be loaned for copying to other monasteries. He also might decide how many copies of a particular work would be needed and would then control production. Holdings tended to be under the control of the designated librarian until the development of schools and universities, when the collection was divided among sections or departments. What began as a tight reign on borrowing gradually became more liberal. By the thirteenth century more books were lent than before. A type of interlibrary loan, founded in the ninth century when books made a regular circuit in various parts of Europe, became common from the thirteenth to fourteenth century. The price of a loan might be the return of the original with a fair copy which the librarian then put into an ever-widening circulation circle.

ISLAMIC CONTRIBUTIONS

During the European Dark Ages, Islam became a force on the world scene. In 622, Muhammed fled to Medina, and his ideas gave the Arab world a sense of identity carried on by Caliph Omar (581–644). By the eighth century the Islamic world was divided by disputes and sects (particularly Sunni and Shiite). Despite setbacks, the Muslims conquered Spain in 715, were stopped from entering the rest of Europe by Charles Martel in 732 and by his grandson Charlemagne some forty years later.

Arabic contributions to the West were staggering, conserving the work of Aristotle and contributing the concept of numbers and optics. Córdoba, by the tenth century, became the Islamic science center. The Arabic influence began to wane with the fall of Spain to Christians and the First Crusade (1096–99). Islamic libraries survived much of the loss. At Cairo a collection of over a million volumes was noted in the eleventh century. Here and particularly in Spain, the Islamic libraries served as a conduit for the passage of Greek learning to the West, replacing what was lost after the fall of Rome.[15]

Lexicography was of great interest to the Arabic world. Work ranged from Koranic lexicology (c. 688–1,000) to didactic poems and collections of scholarly anecdotes. The early Arabic encyclopedias were manuals, produced in the ninth century, to assist public officials. By the tenth century a group of scholars published the first encyclopedia made up of separate articles by numerous authorities. The most important was compiled about 1040 and consisted of essays on human nature, clothes, weapons, etc.

END OF THE DARK AGES

Charlemagne (742–814) reunited Europe into the Holy Roman Empire in 800, and pushed forward education, culture and a concentration on manuscript production. Charlemagne, concerned with correct language usage associated with ancient Roman civilization, promoted schools in monastic centers and episcopal seats throughout his empire. As a devout Christian he was interested in furthering the importance of the Book and literacy—at least among the monks and the court.[16] The educational organization was under the direction of Alcuin. The monk from York is an early example of a humanistic scholar whose genius for creative solutions to difficult problems still commands respect.

Trained in the Irish and Insular movements, Alcuin was persuaded by Charlemagne to establish a palace school at Aachen and later at Tours.[17] A basic system of copying and illuminating manuscripts developed in both centers. Equally, small but much used libraries were established. These might have under 100 volumes with an average of between 400 and 500 books.

A poet, Alcuin saluted the scribes with "May those who copy the pronouncements of holy law, and the hallowed sayings of the saintly fathers sit here." And with that he warned against practices which today make many of the otherwise dull, usually non-illuminated manuscripts, lively. For example, "let them take care not to insert silly remarks." In a triumphant close to his "On scribes," he exclaims: "It is an excellent task to copy holy books. . . . It is better to write books than to dig vines: one serves the belly but the other serves the soul."[18]

TRANSMISSION OF TEXTS

With the revival of interest in government and education, there came the need for more books. Scriptoria, more or less neglected or rarely encouraged, took first place in meeting the need. Publishing gained new importance, and while during the centuries after the fall of Rome there was a scarcity of manuscripts, from the ninth century alone there are close to 7,000 extant works.[19] The great gift of the busy scribes to our day is the fact that almost all Latin texts extant are from copies made in the monasteries during the late eighth and ninth centuries. Only Virgil can be traced back almost in full to manuscript before 800. All the others, all of our classics, are drawn from complete copies made after 800. By the end of the period there were so many copies of books, of authors from Ovid and Martial to Livy and Terence, that there was little danger of their permanent loss. Conversely, some authors such as Pliny the Younger and even Ovid and Tacitus are scarcely available. In some cases only one copy exists from the period.

Many classic texts perished not so much because of Christian opposition, but simply because no one was interested in reading them. Conversely, the major classics were read by both pagans and Christians alike, and the interest insured their survival. After the firm establishment of Christianity the Church rarely imposed censorship, and except for isolated cases (e.g. Jovian in 363–4 burned a library at Antioch, although this is not certain) pagan libraries were neither destroyed nor dispersed. Most of the effort was to eliminate unorthodox Christian works, not the Greek or

Latin classics. Christianity borrowed and modified pagan antece-
dents. A shared culture was evident in the continuities between
the Greek and Latin worlds, as well as between the Christians and
Islam. Knowledge of Greek and Latin was necessary for the
reading of church literature, and a few monks developed profi-
ciency in these languages by working with the classical authors.
They thus created an international literary culture, primarily
religious in character, but maintaining a connection with the
intellectual life of classical antiquity.

"Our times (c. 800) are transformed into the civilization of
antiquity," proclaimed one poet. "The golden age of Rome is
reborn and restored anew in the world." The Carolingian age (so
called from "karling" or French people) marked the end of the
Dark Ages.

NOTES

[1]Terminology and dates vary for the period from the fall of Rome to
the Renaissance, but here (drawn from the *Dictionary of the Middle
Ages*. Scribners, 1987) names and approximate dates of periods covered
include: (1) Dark Ages (c. 400–800). A synonym for approximately this
same period is Late Antiquity. (2) Middle Ages (c. 410–1455), an
inclusive term for both the Dark Ages and the period which followed; or,
from c. 800 to 1455.

[2]In the West the papacy was heir to Rome and followed many of the
same administrative patterns, including a heavy reliance on writing and
literacy among the clergy. As a religion of the Book, Christianity was
dependent on literacy. See Jane Stevenson, "Literacy in Ireland," in
Rosamond McKitterick, *The Uses of Literacy in Early Medieval Europe*
(Cambridge University Press, 1990).

[3]Vivarium (fish pond) was a gorgeous retreat for the veteran statesman
and his followers. Unlike St. Benedict, who was more concerned with
keeping his monks busy than scholarship, Cassiodorus was interested in
preserving the classics and, of course, religious works. With the death of
Cassiodorus (age 95) the fate of the library is uncertain, although much
has been written about its possible dissemination. It is certain that some
of the manuscripts were used as models for copies throughout Europe.

[4]Legend has it that Benedict of Nursia formed his ideas of a monastic
community while in a three-year retreat in a cave near Rome. Over a
period of time he was said to have established 12 monastic communities

each with 12 monks—although, in reality, most were larger. He established his rules at Cassino, where he died. St. Benedict's famous Rule has no direct mention of the scriptorium, although there are commands to study and read. Work hours, too, were established and the implication is that copying religious titles was part of the manual labor. Essentially it was a method of counteracting idleness, and did not serve the broader ends envisioned by Cassiodorus a few years later. Primarily, though, The Rule's ordinances became the code of Western monastic communities. Regulations about copying books were individual matters at, say, Rheims, Bobbio, Fulda, Reichenau, etc.

[5]Cassiodorus Senator. *An Introduction to Divine and Human Readings* (New York: Columbia University Press, 1946), pp. 134–135. These are fat fed lamps which "burned continually with a bright flame." This collection is edited by Leslie Jones and includes considerable information on the man, the monastery at Vivarium and possible book production.

[6]The study of codicology has gained in importance during the past 30 years, and is evident in details found in bibliographies such as *Illuminated and Decorated Medieval Manuscripts in the University Library Utrecht* (Cambridge: Cambridge University Press, 1991) or in the ongoing series initiated by Otto Pacht and J.G. Glaexander which catalogs illuminated manuscripts in the Bodleian Library, Oxford. Discussing the nomenclature of script types often may sound like a discussion of wine; i.e. such terms as "dignity, harmony and destiny" are common, or a script may be characterized as "weaker" stylistically than another.

[7]Marc Drogan. *Anathema: Medieval scribes and the history of book curses* (Totowa, NJ: Allanheld & Schram, 1983), p. 69.

[8]*Ibid.,* p. 19, Prior Petus, eleventh century. See also, Lilian Randall, *Images in the margins of Gothic manuscripts* (Berkeley: University of California, 1966).

[9]*A Celtic Miscellany* (New York: Penguin Books, 1971), p. 279.

[10]The book had intrinsic magic powers, and Bede explains how swallowing bits of an Irish manuscript will cure poison. The *Book of Durrow* barely escaped destruction as it was constantly immersed in water to cure certain cattle diseases.

[11]Ammianus Marcellinus (c. 330–396). The historian of the fourth century whose work traces the history of the Roman empire from 96. Only the last 18 books (of 31) survive.

[12]In spite of the vandalism they have suffered throughout the ages these libraries today still contain great treasures from the early Middle Ages. They preserved the Byzantine cultural tradition, which was later continued in the monasteries at Kiev and Novgorod and in the Balkans,

and particularly in the monasteries of Athos, where the libraries became prototypes for those in Russian monasteries. For a concise history of the monastic libraries, see Michael Harris, *History of Libraries in the Western World* (Metuchen, NJ: Scarecrow Press, 1984).

[13]Later masters of the general encyclopedia often were chastised, as was Varro (116–28 B.C.) for simply copying from other works. After the Republic, they all drew from Varro, Pliny and Verrius Flaccus (c. first century A.D.). The latter is quoted by Isidore, although not a trace of his encyclopedia original work has survived. Isidore quotes, too, the lost work of Suetonius Tranquillus (late half of first century A.D.).

[14]Ernest Brehaut. *An Encyclopedist of the Dark Ages, Isidore of Seville* (New York: Columbia University Press, 1912), p. 31. There are generous samples of Isidore's writings, including (in Part II) "The Etymologies." Grammar and rhetoric are the topics of the first two books, but others include such subjects as "on man and monsters" as well as "on ships, buildings and garments." The latter has information on "bedding, tablecloths and so forth." In "on languages, races and empires" Isidore gives his Shavian views of various nationalities, including "the Britons...so called according to the Latin because they are stupid" (p. 212).

[15]According to a seventeenth-century Moroccan author, in the tenth century Córdoba had a library which "contained no less than four thousand volumes...and there were in the capital many other libraries." Roger Collins, "Literacy and the laity in early medieval Spain," in Rosamond McKitterick. *The Uses of Literacy in Early Medieval Europe* (Cambridge University Press, 1990), p. 109.

[16]Charlemagne (like his counterpart Alfred, who ruled Wessex in England from c. 878 to his death in 879) was instrumental in reviving education in Europe, although he himself probably was close to illiterate. Apparently he was a great listener, particularly to the reading of religious works such as Augustine's *City of God;* e.g. see Betty Radice, ed. Einhard, *The Life of Charlemagne* (New York: Penguin Books, 1969), pp. 78–79. Also (p. 82) he "directed that the old-age narrative poems, barbarous enough, it is true, in which were celebrated the warlike deeds of the kings of ancient times, should be written out and so preserved. He also began a grammar of his native tongue."

[17]Alcuin (c. 730–804) was England's gift to France and the world in that he agreed to a request by Charlemagne (c. 781) to move from York to Aachen to revise and remodel the monastic educational system. From 782 to 796 Alcuin was head of the palace school where Charlemagne, with his family, was a student for a time. In addition to education, Alcuin set in motion the project to remove errors from standard texts. In 796 Alcuin became head of the Abbey of St. Martin at Tours where he lived

until his death. Here he developed the library and a model scriptorium. He composed much poetry—and his own epitaph: "Alcuin was my name and wisdom always my love."

[18]Helen Waddell. *The Wandering Scholars* (London: Constable, 1927), various pages.

[19]Comparatively, there are under 1,800 extant manuscripts, the majority in fragments and parts, surviving from the early Christians to c. 800, primarily from scriptoria and libraries in monastic communities. With the standardization and spread of scriptoria the number of books dramatically increased; e.g., for the ninth century alone there are 6,700 titles surviving. The more famous manuscripts, particularly in terms of glorious illumination, were located at Fulda, Reichenau, and St. Gallen.

CHAPTER FIVE

MIDDLE AGES TO THE RENAISSANCE

> No work arises which age, full of years, does not destroy, nor wicked time overturn. Only things which are written avoid this fate, challenge death. Only things written in books maintain what has been.
>
> —Hrabanus

With the death of Charlemagne (814), the tradition of a modern King David ended. His successor, Louis the Pious (who never showed his white teeth in a smile),[1] moved Europe towards the Ottonian age—roughly from the mid-tenth century to about the middle of the eleventh century. This was the height of feudalism.

By the end of the twelfth century feudalism was on the decline. It gradually was replaced by strong nationalist monarchies which, in turn, encouraged urban centers, trade and business. Numerous other major factors undermined the feudal system. The Crusades (1095–1272) sapped the strength of the lords.[2] The first famine and Black Death (beginning in the fourteenth century) increased the value of labor and to an extent offered peasants more independence. The local systems gave way to more centralized government, and the first indications of limited democracy appeared. Feudalism disappeared, although it maintained a hold in France until the French Revolution and in Russia up to the end of World War I.

Before 1300 there were few places in Europe with more than 10,000 people. It took 100 to 200 years to develop cities and it was not until the mid fifteenth century that towns of 50,000 were usual; even then the largest cities, such as London, had no more than 150,000 citizens. The emergence of urban centers, spurred on by trade developed during the Crusades, became magnets for, first, abbey and cathedral schools and later, universities. Around the universities publishers and specialized groups from doctors and lawyers to business people assembled. By the thirteenth century higher education, systems of European law and scholastic philosophy developed. Architecture, first in the Romanesque cathedrals and later in their Gothic counterparts, took on major importance as did sculpture. Both Latin and vernacular poetry flourished with liturgical drama.

Life became more settled, even civilized, and certainly by the fourteenth century much safer for daily living. Trade encouraged a wider world view which, in turn, helped to set the stage for the Renaissance (c 1350–1600) and the great leap forward in the history of the book when Gutenberg employed movable type to print the Bible in 1455.

THE RISE OF THE UNIVERSITY

The monastery was the single best way for a young person to gain an education, at least from the fall of Rome until the development of abbey and cathedral schools and universities in the twelfth century. Actually, the monastic community continued as an educational force until well into the nineteenth century, but it was particularly impressive during the Dark and early Middle Ages. To study was to join the priesthood, although some ''graduates'' took their vows less than seriously. Many moved on to join the basic bureaucracy in the feudal system's courts or took to the highways as poets and vagabonds.

In about 972 Gerbert of Rheims, later Pope Sylvester II (999–1003), said, ''I have always studied to live well and to speak well.'' And as an early organizer of a cathedral school he marks the turning away from the monastic communities to broader interests which trained both clergy and lay persons for administration.[3] Gradually a renewed focus on the individual resulted in more secular groups. Out of the cathedral schools developed the urban universities at Bologna, Paris, Rheims, Oxford and Cambridge.

A scholastic movement led to a systematization of commentary and texts, as well as translations used in the classrooms. The availability for the first time in Latin and Greek, of Aristotle and other Greek thinkers, had a wide influence. The early notion of scientific analysis (via Aristotle) was manifested in the study of medicine. The curricula in the universities took a pragmatic turn away from the abbey and church schools. The universities concentrated on rhetoric and science, as well as theology, but primarily at an abstract level. Thanks to the need for literate clerics in government and church, the number of university students grew dramatically from the thirteenth to the fifteenth centuries.[4]

Universities, a term used first by Cicero to indicate the whole of the human race, were created out of the nucleus of scholars first gathered in earlier cathedral and canonical schools. The organizational models tended to follow those of urban guilds. As they developed strength (c. 1231+) from Paris to Oxford, they gained support of both central governments and the Church, both of whom wished to be associated with the equivalent of today's "think tanks."

BOOK PUBLISHING

Literacy encouraged interest in owning copies of books. By the sixteenth century a new reading public emerged, made up not only of clerics and court members, but of professional and business people. This and the growth of universities required different approaches to publishing of books. Not only were new types of titles needed—from grammars to basic commentaries—but books were required in quantity for both students and teachers. Out of the need developed an early approach to mass publishing.

By the twelfth century both monastic scriptoria and scribes ceased to be major factors in book production. There were numerous reasons for this shift, but among the more apparent were the lack of interest by the monks and the need for not one or two copies, but numerous copies, which the monastic community was not able to accomplish with limited help. The development did not entirely eliminate monastic scriptoria, which by the beginning of printing were to be found throughout Europe. If anything, they gained strength outside of university towns, but their earlier importance in transmission of texts faded.

Publishing around the universities, from about the mid thirteenth century, was controlled in most cases by licensed publisher—booksellers, i.e. stationers. Each year the university authorities checked the primary copy (i.e. exemplar) and issued an official list of texts and from whom they were available. The number of authorized individual titles varied from 125 to 175. The stationers were appointed or at least controlled by the university. They had to agree to keep in stock correct editions of the books that were used for instruction and to rent them to students for a fixed fee. They could sell books only on commission. Book selling was thus a strictly limited and regulated business, yet it must have paid well, to judge from the large number of stationers that quickly gathered at the new seats of learning, particularly in Paris. Rules for stationers appeared in 1259 in Bologna and in 1275 in Paris. A stationer at a university could sell manuscripts to other universities and to scholars in foreign countries. Books on medicine came primarily from Salerno and Montpelier, scholastic literature from Paris, and law books from Bologna.

SECULAR PUBLISHING

Aside from the official stationers, secular publishing emerged in cities from Florence and Rouen to London. Here the call normally was for books in the vernacular, not in Latin. They were for civil servants and merchants. The more mundane work consisted primarily of copying business and legal documents. Textbooks, even outside of university centers, were popular and included Donatus and the Latin grammar, as well as mathematics and philosophy. Popular works, from *The Song of Roland* (c 1100) to Chaucer's *Canterbury Tales* (1395), also provided work for the private scribes.

The work was subcontracted. An illustrator or scribe might be engaged in doing four or five works, from business documents to elaborate books, at the same period of time. Thus the publishing was spread about so that employment was relatively regular. Individual scribes and illuminators gradually replaced the large abbeys as primary sources of illuminated works.

Authentic unbound copies were available in quires, spread out over a number of copyists. The system worked well enough; the stationers hired scribes, usually students, to strike off a section (quire or pecia). Under this system of "mass production" a text of 312 pages which might take an individual six months or more to copy, could be done in days by scores of individual copyists.

An author seeking to have his work published would at first make a perfect copy, often with notes, and then supervise it through the publisher until a satisfactory exemplar was at hand. Chaucer in the fifteenth century, for example, probably first wrote the books on paper or even waxed tablets. After that it is presumed that a fair copy was made by a professional scribe. The copy was proofread by Chaucer. *The Canterbury Tales* was then copied as sales required. After Chaucer's death, various professional scribes and amateurs made numerous unauthorized copies. These tended to be without comment, on cheap paper and rather rough, although some copies, made for the rich, were quite handsome.

Manuscripts might be copied for friends and the family of the owner of the original manuscript. In England, the fifteenth-century Paston letters give proof of such practices. It was not uncommon, too, for a writer to expect his patron to have multiple copies made of his work and distribute them among friends. In fact, the patron was under some obligation to insure the dissemination of the new work or translation.

The gradual expansion of secular publishing indicates that the two major sources of books from the fourteenth to the sixteenth century were the amateur scribe and the professional scribe/publisher/bookshop. The latter provided an organized approach to book distribution, and there was an increased demand for such services by both clergy and laity. Book peddlers carried manuscripts from house to house, or set up a booth at a local fair. Often they sold used copies of standard works.

The rise of independent publishers resulted in another significant change: the focus on the individual, or at least, at long last the recognition of the individual scribe, illuminator, binder, publisher, etc. by name. What began as an anonymous group effort for the glory of God became by the fifteenth century identified with such craftspeople as those who formed the Scriveners' Guild or Stationers' Company in London in the area of St. Paul's.

Availability of paper, numerous underpaid scribes, and a type of mass production publisher made books relatively common by the fourteenth century. Merchants, otherwise unfamiliar with books, took up their distribution as they would any commodity which might be sold profitably at fairs or in distant communities. The enormous number of translations and copies of Greek manuscripts opened the way for the even greater diffusion of information in the fifteenth century.

SCRIPT DEVELOPMENTS

Until the introduction of the Carolingian minuscule in the late eighth century, scribes throughout most of Europe followed the Roman pattern of capitals or uncial or half uncial, using what was appropriate for the document (Fig. 17). They also had various styles of cursive, although none seemed satisfactory. An unknown individual or group introduced the Carolingian minuscule. It lent itself to the quick, efficient copy of manuscripts, and after its development in the late eighth century it was used widely by Alcuin and his monks at Tours. This natural bookhand was as practical as it was legible and had no real rivals until the introduction of Gothic script in the early twelfth or late eleventh century (Fig. 18).

In the course of the twelfth and thirteenth centuries script underwent a transformation; the letters became narrower and more angular and the contrast between thick and thin lines became more pronounced—the result was Gothic script. Corresponding to the contemporary Gothic style in art, writing evolved from the round Roman arch to the pointed Gothic arch. The letters were written so close together that two adjoining ones were often run into one (e.g., the d and e). In large liturgical manuscripts the letters were usually made quite large and heavy and given a rather decorative appearance; this style was called missal script (from the mass books, or missals); the name lattice script was also given it because the crowded letters made it resemble lattice work. For more ordinary use there was a Gothic cursive, which was the ancestor of the script that is still used in Germany. Gothic was preferable to the Carolingian style because its angularity allowed it to be written much faster. It had a flow which permitted the scribe to write without lifting a pen. The style spread beyond universities as the common writing hand of officials, notaries, business people, etc. (Fig. 19).

XCUIIVIILENTICYCLOPESJUIKMINAMASSIS
CUMCROCIRANPALLITITAVRINISIOLLIBUSAURAS
ACCLIDUNIRIDDUNIQMPALLISIRIDENTIATINGUNI
ALRAINCUGIMLIINCOSIPISINCUDIOUSANIRUM
ILLISINTERSESLMAGNAUIORACCHIATOLLUNI

17. An uncial (capitalis rustica) Virgil manuscript of the 4th century. (Papal Library in the Vatican.) The illustration shows the smithy of the Cyclops and is typical of Roman painting of the classical period.

genera hostium · proponamus; Pagani dicunt; Quid
quodnos ex or recul adq abicias· tamquá multos cole
deos· ecce uos dm qué pdicaus colendú · filium habere
citus· & sine alterius con mixtione sexus· natú ee con
gus, Iudei dicunt; Quomodo unú colitus dm · quand
homine qué patres nri · crucifixerunt · dnm dicent
hominib error queus· ut tamquá filium dei uenerab

18. Carolingian minuscule script in an Augustine manuscript of the 11th century. (After Franz Steffens.)

19. Gothic minuscule script in a manuscript from 1339. (After Franz Steffens.)

Punctuation became more universal and this in turn contributed to the end of reading aloud. Romans were encouraged to read aloud to help memory. The lack of space between words, the lack of punctuation, encouraged oral activity. With the Middle Ages and the wide gap between spoken and written Latin, the Christian codices provided limited punctuation and, more important, popularized the division of words, sentences and paragraphs. By the twelfth century full word separation allowed one to read silently. This was encouraged, particularly where scribes were copying works in a crowded space. It took another 100 to 200 years to make silence a custom. By then word separation and punctuation encouraged an easy understanding of words, if not always the sense of the text, without sounding them aloud.

ILLUMINATED MANUSCRIPTS[5]

Illumination (literally to use gold for brilliance) was a method of applying decoration. Refinements, including illustration or illuminated letters or both, depended on how elaborate and costly the work was to be. Pigments and the gold were fixed to the parchment with egg whites, a practice employed later by the craftspeople and some artists of the nineteenth century. Rubrication (from rubber or red) was employed early to indicate decoration of letters, but by the fourteenth to fifteenth century it became a simple descriptor for illumination or decoration of all types. While it seems probable that both Roman and Greek papyrus rolls were illustrated, none is extant (Fig. 20). In fact, there is little real evidence of illustration except by inference and probability until the fourth to fifth centuries A.D. Scraps and fragments suggest illumination, but only the Ambrosian *Iliad* and two Virgils of the late fourth or early fifth centuries are proof of illustrated books. Scientific illustration, with striking pharmacological work and author portraits, is the focus of the Vienna Dioscorides from the early sixth century. And the great illuminated masterpieces of the Hiberno-Saxon school came 200 or more years later—*Book of Durrow* (c. 650); *Lindisfarne Gospels* (c. 700) and *Book of Kells* (c. 750–830).[6]

Drawing upon Greek and Roman models as well as their own invention, the early Christians quickly learned the importance of drawing. This found form in everything from graffiti to tomb paintings to murals. Eventually books were illuminated.

Pictures of scenes from the Bible, Evangelists or religious events were employed both for aesthetics and for the illiterate. Pope Gregory the Great in the late sixth century declared, ''a picture takes the place of reading.'' The view generally was held that illustration and art were superior to the written word for those who were unable to read or just barely literate. A challenge came when iconoclasts in the Greek church sought to remove art from books and churches.

By the fourth century the illuminated manuscript and wall paintings on churches became common. Nevertheless, rumbles of the iconoclastic rebellion against figurative art can be found in the puritanical attitude of Eusebius of Caesarea. About 327 the early Christian historian reported that pictures of Christ and the apostles could be purchased in Palestinian bazaars, but he suggested that these salespeople couldn't be Christians. They must be pagans. This undercurrent of mistrust of art emerged in the eighth century when the Byzantine Emperor Leo in 726 initiated by edict a full-scale program of destroying religious art. The identification with images and pagans had a measure of truth which fired the

20. Probably a fifth-century illustration from the *Iliad,* this may be a copy of now lost Roman and/or Greek illustration. The charioteer papyrus illustration is all that remains of a codex.

iconoclastic argument in Byzantium until the mid-ninth century when the Empress Theodora restored icons. Fortunately this had little influence in Europe, primarily because, from 590 on, Pope Gregory vigorously defended pictures and images in the Church—a tradition maintained by the West, despite the Pope being a subject of the Emperor in Constantinople through the seventh century.[7]

The use of pictures was an important part of educating illiterate church members and art is often referred to in that role in literature. François Villon (b. 1431, d?) in his famous *Testament* puts words into the mouth of an old woman "'Who knows nothing and can't read/On the walls of my parish church I see/A paradise painted with harps and lutes.'"[8]

The classical Greek-Roman art style gradually gave way in the Christian antique to virtual elimination of landscape and the human figure. The latter's sensuous beauty was eliminated and replaced by outline figures generously covered with folds of clothing. There was little indication of the body under the drapes, as was the case, too, with the mosaics and frescoes of Byzantine art picked up in illuminated manuscripts.

Never faced with the problem of illuminating the manuscripts from nature, but rather mastering traditional descriptive illustrations, the early artists established a group of archetypes and symbols, familiar even to this day. For example, the fish is a symbol of Christ, and Four Evangelists are represented by an ox, angel, eagle and lion. The likeness of a real person was never the object; indeed, this was considered by many heresy. The result is that we lack any accurate portraits from the Romans until late into the Middle Ages. Matthew Paris's portrait of Henry III in c. 1225 and the more ambitious genius Giotto (c. 1266–1337) are among the earliest.

Only a minority (about 20 per cent) of manuscripts were, in the words of John Ruskin, "writing made beautiful." Most lacked ornament and illumination. Those chosen for special care might include brightly painted initial letters, or decorated borders, or small illustrations—or all of these. Most of the decoration, from the basic opening letters, such as R or P, were standardized, although over the centuries they became increasingly ornate and complicated. Other approaches varied from actually painting rather than drawing the miniatures, to using gold, applied over a base of glue and then rubbed to make the page shine. Variations would include staining the whole page a royal purple, letters in alternating colors, and a type of doodling at line ends. At any rate, the purpose of it all was to celebrate the glory of God, and to make it easier to find the beginning, say, of a Gospel.

The primary works which inevitably were illuminated included the Bibles for larger monastic communities, as well as the Gospels. Close behind came the lives of the saints, psalters, and books of hours. Hours, the private devotional to the Virgin Mary, replaced the psalter as the primary book of worship for lay people during the late thirteenth and early fourteenth century. It became increasingly popular, so inexpensive editions were available in the fifteenth and early sixteenth century. Later the missals, used in mass, and antiphonies for the choral parts of divine services became common.

SCHOOLS OF ILLUMINATION

There are numerous schools of illumination, named for the most part in the nineteenth and twentieth centuries. The outstanding ones include:

(1) the Insular and Hiberno Saxon monastic contributions of the seventh to eighth century. In Ireland the *Book of Kells* features stylized, strikingly modern minimalist-looking animals and human figures, usually the Evangelists. Figures wander through the pages and canon tables, which are elaborately patterned with interlocking decorations. Thanks to Alcuin, Charlemagne's court retained much of the insular style of ornamentation and design, yet turned them into more monumental works of art[9] (Fig. 21).

(2) Byzantine book decoration, which reached its highest development in the eleventh and twelfth centuries, was characterized by extensive use of gold, of purple, and of other dark colors. This produced a rather somber and mystical effect at times and it showed the influence of Syrian and other Oriental art.

(3) Influenced, too, by the Byzantine style, the various monastic communities, from Rheims and Tours to Metz and St. Gall, gradually developed a Carolingian image. The illuminations were extended to wonderfully imaginative scenes for the embellishment of the standard classics and pagan manuals and handbooks.

21. Miniature from the *Codex Aureus,* the work of a southern England miniature school, probably at Canterbury, about the year 750. The decoration combines English-Scandinavian features with strong Byzantine traits. (Royal Library, Stockholm, from *Golden Books.*)

(4) Within the Carolingian school there were numerous subsets, some of which helped to form the next great group of Ottonian manuscripts. Major centers from Fulda to Trier and Reichenau drew even more extensively from late antique models and Byzantine examples. The result is distinctive and, among other wonders, includes imperial portraits of Otto II or Otto III.

Prior to the Renaissance, the two marked artistic periods (given the labels in the nineteenth century) include the Romanesque (roughly 1000 to 1200) and the Gothic (from about 1200 to 1500).

(5) The Romanesque style was similar, yet often with striking differences, in England, France and the remainder of Europe. One thing most shared was exuberance, usually oversized illustrations in brilliant colors. The dominance of line and fixed compositional structures set the Romanesque apart, and it dominated monastic output from about the eleventh to the thirteenth century.

(6) By 1200 the now familiar Gothic had captured the European imagination and it would remain all-powerful until the early sixteenth century, when painters turned elsewhere and manuscript illumination gave way to the printing press. Today the Gothic illuminations, strongly influenced by the rise of painting and the shift to realism, seem more realistic. Whether a massive illustrated Bible or a small book of hours, the illuminations have enchanting details and scenes of aristocratic and peasant life which have wide appeal.

The illuminated letters, miniatures and other decoration might be done by more than a single person and, in fact, often were the work of an artist who was not a monk. By the eleventh century the lay artist might be a woman.[10] The illuminators traveled from monastery to monastery in search of work.

Lacking any names of artists, many illuminated manuscripts are identified by "Master of . . . "—such as Master of the Berlin Passion, indicating he or she can be identified by the style employed in the particular work, i.e. the Berlin Passion. With the Renaissance individual artists began to sign their works.

The Gothic marks the beginning of the time when illuminators started to sign their works. In parallel with the importance of the individual, the artists began to emerge as personalities with well defined styles. Jean Pucelle, for example, took pride in his paintings in the *Belleville Breviary,* completed c. 1340. Later in the century the Franco-Flemish tradition reached a zenith with the *Trés Riches Heures* of the Duc de Berry. Pol de Limbourg and his brothers were still illuminating the manuscript when the duke died in 1414. And while illumination continued into the early 16th century, none would surpass, although many might come close to equalling, the work of the Limbourg brothers.

BOOK OF HOURS

The most common illuminated manuscript after the thirteenth century was the Book of Hours. These, usually small, easy to handle works, served as prayer books for lay people. They might be quite simply decorated, but the majority included some illumination. No two Books of Hours are similar, but each had similar sections. The most common included a calendar of the church year, the Hours of the Virgin (a series of short services), the Psalms and the Office of the Dead. The owner was to pause eight times a day and read from the Hours, which, if one were in a hurry, could take all of two or three minutes. Often the single book in a household, it might be used to teach reading. Thousands are found throughout England, Europe and, by now, the United States.

The most famous, by far, was ordered by Jean, Duc de Berry (1340–1416). Six of the fifteen elaborate Book of Hours he had produced by a group of artists have survived, and the most notable is the *Trés Riches Heures,* now at Chantilly.

Books of hours, and particularly the French and Dutch specimens of the fifteenth to early sixteenth century, are notable for their naturalism and genre miniatures. There is a fascination with the daily activities of the people and the bric-a-brac of daily living. The anonymous illuminators, such as the genius of Catherine of Cleves' hours, offered Biblical scenes with elegance and charm, including Jesus toddling about in a Dutch wooden walker. The Master of Catherine of Cleves is only one of a score of geniuses who gave way to the printing press and the larger forces of history and book production before the seventeenth century and painters from Vermeer to Hals and Rembrandt.

Heavily illuminated manuscripts were extremely expensive and were treated as treasures by the nobility who purchased them or, more likely, over a period of years commissioned them from traveling scribes and artists. Valued probably more for their decoration than their content, the illuminated manuscripts not only had early sponsors, but equally early collectors. The Duke of Urbino (1422–82) would not allow a printed work in his library, and four hundred years later Sir Thomas Phillipps amassed an estimated sixty thousand manuscripts, collected in part from a second wife in the early 1840s, who brought him money. With the death of Phillipps, sale of the manuscripts went on for close to 100 years to various museums and libraries throughout the world.

Many of the nineteenth-century purchasers of pieces from the Phillipps collection were other wealthy collectors who prided themselves on building libraries they could not read. The pleasure was not in the book but in the previous owner(s), from Dukes to Kings. The habit has died out, particularly with higher prices and income taxes.

EARLY MEDIEVAL BOOKBINDING

One of the monastery brothers took care of the binding of the books. The oldest type of binding from the Middle Ages, however, was quite different from what we now understand by bookbinding. It was goldsmith's and jeweler's work. In the time of the Empire the wax tablets used by the Romans for short notations were made of ivory for festive occasions, and their outer sides were artistically decorated. There are also several examples of such diptycha from the Middle Ages, when they served as bindings for ecclesiastical manuscripts. They are considered the progenitors of the gem bindings of the early Middle Ages, which consisted of flat wooden boards embellished with reliefs in ivory or in hammered silver and gold, and sometimes with precious stones, pearls and enamel work. These bindings were made chiefly for the so-called altar bindings. Often the front side, which lay uppermost, was more richly decorated than the back. The motifs for the reliefs were usually taken from pictures in the manuscript itself and represented episodes from Bible stories, with perhaps a crucified Christ as the central figure. In the surrounding border stylized flower and leaf ornaments were often used (Fig. 22).

These fine bindings, in common with the miniatures in the manuscripts themselves, exhibit various styles according to the time and place where they were made. Thus there are characteristic Byzantine enamel bindings, silver and bronze bindings with the easily recognizable Irish dragon patterns, ivory bindings that show the marks of Carolingian art, and others that are just as clearly in the Romance style. There are bindings in which the

22. Jeweled binding from the 10th century, containing the *Echtenach Gospels* (Landesbibliothek, Gotha).

borders set with precious stones are the most conspicuous feature, and others in which the central panel, with its high relief in hammered gold, dominates. A multitude of artistic fantasies is represented in these bindings, which are still preserved in quite large numbers in libraries and museums, though many have been robbed of their gold and precious stones.

In contrast, ordinary monastery manuscripts had either a plain parchment cover or a leather binding. In the course of the 14th century, jeweled bindings became scarcer. Many liturgical books were made of velvet or leather, with metal limited to the corner pieces and the bosses that came into use in the late Gothic period. The book could rest on those bosses when it lay flat and the face of the binding would not be scratched.

Leather binding, although known in ancient times, did not come into general use in Europe until the Middle Ages. The covers of books were usually made of beech, oak or maple wood, across which leather was stretched. Dark brown calfskin was commonly used and it could be decorated in various ways. There is evidence that deerskin and the skins of other wild animals were used.

From the older medieval period there are a number of bindings embellished with leather tooling: a pattern was drawn on the damp leather and the lines were cut into the leather with a knife and then spread or punched out with a blunt tool. The technique of leather carving was used in the Coptic monasteries, but its flourishing came in the 15th century, when its home seems to have been primarily in southern Germany and Austria. The decoration usually consisted of plant designs and grotesque late Gothic animal figures, but included representations of angels and saints, and later of knights hunting or of love scenes.

Far more common, however, are the pressed leather bindings, which did not require as fine a touch as leather carving. Hot stamps with the designs engraved on them were pressed down on the leather to make the ornamentation stand out in relief. No gilding was involved in the process; this was called blind stamping. Blind-stamping is also found in the early bindings from the Coptic monasteries. The basic pattern consisted of a series of borders composed of small square, triangular, round or heart-shaped figures. As a rule there was a difference in the design of the outer borders and of the middle section, where the stamps were either arranged in small geometric groups or in less formal patterns. In the Carolingian period the variety of stamps was rather limited, but in the Romance period the number increased considerably, with the sides of the binding filled with plant and animal designs, figures of saints, knights and other human forms. In the gothic period the trend was back to simpler decoration.

The corners of the binding were, as before, usually protected by brass mountings with bosses, and the book was kept tightly closed by metal clasps. In the later Middle Ages, iron chains were attached to the upper or lower edge of the binding to fasten the book to the desk or the shelf, so that it could not fall down or be removed. No importance was attached to decorating the spine of the book; the books usually lay on a desk. If they stood on shelves it was with the spine toward the wall; our practice of placing them with the spine forward dates from the 17th century. The title of the book was therefore often written in ink on the bottom edge, where it could be seen when the book was lying down, or on the fore edge, where it could be seen when the book was standing on the shelf.

It should not, of course, be assumed that all the bindings made in the monasteries were as artistically executed as those described here; many were quite plain, and not all the monks who acted as ligators were above the level of dilettantes. But in just as many instances the artistic sense and precise workmanship exhibited in the use of stamps seem marvelous (Fig. 23).

MEDIEVAL LITERACY

There are definite clues as to the number of people who were literate by the close of the Medieval period. One suspects the poor and the agrarian population was no more literate than before, but there is too little real evidence. As for today's equivalent middle and upper classes, one may turn to letters for some indication of literacy.

By the fourteenth century the number of letters increased dramatically, and the need and desire to write, if only for business and government, indicates a relatively high rate of literacy, at least among the men. The range of correspondence became wider in the

23. Late gothic binding: blind-stamped squares and circles inside rhomboids; corner bosses and chain. (Royal Library, Copenhagen.) The decoration shows that it was made by a rather unskilled monastery binder.

fifteenth century, and personal letters more detailed. Among the educated Europeans, who were almost exclusively noblemen and middle- to upper-class monks, government employees and business people, the letters show, too, a growing involvement with reading books.

Schools, in and out of monastic communities, continued to teach Latin, but by the twelfth century in universities much of the law, medicine, literature and even theology was taught in the vernacular. By the Renaissance, only the elite and well educated knew pure Latin, and by stressing the need to keep it classically pure, they signed its death warrant as a universal method of communication.

A similar fate befell Greek, the common language of the eastern remnants of the Roman empire. The Byzantine language of the street was soon quite different from that of the classical or hellenistic authors. At the same time in the Byzantine academies ancient Greek, and particularly Homer where 20 to 40 lines might be memorized each day in school, outranked the vernacular. Soon popular speech and the demonic elements took charge, and classical Greek, like classical Latin, became the province of only the better educated.

The better educated continued to master Latin—right up until World War I in England—but French became the key to diplomacy and trade. And, more to the point, the local language increasingly dominated daily documents and literature. By the sixteenth century, thanks in no small way to printing, books in the vernacular were common, thus appealing to a wider audience, particularly those not trained in Latin or familiar with French or diplomacy.

The wandering scholars, or goliards, carried the vernacular throughout Europe, often translating from the Greek and Roman classics as well as composing individual verse. The members were primarily students and ''hedge priests'' who took to the roads instead of the cloisters. Their songs and ways were in reaction to the ascetic notions of the Church. Many of their songs took the form of satire and lusty tributes to love, wine and the free life.

The Church became exasperated with the wanderers and by the fourteenth century the world ''goliard'' became equivalent to the brothel-keeper. Nevertheless, the learned tramps, who wandered the highways of central and western Europe, introduced a rough literature to many.[11]

The troubadours, almost exclusively from Provence in Southern France, tended to be of noble birth and more concerned with romantic love than their less gentlemanly goliards. The much illustrated manuscript, *Romance of the Rose,* grew out of the troubadour tradition and the book (c. 1230–1265) was a popular treasure trove of amorous doctrine.

Oral communication was by and large the most common way of "publishing" a vernacular work before the spread of printing. Oral dissemination of popular texts proved as important in the late Middle Ages as in earlier times. A new epic or poem was recited, copied and recited again and again from the single copied work which was memorized. Each recitation differed a bit from the original and from these another copy might be produced. The type of chain-letter approach was the rule rather than the exception. Professional reciters were more important to the average individual than the scribe or the early printer.

LIBRARIES

The Benedictines placed special emphasis on literary activity, and in the twelfth century the oldest of their monastery libraries, Monte Cassino, attained high renown. Other monastic orders also made their contribution. Among these was the Cluniac offshoot of the Benedictine order, whose principal seats were Canterbury and the Abbey of St. Albans in England. The new monastic orders of the later Middle Ages, the Carmelite brothers and the mendicant friars, the Franciscans and the Dominicans also took part in this work. In England, where the mendicants came in 1224, they built up large collections of books at London and Oxford.

The device now known as a union catalog was compiled at that early time by the Franciscan monks. At the end of the fourteenth century requests were sent out to no less than 186 English monasteries for information concerning their book stocks, and on the basis of the replies there was formed the *Registrum librorum Angliae* (catalog of books in England), which is now in the Bodleian Library at Oxford. It is the oldest known attempt at compiling a common catalog.

Libraries were small by today's standards.[12] Founded in 909, the library at Cluny had a collection of only 570 volumes by 1100; and even the Sorbonne by the mid fourteenth century could claim only a maximum of 1,700 books. Merton College (at Oxford) was more typical with, by the late fourteenth century, a total of 570 volumes. Private collections often were larger. Petrarch (1304–1375) bequeathed his library to Venice and it was said to have been comprised of 1500 works (of which a mere 45 survive).

Often subdivided into a working and research library, a university collection would include duplicates and non-exemplar copies for student use. As in the monastery libraries, the books of the university collections were chained to their places (Fig. 24). If a book was borrowed, another book had to be left as security. Additions to the collections came through gifts by royal persons or other prominent individuals, from high ecclesiastical officers or from professors.

The first national library, which would become the base of the Bibliothèque Nationale, was established in the second half of the fourteenth century in Paris by Charles V. The library was part of the palace, i.e. the Louvre, and most of the texts were in French, often representing translations from the Latin and, later, the Greek. The idea spread throughout Europe and by the sixteenth century most countries has a royal and/or an equivalent national library.

Reference services first appear parallel with the growth of universities. Chained books allowed the reader dependable, easy access, while at the same time assuring that the book remained in the library. In addition, a librarian would have a classified catalog of holdings—including works which might have a limited circulation. This, in turn, showed the way for the ever-growing archives in government, church and trade.

Most of the tools associated with modern reference service were invented and refined in the Middle Ages. The encyclopedia was passed on through the period by Vincent of Beauvais.[13] Dictionaries, from Carolingian times onward, were the concern of those trying to standardize Latin and revive Greek, as well as fix the vernacular. The encyclopedia and dictionary were often merged to form the alphabetically arranged encyclopedic dictionary. The synoptic reached wide popularity with the Catholicon in 1286. Gradually, access to material moved from alphabetization

24. Late medieval library interior at Zutphen, near Arnhem in Holland, showing books chained to desks.

to tables of contents, indexing and annotated bibliographies. Reference or tertiary works became so common by the thirteenth century that they virtually took over the labors of many monasteries, as well as university centers.

LITERARY CULTURE

In the Middle Ages literary culture belonged to the upper classes, and the practical reason was the high cost of books. Here one speaks of collectors, not those who read as a necessity of their occupation. Students and teachers in particular did have access to relatively inexpensive copies, which were passed on from individual to individual. But book collectors as such discovered vellum was expensive. Often several texts were written in a single codex in order to use all the sheets. Copying was a tedious task that could not be performed by cheap labor, such as the slaves of ancient Rome. In the tenth century a countess of Anjou is said to have given 200 sheep, three barrels of grain and some marten furs for a single luxurious book of sermons; at the end of the fourteenth century an illuminated prayer book in two volumes was bought by the Duke of Orleans for 200 gold francs.

It was not until the fourteenth and fifteenth centuries that the middle class attained a cultural, social and economic level that made it possible for them to own books. These bourgeois book collections were not predominantly Latin, like those in the churches, monasteries and colleges. Books in the national language of the country, law books, medical and herb books and the emergent poetical literature were by no means unknown in the institutional libraries, but they predominated in the bourgeois collections.

The English bishop Richard de Bury (1287–1345) expressed himself dramatically about the decline in book culture and respect for books. He was a great favorite of Edward III, whose teacher he had been, and held important civil and ecclesiastical positions, becoming both Royal Chancellor and Bishop of Durham. An ardent desire to collect books had early taken hold of him, and on his diplomatic missions in Europe he had ample opportunity to satisfy this desire. Paris, with its many book treasures, was for him an earthly paradise. As bishop he received many gifts of books from monasteries throughout England, and as chancellor he likewise received valuable additions to his library. It was known that he would rather have a valuable old manuscript than a sum of money: "decrepit folios and old quartos came creeping to me instead of the usual fees and New-Year's gifts"[14] (Fig. 25).

BEGINNINGS OF THE RENAISSANCE

Variously described as "the spirit of the Renaissance" and "the first modern man," Petrarch (1304–1375) turned the thinking of Europe from the dry scholastic to the humanistic. It was he who devised the sonnet form, and, when not acting as the Poet Laureate of Italy and Avignon, he was a teacher, diplomat and avid bibliophile. His personal library, one of the largest of the time, if not the largest, was left by him to the city of Venice. Essentially though, he celebrated the delights of Greek and Latin literature, which emphasized the importance of classical learning, and along

Ripes uocatur. quod fit animal pen
natum & quadrupes. hoc genus fera
rum in hiploreis nascitur locis uel monti
bз. omni parte posterion corporis leoni. alis
& facie aquilis simile. equis uehementer in
festum. nam & homines uisos discerpit.

Est animal quod dicitur elephans in quo
non est concupiscencia coitus. Elephā

25. This leaf from an English bestiary (c. 1225–1250) might have been the
type of material beloved of de Bury. The elephant and the armored howdah
are obviously drawn from an account rather than from observation.

with it, the importance of the individual. He showed the world its future self, while at the same time demonstrating the delights of the past and its focus on the good life. Translation became increasingly important as more classical works were rediscovered, and one imagines that the Genoese Columbus learned the world was round from a Latin translation of Ptolemy's geography.

Petrarch's desire was carried on by Florentine collectors of manuscripts. Many such libraries were founded. The most famous was that of Lorenzo de Medici. In Rome the Farnese family library gained equal fame and to this day makes up a special section of the Vatican library.

At first limited to Italy, the humanistic spirit spread through France, Germany and then England. It was carried by the disciples of Petrarch, and by the fifteenth century through the spread of printing and such humanists as Erasmus (1466–1535) and the ill-fated adviser to Henry VIII, Thomas More (1478–1535).

The visible signs of the Renaissance included a return to humanistic art, with the individual as the center of interest, e.g. from the beginning of Giotto (1266–1337) and Duccio (1250–1315) to Dürer (1471–1610). The influence of these artists was seen first in the luxuriously illuminated manuscripts and later in the more modest, although often as imaginative, woodcuts and wood engravings in early printed books. The printed works, too, followed the progress of science, such as the published theories of Copernicus (1473–1543) and Galileo (1564–1642). Other books celebrated such events as the development of the rifle (c. 1475) and an English coach with a suspension system (c. 1580).

Letters, memoirs and diaries indicate that by the fourteenth century there was more emphasis on the individual and individual privacy and reading. Self consciousness was reborn, although usually with reference to family and to group. This is evident in late medieval painting where the studied background of scenery gives way to a closeup of the individual, often in a family setting. The Renaissance was in full bloom.

NOTES

[1]Helen Waddell. *The Wandering Scholars* (London: Constable, 1927), p. 51. The words of a contemporary Puritan chronicler.

[2]The Crusades, more important for modern readers, gave an excuse for countless films, novels and histories. They shaped, too, as Edmund Wilson and others have pointed out, the myth of the Southern gentleman before the Civil War—a myth gained by careful reading of Sir Walter Scott's novel *Ivanhoe* and related works. "Curiously enough Scott, mingling Froissart's *Chronicle* and the *Arabian Nights,* produces a literary picture of the Middle Ages not too remote from that displayed in the authentic poetic Romances. Scott's lush orientalism can be paralleled in Wolfram von Eschenbach's *Parzival,* finished in 1211." George Henderson. *Gothic* (New York: Penguin Books, 1967), p. 192.

[3]Sylvester was the first French Pope, but, more important, was influential in the organization of early cathedral schools; he was also a brilliant mathematician.

[4]Too much stress can be placed upon literacy in a culture where oral communication and memory were equal to, if not more important than the ability to read and write. Monks, for example, were expected to memorize the Psalter (which might take two or three years). The reliance on memory continued through the Renaissance and well into the seventeenth century. See Mary Carruthers, *The Book of Memory* (Cambridge University Press, 1990).

[5]David Diringer. *The Illuminated Book* (London: Faber and Faber, 1967). A virtual catalog of the subject, this details the various schools, artists, etc. An abbreviated version by the author: *The Book Before Printing* (New York: Dover, 1982). (Originally titled, 1953, *The Hand-Produced Book*).

[6]There are scores of articles and monographs on these three manuscripts and the schools where they originated. One of the best overviews, with helpful readings, is Carl Nordenfalk's, "Before the Book of Durrow," *Acta Archaeologica,* Vol. 28, 1947.

[7]The struggle between the importance of words and pictures was an important aspect of arguments in support of Christianity. Pictures brought the Bible to those unable to read. Conversely, as most written texts were read aloud there was no particular reason for pictures. The didactic importance of art, therefore, can be overemphasized by today's critics, who fail to allow for the importance of oral communication. For a discussion of the iconoclastic debate, see Henry Chadwick, *The Early Church* (New York: Penguin Books, 1967), pp. 277–284; and Peter Brown, *Society and the Holy in Late Antiquity* (London: Faber and Faber, 1982), pp. 251–301. Fortunately, important Christian art survived the debate, from the Rossano Gospels (c. 500) and the mosaics of the churches at Ravenna and Rome to the Syriac Gospels of 586.

[8]*The Poems of François Villon.* Trans. by Galway Kinnell. (London: University Press of New England, 1982), p. 83.

[9]The iconography of the illuminated manuscripts is a vast subject and the illustrations were part of the sacred writing. Every artist was aware of the characters. He had to know, for example, that "a hand emerging from the clouds, making the gesture of benediction with thumb and two fingers raised . . . was recognized as the sign of divine intervention, the emblem of providence. Little figures of nude and sexless children, ranged side by side in the folds of Abraham's mantle, signified the eternal rest to come." Emile Male. *The Gothic Image* (New York: Harper & Row [Icon edition], 1972), p. 2. This classic offers hundreds of examples of iconography. See, too, as another example of the genre, Stephen Nichols, *Romanesque Signs: Early medieval narrative and iconography* (New Haven: Yale University Press, 1983).

[10]By the middle of the Carolingian renaissance, in the late eighth and the ninth centuries, nuns were an important part of book production, at least at certain centers. They would spend a portion of each day as scribes or illuminators. The women became key figures because of the increased need for books in the ever increasing number of religious centers. See John A. Nicholas and Lillian Shank, *Medieval Religious Women,* 1984.

There were, too, numerous woman writers during the Middle Ages. For example, Marie de France (late twelfth century) is the earliest known French woman poet. More famous was Christine de Pisan (c. 1364–c. 1429), one of the most prolific and versatile French writers of the Middle Ages. Her *Treasure of the City of Ladies* (c. 1405) gives a vivid account of what was expected of women of every social order.

[11]The poets were the ecclesiastical equivalent of court jesters. They flourished from c. 1100–1300. See George Whicher, ed., *The Goliard Poets* (New York: New Directions, 1949). The poets were so called because they were equated with "gula" as well as other associations (see Whicher pp. 2–5). They are best known for the "Carmina Burana." A typical short poem (p. 109) captures the spirit of the group: "Little hope of heaven I boast, Charmed by pleasure's motto: Since the soul is bound to roast/Save the skin's my motto."

[12]Efforts to estimate the number of books in libraries from the Carolingian period to the Renaissance are difficult in that lists are missing, catalogs are uneven (counting a book not at all, or several times), and little attention seems to have been paid to books out on loan. Worse, there is no record of what might have been lost—probably as many as 300,000 manuscripts, as compared with about 4,000 accounted for in English monasteries before the sixteenth-century suppression. R.M. Thomson's *Catalogue of the manuscripts of Lincoln Cathedral Chapter: Library* (Woodbridge: Boydell and Baker, 1990) suggests the size and type of collection of the smaller monastic libraries in England

and throughout Europe. About 100 manuscripts constituted a significant proportion of the average collection. Despite the evidence, the notion of large, equally mysterious libraries, is favored by numerous writers, from Jorge Luis Borges' short story, "The Library of Babel," to Umberto Eco's *The Name of the Rose* where the vortex of action takes place in a monastery with well over 6,000 volumes.

[13]Beauvais' *Speculum Majus* is an important addition to the number of medieval books, summae and encyclopedias which go back to the Romans. The various reference works emphasized the "pagan" as well as Christian religious belief that all things, from books to plants and animals and humankind, were linked in an intricate system of related meanings. All were part of God's great design for humankind. See Jesse M. Gellrich, *The Idea of the Book in the Middle Ages* (Ithaca: Cornell University Press, 1985).

[14]De Bury's name has come down to our time through the treatise that he wrote in his later years under the title *Philobiblon*. It was published for the first time in 1473 and since then has appeared in various editions. In it the bishop gives expression to his love of books in clever and picturesque language. *Philobiblon* is primarily a paean in praise of the book, but it also tells how de Bury collected his books, and thus provides a sort of guide to the methods of the bibliophile. It is here that he makes his pointed comments about those who mistreat books. In one of the chapters he has the books accuse the "degenerate race of monks"; he attacks particularly the students in the monastic schools who use the books with dirty hands, let their "vile nose drippings" fall on the pages, and use grass straws as bookmarks.

CHAPTER SIX

PRINTING AND THE RENAISSANCE

> He who first shortened the labour of the copyists . . .
> [created] a whole new democratic world: he had invented the
> art of printing.
> —Thomas Carlyle

The world of intellectual excitement, artistic adventures, new ideas and the examination of self is referred to as the Renaissance. Definitions and achievements aside, the Renaissance is a convenient way of marking the cultural revolution which took place in Italy in the fifteenth century and spread throughout Europe in the sixteenth century. More important for this text, the Renaissance marks the invention of printing. Although type allowed more rapid publication, and, of course, precise, exact copies of a book, it remained a relatively slow process. It was not until the early nineteenth century that the advent of steam presses and other technologies increased production a hundredfold.

Writing at the height of the period in 1517, Erasmus saw the dawn of "a golden age." By 1526 Martin Luther had another view of the times, confessing a need for change to meet "the irremediable confusion of everything." If the new interest in ancient texts and learning sparked the Renaissance's stimulating confusion, Luther led the Protestant Reformation. The Catholic countries struck back with a counter-reformation. The far-reaching consequences of exploration, both of the mind and of the globe, and the new spirit of freedom explains the extraordinary advances in science, humanism and political advancement.

In spite of the plague, the One Hundred Years' War and countless natural disasters, the move toward national sovereignty continued and the centralized monarchies gained almost complete control. At the same time explorations opened the East and West to trade and conquest. Of more importance was the Hapsburg dominance of what had been much of the Holy Roman Empire, and the division of Europe pitting the Spaniards, English and French against one another. The fall of Constantinople to the Ottoman Turks in 1453 brought an end to the Mid-Eastern remnants of the Roman Empire. At about the same period Lorenzo de Medici ruled Florence and raised the arts to a new position of honor. (Some think Lorenzo as patron was more Medici propaganda than reality. This is a single example of the countless conflicts whirling around the Renaissance.)

Thanks to international commerce and centralized governments, no matter how often at war, the Renaissance gave birth to what Albrecht Dürer (1471–1528) called "noble and beautiful cities." By the seventeenth century, the urban centers from London to Antwerp to Paris to Florence and Rome were flourishing. The cities were rich enough to sponsor printers and artists.[1] The combination of better educated, certainly better-off individuals created a public in increasing numbers for the printed book. For the first time the individual's hope for a home was possible, and in that home was the type of lighting required for extended reading. While many now shared a confidence in the powers of education, there was hardly a consensus as to the best method(s) of achieving the state of being educated. The roads were as many as printed books.

At the core of most educational solutions remained the lost world of the Greeks and Romans. Some classics, from Homer to Cicero and Virgil, came down through the Middle Ages as part of Christian literature, usually as examples or as supporting evidence for a Christian theme. Only with Petrarch was there a general movement to accept the classics in themselves. The renewed interest in the pervasive classical mode did much to shape the ideas and ideals of the Renaissance.

The Renaissance came to an end about 1600, or 12 years after the Spanish Armada defeat and the subsequent gradual decline of Spanish power. Highlights of politics over 200 years hardly indicate the depth and importance of the cultural revolution which followed no set timetable.

PRINTING APPEARS

Printing made many of the intellectual developments of the Renaissance possible. Without the relatively rapid production of books, replicated in countless numbers, much of the forward movement of the period would have dissipated.

(1) Print allowed the preservation of the text as offered by the author and not as laboriously copied by hand by numerous scribes. Generations of copied manuscripts might be, because of mistakes, deletions and even awkward additions, a far distance from the author's original ideas. Furthermore, multiple copies insured the preservation of the text regardless of man-made or natural disasters.[2]

(2) Standardization of texts, i.e. the ability to print copies which were exactly alike, allowed many people to study and comment on the same text. More important, scholars could build on work readily available to them instead of trying to find books here and there.

(3) Books could be purchased in greater number at prices considerably lower than the hand-copied works. Fair to good distribution made it possible to buy books for study. Heretofore the student often had to go from place to place to read the original in manuscript form.

(4) New genres of literature, from Montaigne's personal essays to fiction, were now possible thanks to standardized texts and the ability to reproduce the same work—often in vernacular translations, as well as in Latin.

(5) Libraries, primarily private, allowed the scholar to examine various texts of the same work and to compare different theories and ideas in the same field of interest.

(6) The revolutionary developments which followed Luther's fight against the Church of Rome left deep traces on the history of the book. It has been said, with some justification, that the invention of printing was the basis of the rapid triumph of the Reformation. Luther's appreciation of the powers of the printing press, as well as his followers' fascination with publicity, made the rapid spread of Protestantism possible in Europe. The ideas, to be sure, were of first importance; but without a method of making them readily available it may have taken generations or a century

or more to accomplish what was done during Luther's lifetime.[3] Attacks on the Catholic church and clergy became a common feature of broadside illustrations as well as easy-to-read tracts. Printing was an effective weapon because in addition to scholarly works, the public could be reached through ephemeral literature. Poor quality paper was used; type, in anything but flawless form, took the place of the older black-letter type; the same worn-out woodcuts were used in one publication after another; and the workmanship became more and more routine. The products acquired an almost factory-like appearance, but they were relatively cheap and marked a hitherto unknown democratization of the book.

PRINTING BASICS

The principle of printing originated in China around the end of the second century. The Chinese had the paper, the ink and the skill of xylography (i.e. the art of printing from a woodcut or wood engraving).[4] In about 1050 Pi Sheng apparently developed movable type. The problem was that at least 80,000 separate characters were needed. Be as that may, by the early thirteenth century movable type spread to Korea where it was cast in bronze. The invention never reached Europe. It was reinvented by Gutenberg in the mid fifteenth century.[5]

Block or relief printing was used rather extensively in Europe before the invention of movable type. It probably first was used in Italy to stamp patterns on children's clothes. The blocks have been destroyed, and the earliest extant one is part of a Crucifiction of c. 1400. By far the most famous extant block is the St. Christopher of Southern Germany of 1423.

The prints were often sold with a simple line or two of words at the bottom. A more elaborate use was in block books (c. 1450–1515). Made up of dramatic woodcut pictures and a few lines of text, these include the *Biblia Pauperum* and the *Ars Moriendi*—or the art of dying (Fig. 26).

Invented in China about 240 B.C., paper only slowly made its way to the west. Taken from the Chinese by the Muslims, papermaking was established in Baghdad in the late eighth century. From there its production secrets moved with the Muslim

Dauid·Tu vero diffuliſti
rriſtum tuum
zacharias·
Factus eſt ob
probrium viɔ
nns ſuis·

ſaias·De⁹ poſuit in ro ſ-
iqtates ōm nſm dabit ipi-
os ꝓ ſepultura·
Amos·In die
illa occiɔet ſol a
facie dīi contre-
mut ſol ꟾ luna·

De triſte munda·cū ſanguine pſunt unda·

Legit̄ geneſi tu ex latere aɔ dormiētis ē mulier ex roſtis
Sic ɔe latere viri aɔ·i·xp̄i format⁹ ē in apitione late-
ris tot⁹ robur et viror ſacramēti ex aqua ꟾ ſanguine
Legit̄ exoɔo q̄ cū moyſes ꝓplm̄ ꝑ ɔſertū ducret ſitiēs
nūꝗ poterim⁹ ɔe petra har·Ait dīe oſtēɔe eis theſau-
rū tuū fontē aque uiue ut ſitiēs reſſet murmur·Cū āt
iuſſu dīi uirga tāgeret ſilicē egreſſe ſunt aque largiſſie
ut ipi et iumēta biberūt·Silex xp̄m ſigt q̄ pꝛaſſus in
latus egreſſus ē ſaguis ꟾ fons uiuus et ſignū baptiſ-
mum et ſacramēti emunɔationem·

26. Page from a block book containing the *Bible Pauperum*, issued in Bamberg in 1461, with hand-colored illustrations. This Bible is known from many medieval manuscripts; it contains scenes from the life of Christ. Since it was used as an instruction book and was not intended for poor people, its name is misleading.

conquests, across North Africa and up through Spain. By the mid-eleventh century a paper mill was a part of the Valencia landscape. The first paper mill outside of Spain was constructed in Italy at Fabriano by c. 1270. Fine paper still is produced there as it is in much of Italy, where papermaking rapidly spread during the fourteenth century. Other mills were built, always near a supply of water, throughout Europe. By the invention of printing there was an abundance of paper for the new presses.[6]

GUTENBERG AND COMPANY

The father of printing in the West remains an illusive, shadowy figure. Johann Gutenberg's (c 1394/5–1468) primary invention was not the printing press, but movable type. He mastered the art of casting single letters which could be multiplied as needed. The type was combined and recombined into words, sentences, paragraphs, pages and books. He modified a wine press to be used as a printing press, and assembled the other necessary materials. Oddly enough his name does not appear on any of the books he printed, from the famous 42-line (i.e. Gutenberg) Bible of 1455 to earlier ephemera such as an Astronomical Calendar of c. 1447.

More is known about the details of Gutenberg's invention than about the man himself. He belonged to the distinguished Gensfleisch family of Mainz. His parents lived on one of the family properties called zum Gutenberg, and this name he took for himself. He was presumably trained as a metalworker or goldsmith. During the troubles in the 1420s between the craftsmen and the old bourgeois families he left Mainz and in 1434 was living in Strassburg. Here he went into partnership with three men who advanced him money in return for his teaching them his "arts and skills." Assuming that the reference was to his printing, Gutenberg was already working on his invention about 1438. After one of the partners died owing Gutenberg money, a lawsuit was filed in 1439. In the documents still preserved we find mention of lead, a press and various "forms," and one of the witnesses speaks about "that which belongs to printing." How far Gutenberg developed his invention during the Strassburg period, which lasted at least to 1444, we do not know.

Back in Mainz, in 1450 he borrowed money from Johann Fust,

(c. 1400–c. 1466) and because of other loans, by 1455 he lost control of his publishing to Fust and Fust's son-in-law, Peter Schöffer (c. 1425–1502). By 1460 Gutenberg gave up printing, possibly because of physical problems, and shortly thereafter received a pension which he lived on until his death in 1468.[7]

The basic printing process changed little until the early twentieth century. The printer took the cast type from a case, letter by letter. The individual pieces were arranged by words, sentences, and possibly paragraphs on a stick. When the stick was full the pieces were transferred to a frame from which, when ready, the type was put on a press and the full page or pages of a book or whatever was printed. Illustrations might be added with the type in the form.

Gutenberg's heavy and hard-to-operate press consisted of little more than a bed (lower surface) and a platen (upper) which put pressure on the paper to be printed. The platen was literally screwed down to the bed and the type. Later the screw was improved so that it required little pressure to operate and would spring back. By the mid-sixteenth century many of the wooden parts were replaced by metal, although it was not until 1795 that the first completely metal press was built. Finally, steam and later electricity allowed the power necessary to run mechanical presses. Modified since the nineteenth century, today's presses operate at speeds a million or more times that of Gutenberg's first effort (Fig. 27).

The first major work pulled from Gutenberg's primitive press was the 42-line Bible printed between 1452 and 1456. It is often called the 42-line Bible as a majority of the pages have that number of lines in each column. Most people, of course, know the two volumes simply as the Gutenberg Bible. The letters are Gothic, in the style of writing found in the magnificent liturgical manuscripts of the late Gothic period. For headings, initials and borders the printer left blank spaces to be rubricated later. In some copies a few headings are printed in red ink (Fig. 28).

Forty-six copies of the Gutenberg Bible are known, twelve of which are on vellum. The entire edition presumably consisted of about 120 copies. On the rare occasion when this Bible has come on the market it has brought fantastic prices. In 1897 at an auction in London a copy was purchased for the equivalent of about

27. Typecaster pouring lead into the casting matrix. In the basket at the left
are finished types, which will be worked over with a file before being used.
Woodcut by Jost Amman in the book *Beschreybung aller Stände* (1568),
with verses by Hans Sachs.

28. Page from Gutenberg's 42-line Bible, with hand-painted border and initial.

$12,000. In exactly 100 years the price rose to $5.39 million at Christie's New York. This set a world record price.[8]

AFTER THE BIBLE

When Fust came into possession of part of Gutenberg's equipment he started a printing business in partnership with a former scribe and initial-designer named Peter Schöffer, who undoubtedly had worked for Gutenberg. As early as 1457 Fust and Schöffer were able to issue a large Psalter, in which early printing reached its highest level. It is also the first printed book to contain a notation of when and by whom it was printed; its closing lines (colophon) can be translated briefly as follows: "This Psalter has been produced by the ingenious process of printing and forming letters without any writing by hand, and was completed with diligence for the glory of God by Johann Fust, a citizen of Mainz, and Peter Schöffer of Gersheim in the year 1457, the eve of Ascension Day [i.e. Aug. 14]." There is much to indicate that Gutenberg had started this work and that it was merely brought to completion in Fust and Schöffer's workshop (Fig. 29).

The Psalter was followed by a long series of notable works, among them a magnificent Bible issued in 1462. All bear witness to Schöffer's unusual ability as an artist. He was the moving spirit in the undertaking, while Fust mainly provided the money. After Fust's death, Schöffer continued the business alone for many years until his death in 1502 or 1503. Like the other early book printers, Schöffer cast his own types, which surpassed even Gutenberg's in accuracy and appearance.

The earliest printed books, or incunabula, intentionally looked like manuscripts, and the Gutenberg Bible was printed in a type which reproduced manuscript handwriting.[9] Furthermore, the large initials were duplicated by manuscript illuminators. All of this was done not to deceive the purchaser, who would know the difference anyway, but simply because the manuscript was the only model the printer could follow. Only gradually did the printed work take on its own individual characteristics, with its own type and decorations, as contrasted with medieval copies.

Still, it took more than a century for the idea of the printed book to triumph over the hand-written and hand-illuminated book.

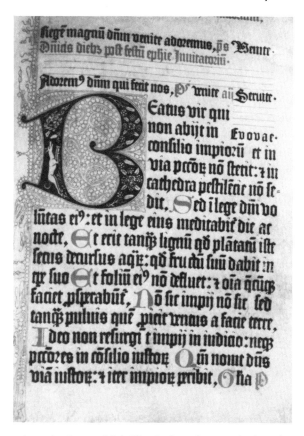

29. A page from the Fust and Schöffer Psalter of 1457. The large letter B was inked separately in another color and dropped into the form to allow two-color printing.

Renaissance princes and theologians insisted on richly decorated titles beyond the powers of the average printer. Federigo da Montefeltro boasted that his princely library contained only books written with a pen, "and had there been one printed volume it would have been ashamed in such company." In 1482, some thirty years after printing, the Duke of Urbino described his library as "of perfect beauty, all written by skilled scribes on parchment and many of them adorned with exquisite miniatures. The collection contains no single printed book."

The esthetics of the printed book were challenged often by those who had grown accustomed to elaborately illuminated manuscripts. It is easy to forget that the vast majority of manuscript works were poor in quality and appearance. As working tools they were equally inaccurate. Early printed books, and particularly those which used Roman type, could be (depending on the printer's skill) better looking and certainly more reliable than the manuscripts they replaced. It is true, not all printers were an Aldus or a Froben, and it is true in England particularly, that many printed works well into the eighteenth century were less than handsome, but they surpassed the earlier manuscript workaday titles. And as one modern critic puts it: "It is impossible to believe that the writers of the sixteenth and seventeenth centuries did not feel sensuous pleasure at the sight of their work in print. . . . The smell of the paper, the ink and the glue have not (thank heaven) been distilled and bottled in Paris or New York."[10]

Unable to compete, to supply the greater demand for new books, the scribes and illuminators faded away, or, more likely, adapted their skills to printing. This was particularly true for illuminators who turned to illustrating the printed books. The scriptoria virtually disappeared in the early 1500s. Even the universities turned from the scribes and commenced to license printers for their needed volumes. In many cases, of course, the stationers serving the university simply set up printing establishments and continued.

SPREAD OF PRINTING

There were other practitioners of the art of printing in the various towns in southern Germany in the 1460s. One reason for this was the attack on Mainz, during which a large number of the inhabitants were exiled or fled. The journeymen printers also left, Schöffer going to Frankfurt. Thus, destruction of Mainz contributed to the rapid spread of the art. Printing followed the old trade route of the Rhine; Strassburg became one of the chief centers of printing, but Cologne, Augsburg and Nuremberg soon had printing shops as well, in some instances rather large establishments.

Printing spread relatively rapidly beyond Germany. Although the technology remained much the same throughout Europe and the world, the actual appearance of the book differed depending upon the skills of the printer/publisher and the amount of time, effort and money involved in the particular title. By the early 1470s, printing had reached most of Europe. Caxton set up his printing shop in the precinct of Westminster Abbey in late 1476. Printing crossed the Atlantic in 1540 to Mexico, but it was not until 1563 that a press found its way to Russia.

Italy, with its rich literary culture, naturally attracted printers. In 1465 two pupils of Schöffer, Conrad Sweynheim (d. 1477) and Arnold Pannartz (d. 1476), started a printing shop at a monastery in Subiaco near Rome.[11] Sweynheim and Pannartz stayed only two years at the monastery. As any business person, the printer went where a market existed. In the beginning this tended to be religious organizations. Eventually, the printer moved on to a large urban center, from Paris to Venice to London, where government, business and universities proved natural customers. The better educated, too, were found in cities. Sweynheim and Pannartz followed the familiar pattern in that they left the small religious community for Rome. Not only was Rome the center of business, but the church provided countless work—from papal bills and administrative papers to indulgences—which heretofore had been the monopoly of scribes.

The two German printers' records indicate what was probably a pattern. Their press runs were about 250 to 300 copies for each of the 46 volumes (actually 28 separate titles) they printed. Most of the titles were religious, with a dash of secular Latin. Gradually emphasis on religious titles changed. In Rome alone, before 1500 a wide variety of titles was available, from music and travel books to Latin and Greek classics. While theology and law had dominated the subject matter of manuscript books, by the late sixteenth century one could purchase any of the extant classics in print, as well as well-edited editions of Renaissance writers in every subject field. Also, most were available in the vernacular as well as in Latin. Throughout the Middle Ages, by and large the most popular secular work was Virgil. Sweynheim & Pannartz printed the first Aeneid in Rome in 1469. Before the end of the fifteenth century over 100 separate editions of Virgil had been printed. The most important edition was published by Aldus in 1501—the first pocketbook and one of the best edited.

During the next decades many other German printers followed

Sweynheim and Pannartz to Italy and settled there. The great trade center of Venice offered the most favorable conditions, and from 1469 on attracted a large colony of printers. Many of them made names for themselves, such as the brothers Johann and Wendelin of Speyer, who printed one of the first books in Italian, a volume of Petrarch's sonnets.

Then there was the French engraver, Nicolas Jenson (c. 1420–1480), who had been sent by King Charles VII to Mainz in 1458 to learn the new art.[12] He later emigrated to Italy and may have cut Sweynheim and Pannartz's roman types. Jenson worked in Venice, where still another German, Erhard Ratdolt from Augsburg, established a printing shop in 1476. Ratdolt, together with Jenson and the brothers Johann and Wendelin of Speyer, contributed to giving the city its position of leadership in the first period of Italian book printing (Fig. 30).

TYPEFACES AND TITLE PAGES

Most printers by the early sixteenth century relied on two basic typefaces, as contrasted with dozens of forms used until that time

nihil iis fegetibus : quæ deiceps in eo loco feminari debent:profuturum fit. Ac de iis quoq; leguminibus:quæ uellunt:Tremelius obeſſe maxie ait folo uirus ciceris & lini:alterum quia fit falfæ:alterum quia fit fer-uidæ naturæ. Quod etiam Virgilius fignificat dicendo:
Vrit enim lini campum feges:urit auenæ:
Vrūt læteheo perfufa papauera fomno. Neq; enim dubium quin & iis feminibus infeſtetur ager:ficut & milio & panico : fed omni folo quod prædictorum leguminū fegetibus fatifcit:una præfens medicina eſt:ut ftercore adiuues:& abfumptas uires hoc uelut pabulo refoueas. Nec tā-tum propter femina quæ fulcis aratri committuntur:uerum etiā ,ppter arbores & uirgulta : quæ maiorem in modum lætantur eiufmodi ali-mento. Quare fi eſt ut uidetur agricolis utiliſſimū:diligentius de eo di-cendum exiſtimo:cum prifcis auctoribus quãuis nõ omiſſa res:leui tā-men admodum cura fit prodita.

30. Nicolas Jenson's roman type.

to reflect the work of scribes. Roman and gothic were the favored styles, the former preferred by Jenson in 1470, the latter from about 1480 in Germany. Gothic characters might be employed for law and scholarly works, while Roman types were used for humanistic titles. As independent type founders took over from individual printers a universal style of type (usually Roman) prevailed. By the end of the sixteenth century there was considerable uniformity in type styles. In most of Europe Roman was favored and by the end of the sixteenth century the small, light letters dominated book production. Esthetics aside, "the great change was the result of a basic change of attitude toward the past. The gothic letter was rejected by modernists . . . because "[gothic] symbolized a long intellectual deviation which was repellant because it separated [the Renaissance] from the standards of the classical age."[13]

The title page, a familiar part of any book today, developed slowly. At first the colophon, i.e. the statement at the end of the book, served to inform as to the name of the book, its author, date of publication, printer, etc. An identifying printer's mark or device usually followed the colophon[14] (Fig. 31). Actually, before printing few scribes bothered to identify the book by title, or more or less indicate the author. Apparently the earliest title page was an effort to protect the contents of a broadside rather than to pioneer a new format. Peter Schöffer in 1463 used a title for a papal bull, but went no further. Erhard Ratdolt was the first, in 1476, to design a proper title page with all the required information. Printers soon discovered the obvious: a title page, often with a

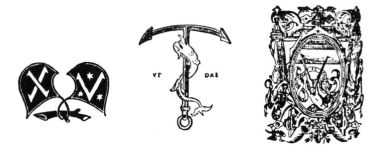

31. Three famous printers' marks: Fust and Schöffer, Aldus Manutius and Christophe Plantin.

colorful frame or other types of decoration, served as a good advertisement for the book. So, by the sixteenth century, the title page was a permanent addition to book design. As a reflection of contemporary feelings about design, forms of art reproduction, typography and attitudes towards books themselves, the title page throughout the ages has proven a valuable key. For example, one may follow the development of illustration from woodcuts and wood engravings to desk-top computer figures by a study of title pages from 1500 to the present.

KOBERGER AND ALDUS

Anton Koberger (1445–1513) was the first large scale commercial printer-publisher. Recognizing the business possibilities of Nuremberg, major capitalistic center in Europe, he established himself there in 1470. Before long he had one of the biggest firms in the city, with over 24 presses and 100 workers. He sold his books throughout Europe, and maintained agencies in major cities. Forced by the guilds to leave printing, he turned entirely to publishing and in so doing was among the first to make what became a common division between printer and publisher. With his death the firm gradually fell apart.

Of the more than 200 titles Koberger published, the most famous is Hartmann Schedel's *Nuremberg Chronicles* (1493), the leading illustrated printed book of the fifteenth century. Although there are 1809 separate illustrations, representing cities, rulers, scenes of conflict, animals and the like, they are reproduced from only 645 wood blocks. As representation of cities and personalities, it made little difference to the illustrator, printer, or reader that one cut might be employed over and over again with different names. The close to 600 portraits of kings, popes and prominent men are clearly identified in print, but as only 72 woodblocks were used, the same face appears eight or a dozen times for as many different people. This is true of cities and views of Rome and Paris, which on following pages become Jerusalem and Bologna (Fig. 32).

Aldus Manutius (1450–1515) is considered to be the most important printer-publisher of the sixteenth century. The Venetian printer's fame is based primarily upon his attention to scholarly

Engelland ist ein innsel. die die alten von ettlichen weissen bergen. die den ihenen so dahin schiffen vor erscheÿ
nen Albion genennt haben. ettlich nennen sie Britaniam nach Bruto siluy des konigs der lateinischen sun. d
dieselben innsel albionam darinn die rysen woneten eroberte. vnd sie britaniam nach ime nennet. vnnd diss hiess
das grösser Britania zu vnderscheid des kleinern Britania das an Galliam stösset. Aber mw ist es von einem mech
tigen englischen könig bis auff disen heutigen tag engelland genant. Dise insel ist dreieckt vn zwischen mitternacht
vn dem nidergang gelegē. die von allen darumb gelegen örtern abgeteylt ist. dan sie fahet sich an ein nidern teil
schem lannd vnd raichet hin bey Gallia oder franckreich vnd hispania gegen dem nidergang. Aber als Brutus
der römer ime ein wonung oder bleybung in Britania oder Engelland erwelt het. do pawet er bey dem fluss ta
mesis die stat Trinoanten gar wol gefestigt vnd an allen notturftigen dingen fast fruchtper vnd d gedechtnus d
alten Troya wol zegleichen. Derselb Brutus hat (als sie sagen) geporn drey süne. Lotrinum Albanetum vnd Cā
brē. die habē erstlich dise insel vndsich geteylt. vn Lotrino als dē eltern ist d halbteil gefallē vn nach ime lothria ge
nāt wordē. vn man sagt dz die stat Lundinū nochmals darñ sey. die von kauflewte vn mit häutirung vn gewer
be garfast besucht werd. darinn nochmals die kong vnd fürsten zu engellār vnbie ratgebē des volcks musampt
den kauflewten offt zesamen komen. Vnd Albaneto wardt der vierd teyl der innseln vn albania nach ime geheissē
die wirdt yetzo Scocia oder schotten land genant. vnd ist der ober teyl gegen mitternacht mit kleinen flüssen. vnd
einem berg von engelland vnderschiden. Aber Cambri dem dritten sun gefiel Cambria yetzo Tyle genant ein insel
zwischen mitternacht vnd dem nidergang gelegen. vnd die letst auss den die von den römern erkant warden. weñ
sich die sun im sumer wendet so ist daselb kunn kein nacht. vnd zu winterlicher sunwendung kein tag. Der gröst
teyl diser innseln ist fruchtreich. vn an vihe. gold. silber vn eysen habhaftig. vnd dannen herauss werdē gebracht
rawhe war. vihe. thier. vnd die aller geschicktsten iaghund. Dise insel ist mit vil mit vnedeln inseln vmbgeben. der
selben eine ist hibernia die sich in der grösse engelland nehmet. vnd douon mit einē kleinē meer vnderschaidet. Da
rvmb sind auch gelegen die kleinen inseln Orchades. Der hailig babst Gregorius der ander hat durch ettwieuil da
selb hin geschickt man bewerts lebens zn erst engelland zum glawben bekert. vnd vil könig dariñ habē darnach
in wunderzaichen geleuchtet. do sind auch vil vnd gross flüss. vnnd auch darzu vil vnnd mancherlay metals.

Engellannd oder Brittania

ANGLIE PROVINCIA

32. Hartmann Schedel: *Das Buch der Chroniken* (*Nuremberg Chronicles*),
published by Anton Koberger in 1493.

editions of Greek and Latin classics, and particularly to the pocket-sized "Aldines" which were the equivalent of modern paperbacks. Aldus turned from publishing almost exclusively religious works to what, for the time, might be considered popular books. The press run was raised from the normal 200 to 300 copies to over 1,000, with the text crammed on the small pages. The books were easily recognized by their limp leather covers, their relative low price, and the now familiar printer's device of a dolphin and anchor. The format was copied throughout Europe, although never with such attention to editing and accuracy as well as quality of printing. As his publishing business grew, Aldus employed a whole company of scholars, including, for a time, Erasmus.

Aldus introduced a Greek type cut on the pattern of contemporary Greek handwriting with its many abbreviated forms. In a Virgil edition of 1501 he broke completely with tradition and started printing the classics in an entirely new typeface adapted to the reduced size of the page. This type imitated the humanistic cursive handwriting. It can best be described as a form of roman type that slopes slightly to the right. Called italic, or cursive, it has continued to the present day, although it is now used mainly for emphasizing individual words or lines (Fig. 33).

The italic typeface was not Aldus' only contribution to printing. His time is referred to as the Aldine period because he was particularly successful in giving a classical character to the initials, borders and friezes with which he, always in judicious moderation, decorated his books. While Ratdolt's ornaments were mainly executed in white on a black background, those in Aldus' books were all line drawing without any filling-in of the background, giving a facile and bright appearance equally well suited to italic type of Greek letters. Every one of Aldus' friezes and initials is a small masterpiece, whether it is made up entirely of entwined plants or grotesque masks and other classical features, or it shows Oriental influence in its interlaced bands and ribbons.

Aldus reached his high point in 1499 when he issued the allegorical romance of Francesco Colonna, entitled *Hypnerotomachia Poliphili*. This depicts, in dream visions, the realm of classical art. The book contains some 70 illustrations, mostly line drawings, done in true classical style but with their own special character. However graceful and poetic these pictures and the

IVNII IVVENALIS AQVINA
TIS SATYRA PRIMA.

EMPER EGO AVDITOR
tantum?nunquám ne reponem
S   V *exatus toties raua theseide*
Codri?
I *mpune ergo mihi recitauerit ille*
togatus?

H *ic elegos?impune diem consumpserit ingens*
T *elephus?aut summi plena iam margine libri*
S *criptus, et in tergo nec dum finitus, Orestes?*
N *ota magis nulli domus est sua, quàm mihi lucus*
M *artis, et aeoliis uicinum rupibus antrum*
V *ulcani · Quid agant uenti, quas torqueat umbras*
A *eacus, unde alius furtiuae deuehat aurum*
P *elliculae, quantas iaculetur Monychus ornos,*
F *rontonis platani, conuulsáq; marmora clamant*
S *emper, et assiduo ruptae lectore columnae ·*
E *xpectes eadem a summo, minimóq; poeta ·*
E *t nos ergo manum ferulae subduximus, et nos*
C *onsilium dedimus Syllae, priuatus ut altum*
D *ormiret·stulta est clementia, cum tot ubique*
V *atibus occurras, periturae parare chartae ·*
C *ur tamen hoc libeat potius decurrere campo,*
P *er quem magnus equos Auruncae flexit alumnus,*
S *i uacat, et placidi rationem admittitis, edam.*
C *um tener uxorem ducat spado, Meuia thuscum*
F *igat aprum, et nuda teneat uenabula mamma,*
P *atricios omnes opibus cum prouocet unus,*

A ii

33. Page from Aldus' edition of Virgil, 1501, printed in italic type. Space has been left for painting in the initial S.

accompanying friezes and vignettes, it is the balance between them and the text that places this book so high[15] (Fig. 34).

Johann Froben (1460–1527) of Basel was another major scholar printer who also had the good fortune to have Erasmus as a literary editor. Erasmus edited the Greek New Testament in 1516, best known today as the base upon which Luther built his vulgate edition.[16] Froben printed Luther's early work from 1518 to 1520 and sold Latin tracts throughout Europe.

Hora quale animale che per la dolce efca,lo occulto dolo non perpen de,poftponendo el naturale bifogno,retro ad quella inhumana nota fen cia mora cum uehementia feftinante la uia,io andai. Alla quale quando effere uenuto ragioneuolmente arbitraua,in altra parte la udiua, Oue & quando a quello loco properante era giunto,altronde apparea effere affir mata. Et cufi como gli lochi mutaua,fimilmente piu fuaue & delecteuo- le uoce mutaua cum coelefti concenti. Dunque per quefta inane fatica, & tanto cum molefta fete corfo hauendo,me debilitai tanto, che apena poteua io el laffo corpo fuftentare. Et gli affannati fpiriti habili non effen do el corpo grauemente affaticato hogi mai foftenire,fi per el tranfacto pa uore, fi per la urgente fete, quale per el longo peruagabondo indagare, & etiam per le graue anxietate, & per la calda hora, difefo, & relicto dalle proprie uirtute, altro unquantulo defiderando ne appetendo, fe non ad le debilitate membra quieto ripofo. Mirabondo dellaccidente cafo,ftupido della melliflua uoce,& molto piu per ritrouarme in regio- ne incognita & inculta, ma affai amaerno paefe. Oltra de quefto,forte me doleua,che el liquente fonte laboriofamente trouato,& cum tanto folerte inquifito fuffe fublato & perdito da gliochii mei. Per lequale tu- te cofe,io ftetti cum lanimo intricato de ambiguitate,& molto trapen- fofo.Finalmente per tanta laffitudine correpto,tutto el corpo frigefcen-

34. Page from the *Hypnerotomachia Poliphili* of Francesco Colonna, 1499.

DEVELOPMENT OF PRINTING IN OTHER COUNTRIES

France did not receive the art of book printing until 1470, when two professors in Paris called in three Germans to set up a typographic shop near the Sorbonne.[17] Here they printed a series of Latin texts for use at the University. Thereafter the new art expanded rapidly in France, and around 1500 Paris had close to seventy printing establishments. Jean Dupré was responsible for the first printed Books of Hours (1490) which in their general features imitated the handwritten ones as much as possible. They were often printed on vellum and supplied with borders and illustrations, which, although printed from wood or metal cuts, kept very close to the illuminated manuscript tradition, and were even painted in colors and gilded. Around the end of the fifteenth century hundreds of these delightful and popular prayer books were printed.

The art of printing spread from Germany and Italy in the years following 1470. In the Netherlands the first books were presumably printed in Utrecht, but they carry neither date nor printer's name. These Dutch books, like the German, were printed in various forms of black-letter type.

The first English printer, William Caxton (c. 1420/4–1491) was originally a merchant, and for some 30 years was at Bruges, then one of Europe's major market centers.[18] In semi-retirement he turned to translating a popular romance *Le Recueil des histoires de Troie,* but he failed to find a printer skilled enough to publish the work. Hardly set back, he went to Cologne to learn enough of the trade to print the book himself and to finish the translation in 1471. A year later he was back in Bruges where he set up his own press, printed his translation and went on to publish four other books as well—three of which were the first to employ French in print.

Returning to London in 1476, Caxton established the first English press in the Westminster precinct. A year later he published the first book printed in England—the *Dictes or Sayengis of the Philosophers.* From then until his death, Caxton published some 90 books, most noteworthy for the fact that the majority were in the vernacular, often English translations by Caxton himself. An exception was Chaucer's *Canterbury Tales,* which was published in its original English form in 1478. Another English title, equally famous, was *Le Morte D'Arthur,* issued in 1485.[19]

GROWTH OF THE VERNACULAR

Unlike the rest of Europe, England tenaciously stuck to the vernacular throughout the Middle Ages. When Caxton struck off the first books in English it was more in keeping with tradition than in opposition to Latin.[20] And Caxton, as many printers before and after, went one step further by setting rules for English vocabulary, syntax, grammar, and punctuation. Printing served to revive and spread the poetry and prose of the spoken languages, not only in England, but throughout Europe. Prior to about 1500 the various scribes used grammatical rules, punctuation and spelling more or less as expressed (i.e. heard) in the spoken word. The result was chaotic. Chaucer, and his companions in other countries, helped to set the rules for the vernacular which hold to this day. Spelling and grammar reformers, from the Simplified Spelling Society to G. B. Shaw, have tried to impose schemes; but the rules first established by early printers have changed little.

A peculiar, long lasting aspect of the English, as reflected in early printing, is the emphasis on isolation from Europe. By the early sixteenth century the British looked inward rather than to European markets for the sale of books. It was for this reason that there was so much emphasis on the vernacular. Furthermore, most of the book trade for that century, and well into the next, was concentrated in London, which allowed for closer control, among other things, by the monarchy. "By the late 1550s there was a clear community of interest between the crown, with its desire to control the press, and a small group of printers eager to obtain and to defend special privileges."[21]

The Reformation was a major element in the spread of the vernacular. By the early sixteenth century, religious works were hardly read by anyone but clerics. Then, in 1517 Luther and the Reformation urged individuals to read the Bible. Most of the Bibles were published in the vernacular of the country and/or region, and this, coupled with public readings, brought the

Lutheran version to millions who heretofore had been unable to understand Latin.

Interest in other books, for and against Protestantism swept Europe. Luther and Calvin also helped develop the equivalent of today's newspaper—the poster or broadside, which gave arguments for the new religion. Ephemeral leaflets and pamphlets carried the message, too. First the demand was centered in Germany, and particularly for Luther's Theses, which were distributed throughout Germany within days of his Wittenberg posting on October 31, 1517. The Papacy fought back. Many a press in Germany and in other parts of Europe was closed or threatened with closure, although this had little effect.

A more practical method of checking Luther was to turn to censorship. This was a common cousin of any form of the book. The *Index Librorum Prohibitorum* was an important development of the Reformation and Inquisition. It was first issued under papal authority in 1559. As an official catalog of what the Church considered dangerous or heretical writing it was a major censor's tool until well into the twentieth century (1966), when it finally ceased publication—much to the relief of most Catholics and the disappointment of others who used the listings as a sales aid and an indication of at least thoughtful writing. Over the centuries the List had become slightly ridiculous in its narrow definition and for its inclusion, in part or in whole, such writers as Chaucer, Milton, Gibbon, Descartes, Voltaire and even Locke.

Despite, or often because of bans and condemnations of the new Protestant faith, editions multiplied and were distributed whether they were Bibles or one page broadsides. Censorship and legislation simply could not stop what printing brought to millions. If a public press was halted, a secret, underground press continued the work. It is not easy to determine how much was published and distributed by the clandestine press, but the authorities were unable to halt such publications.

The political paradox of printing is that while relatively inexpensive books encouraged literacy and a wider understanding among peoples, it equally fostered the concept of nationalism by stressing books in the narrow vernacular of each country rather than in international Latin. The wide distribution of books in the vernacular, primarily after the mid-sixteenth century, doomed Latin as an international language. True, Latin continued to be basic to professions, from theology to medicine, up to the twentieth century, but by the end of the seventeenth century it no longer was indispensable or even the mark of an educated person.[22]

PRINTER TO PUBLISHER

The only printers who could make a profitable business of their trade were those who operated on a large scale and could afford to maintain stocks in the larger cities, as Schöffer did in Frankfurt and Paris. In the early years of publishing, the printer was at the center of publishing. He provided the type and press, and decided what to publish, how many copies, and where to distribute. Also, he was the copy editor and might even serve as a bookbinder, although normally this was done by someone else. Only the paper came from an outside source. The separation of printer and publisher was gradual, growing and shaped by economic developments. With the end of the incunabula period (1501) business dictated larger and larger printing-publishing-bookselling firms. By the turn of the seventeenth century there were major publishers in France, the Netherlands and throughout Europe. Most included their own large print shops, but the printers were hired and separate from the business-publishing side. Publishers emerged who would contract out the printing, the binding, etc. By the mid-nineteenth century printing and publishing were fairly well separate endeavors, as they are in most cases today.

Robert Estienne (1503–1559) was among the first of the major sixteenth-century publishers. Built on an interweaving of marriages, deaths and births, the French Estiennes' publishing firm proved a financial success. They gained fame as France's finest printers, particularly from 1515 to 1547, the golden age of typography in France. Geoffroy Tory, Simon de Colines and Claude Garamond among others established type faces which still are used and praised. The Estiennes held to quality and in the steps of Aldus established themselves as Europe's leading scholar publishers.

Supported by King François I, the house flourished. The King recognized the importance of printing to spread government propaganda. He was the first ruler to exploit the principle of wide, cheap publication. He, too, proved a friend to readers in that in

1538 he established a national library. Estienne, and later other publishers, were ordered to give one copy of every book published to the royal library. With the death of François in 1547 the Estiennes carried on, sometimes in difficult times, until the late seventeenth century. They stand as one of the longest lived houses of the period, a claim made even more remarkable because through the whole time they stressed quality publishing.

When Geoffroy Tory (1480–1533) became the first "royal printer" in Paris, in 1530, the gothic style was still dominant in French books, but the Italian influence had begun to make itself felt and the roman type gradually found its way into French books. It was used to print numerous works of Erasmus and other great humanists of the period. However, when Tory in the years following 1520 turned from scholarship to art and developed his remarkable talents as a designer and stampcutter, roman type and Renaissance book decoration experienced their flowering in France. Outstanding among Tory's work is a series of Books of Hours which he decorated with illustrations and single-lined borders that harmonized well with the roman type of the text. The most famous of his works is *Champfleury,* issued in 1529—a book that concerns itself with the question of orthography and the esthetics of typography. In designing his type Tory drew the letters within a square that was divided into smaller squares (Fig. 35).

Among those who followed Tory were Simon de Colines (1480–1546), who published small editions of the classics patterned after those of Aldus and printed in three italic typefaces cut by himself; and Robert Granjon (c. 1513–1589), who was active in Lyons from 1557 on as a printer and as a type cutter. Granjon supplied large quantities of type to famous European presses. He created his "civilité" type from an expanded italic. This type gained wide acceptance, and Granjon's composite flower and leaf ornaments also became standard equipment in printing shops.

PLANTIN OF THE NETHERLANDS

Christophe Plantin (c. 1520–1589) is considered by many as the single greatest commercial printer of the sixteenth, or for that matter any, century. Born in France, he learned bookbinding there

35. Final page of Geoffroy Tory's *Champfleury* (Paris, 1529) with his mark and a decorative border. Tory's mark (a broken vase, *pot cassé*) is an imitation of a woodcut in *Hypnerotomachia Poliphili*.

and in 1549 established a shop in Antwerp. By 1555 he turned to printing and almost from the beginning his publications were known for their high level of scholarship and aesthetic delight. His best known, almost financially disastrous work, was the *Biblia Polyglotta* (1569–72) which was to fix the text of the Bible in four languages and filled eight volumes (Fig. 36). Plantin issued over 1,600 works in the course of the forty years or so before his death in 1589. Few printer-publishers have had as a wide a market as he; his publications were sold in Germany and Scandinavia, in France, Spain and England, and he had branches in Leiden and Paris. He printed scientific works on philology, law, mathematics, etc., as well as classical authors, French literature, theological works and a series of large liturgical works. His mark was a hand with a pair of dividers, and his motto was ''labore et constantia.''

Plantin's broad and heavy roman type was cut by Granjon and other French artisans, and his italic almost surpassed that of Aldus. Like his predecessors, he had scholars in his service. Plantin's great business brought together a whole colony of printers, typecasters, punch-cutters, illustrators and bookbinders. Plantin used woodcuts generously. Since the art of wood carvings was on the decline, he also made considerable use of the new process of copperplate engraving.

After paying a heavy ransom to the plundering Spaniards in 1576, Plantin established an office in Paris and by 1583 was at Leiden as a printer for the new Holland and its university. His sons-in-law took over the business in Antwerp, and the firm carried on until almost the end of the nineteenth century.[23]

TRANSMISSION OF TEXTS

Petrarch described creative writing as a contagious disease which swept through the Renaissance. Sometimes printers waited, literally, for the author to deliver works as written. The new titles were attempts to meet the one unifying intellectual manifestation of the Renaissance, the sheer wish to know everything. Here, of course, the personification of this driving force is the quintessential Renaissance person, Leonardo da Vinci (1452–1519), who set out to find out what truth was through question and experiment. That basic idea runs through most of Renaissance literature, whether it

E S A I A S. CAPVT I

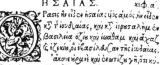

IS IO quâ vidit Esaias filius Amos, quam vidit contra Judæam & contra Ierusalem in regno Oziæ, et Ioatham, Achaz et Ezechiæ, qui regnauerunt in Judea.

Audi cælum, et auribus percipe terra, quia Dominus locutus est : Filios genui & exaltaui, ipsi autem spreuerunt. Cognouit bos possessore, & asinus præsepe domini sui, Israel autem me non cognouit, & populus me non intellexit.

Væ genti peccatrici, populo plene peccatis, semen nequam, filij iniqui dereliquistis Dominū, & ad iracundiam concitastis sanctum Israel : alienati sunt in retro.

Quid vltrà percutiemini addentes iniquitatem? Omne caput in laborem, & omne cor in tristitiam. A pedibus vsque ad caput non est in eo sanitas: vulnus, liuor, plaga tumens, non est mal-igna imponere, neque oleum neque alligaturæ. Terra vestra deserta, ciuitates vestræ succensæ igni: regionem vestram coram vobis alieni deuorant eam: & desolata est subuersa à populis alienis.

Derelinquetur filia Sion sicut tentorium in vinea, et sicut pomorum custodia in cucumerario, sicut ciuitas obsessa. Et nisi Dominus Sabaoth reliquisset nobis semen, quasi Sodoma vtique facti fuissemus, & quasi Gomorra vtiq, assimilati essemus. Audite verbum Domini principes Sodomorum, attendite legi Dei nostri populus Gomorra. Quid mihi multitudo victimarum vestrarum, dicit Dominus: plenus sum holocaustis arietum, et adipem agnorum, & sanguinem taurorum & hircorum non volo.

Neque veneritis apparere mihi: quis enim quæsiuit hæc de manibus vestris calcare atrium meum? Non apponetis, si obtuleritis similginem, vanum: incensum abominatio mihi est. Neomenias vestras & sabbata, & diem magnum non feram: ieiunium & otium.

INTERPRETATIO LATINA TRANSLATIONIS CHALDAICAE IN ESAIAM.

Ex Complutensi Bibliotheca, ad Hebraicam & Chaldaicam vntatem à B. Aria Montano correcta.

ROPHETIA Esaiæ filij Amos, quam prophetauit super viros Iuda, & habitatores Ierusalæ in diebus Oziæ, Iotham, Achaz, Ezechiæ, regum domus Iuda. Audite cæli, qui commoti estis, quando dedi legem meam populo meo, & auscultا terra, quæ contremuisti à facie Verbi mei, quoniã Dns locutus est. Populus meus domus Israel, quos vocaui filios, & dilexi eos, & honorificaui eos, & ipsi rebellauerunt in verbum meum. Cognouit bos emptorem suum, & asinus præsepe domini sui, Israel autem non didicit vt sciret timorem mei: populus meus non intellexit vt conuerteretur ad seruitium meum. Væ eis qui vocati sunt populus sanctus, & peccauerunt, congregatio electa, & multiplicauerunt delicta: cognominati sunt semen electi, & malè egerunt, & dicti sunt filij dilecti, & corruperunt vias suas, dereliquerunt cultum Domini, derestati sunt timorem Sancti Israel, & propter opera eorum praua suarti sunt, & facti sunt retrorsum. Non animaduerterunt, dicentes: Propter quid percussi sumus? adhuc addunt peccare, nec dicunt : Quare omne caput languidū, & omne cor moerens? A reliquo populo vsque ad principes, non est in eis qui perfectus sit in timore mei: omnes sunt cōtumaces, & rebelles, coinquinati sunt in peccatis suis, sicut plaga vlcerosa, nō dimittunt superbias suas, nec desiderant agere pœnitentiam, neque fuit in eis iustitia quibus protegantur. Terra vestra deserta, ciuitates vestræ succensæ igni: terra vestra coram vobis populi possident eam, & propter peccata vestra deserta est terra, & transit in est ad alienos. Et relinquetur cœtus Sion, sicut vmbraculū in vinea, postquam vindemiarunt eam, sicut tugurium mansing in cucumerario quod pullulum legerunt cucumeres ab eo, sicut ciuitas quæ obsidetur. Nisi superexcedens bonitas Domini exercituum reliquisset nobis redemptionem in miserationibus suis, peccata sunt in nobis propter vias suas Sodomæ perijssemus, & quasi habitatores Gomorræ continuati sumus. Audite sermonem Domini principes, quorū opera similia sunt principum Sodomæ, auscultate legem Dei nostri populi quorum opera similia sunt populo Gomorræ. Non est beneplacitum coram me in multitudine victimarum vestrarum, dicit Dominus: satiatus sum abundantia holocaustorum arietum, & adipe pinguium, & sanguine taurorum, & agnorum, & hircorum quia in eis non est beneplacitum coram me. Cum veneritis vt appareatis in conspectu meo, quis quæsiuit hoc de manibus vestris, vt veniatis ad conculcanda atria mea? Non addatis vltra offerre oblationem ex rapi-na, sacrificium abominabile est coram me, & neomeniæ & sabbatha cœtus congregationis vestra, quonia non relinquitis peccata vestra, vt exaudiatur oratio vestra in tempore congregationis vestræ.

be religious tracts, Machiavelli's *The Prince,* (1513), Italian comedies or Rabelais' *Gargantua* (1534).

At the same time there was a renewed interest in the classics, and in their languages, from ancient Greek to Hebrew and Latin. The urge was to get back to the original, or as close to the original text as possible, which in turn required a thorough knowledge of classical languages. Professional bibliographers and book collectors searched for new approaches to texts and hence was born classical scholarship in the sixteenth century. Virgil continued to be the most popular of Latin authors through the Renaissance, and, for that matter, until the early twentieth century. Others favored for constant new editions included Ovid, Juvenal's *Satires,* the historians Livy and Sallust, as well as the philosophers and masters of rhetoric, Seneca and Cicero.

Compared to works in Latin, Greek was poorly represented except for Homer and Plato, although the popularity of the Greek authors required more and more printers to incorporate Greek types in their shops. As a result, by the mid-sixteenth century the knowledge of both the Greek classics and the language spread among the educated.

Why did some classical works survive to our day and others disappear? The answer is complex. Essentially, though, it depended upon interest. If Virgil was unquestionably the most influential Latin author, and therefore throughout the ages guaranteed transmission, many of the Greek and Latin writers enjoyed little popularity. Their work died from lack of use or interest; and while physical destruction played a part—such as the decay of the library at Alexandria—this was only one factor.

Although the Reformation gave rise to flourishing literary activity, it also became the occasion for the destruction of many books already in existence. In the fight against the Church of Rome Protestants turned against Catholic literature. Many old monastery manuscripts and incunabula suffered a sad fate. During the peasant uprisings in Germany in 1524–25, German monastic libraries suffered great losses, just as French monastic libraries did later, during the Huguenot wars. Nevertheless, it is unjust to ascribe to the followers of the Reformation the chief blame for the fact that so little of the great book treasures of the Middle Ages has been preserved. A great deal was destroyed by the fires which ravaged churches and monasteries, and by the monks' own carelessness. Wars in more recent times added to the loss.

DISTRIBUTION AND PUBLISHING

In the beginning the printer usually sold the books he printed. Before long booksellers traveled about from town to town and offered for sale books that they had bought from the printers; they took advantage of church festivals, trade fairs, markets or other community events. The ability to produce numerous copies of books necessitated widening the channels of distribution, from the few who bought ordered copies of works to the masses of literate and semi-literate who might be persuaded to purchase a new work. Potential customers were sought with advertising (handbills, broadsides, catalogs, circulars, etc.), book fairs and shops—usually in conjunction with the printing establishment where books were displayed. Available copies of advertising sheets used by these dealers date as far back as 1470; the sheets announced the sellers' arrival in the town, listed the books they had for sale, and invited the public to examine the books at some particular inn.

Little of the early published works might be termed popular. Official government printing made up a large part of early publishing, as did textbooks, grammars and theological titles. One of the latter, Kempis' *The Imitation of Christ* (1473), became a type of religious best seller, exceeding over 100 editions in various languages before 1500. (The fact that he may not have written the book is another matter.) The work continues to be popular and as of 1992, can claim well over 3,200 editions. Erasmus' *In Praise of Folly* (1509) and *The Education of a Christian Prince* (1515), an early work on etiquette, proved to be equally well read. Luther's many books were popular, and various vernacular editions of the Bible then, as now, outsold all secular works.

Turning to non-theological works, they were few and far between in the fifteenth-sixteenth centuries, although *Canterbury Tales* (c. 1400) and Ariosto's *Orlando Furioso* (1532), the best known Italian romantic work, were reprinted scores of times. Ephemeral street literature grew up with the more formal book trade. Here the focus was on easy to read, often crudely illustrated almanacs, broadsides, calendars and propaganda pamphlets for everyone and everything, from Protestants to entertainment.

How many books were printed in the first years, that is, in the incunabula period from about 1450 to 1500? Statistics vary, although estimates are that there were 10,000 to 16,000 different titles and about two to three times that number of different editions of the various titles. If one agrees that the average press run was about 500 copies, then about 20 million different books were printed prior to 1500. It was over production. The European population was relatively small and the number of literate considerably fewer. Little wonder, then, that so many printers-publishers went out of business so quickly.

LITERACY

The exact extent of literacy in Europe by the turn of the sixteenth century is baffling. Records available permit generalizations: (1) Thanks to the wider distribution of books and to a growing attention to education, the percentage of literate men rose to about 25 per cent in 1500. Thomas More's famous claim in 1533 that half the population of England was literate was exaggerated. Still, an appreciable number of the male population did have some ability to read and write—a contention based on the production of records which required at least basic literacy.

(2) This, though, is to focus on men. Women's literacy rate was much lower. Inequalities are apparent, too, between different types of trades and professions; between urban dwellers and those living on a farm. Also, the ability to read varied from country to country and in regions within those countries.

(3) Pragmatic literacy, or learning just enough reading and writing to carry on a trade, became more evident by the fifteenth–sixteenth centuries. It was no longer totally confined to the clerics (in or out of the monastic community). Moving from the ability to sign a document, to understanding a simple broadside, to analyzing a scholarly work indicates the problem with gross percentages. For example, by the 1800s over 88 per cent of American men signed their wills, but what percentage were able to read a newspaper or an English literary journal is not clear.

(4) Among some of the uneducated, as today, there was a

mistrust of learning and often of writing and books. Depending on the period, the country and the leaders, this might be more a reflection of distrust of church, government or employer than any real hostility to literacy.

Although there is no precise way to describe the literacy rate in any given country, more or less throughout Europe, by the end of the fifteenth and sixteenth centuries, the reading public profile is relatively clear. It was made up, as before printing, of clerics, teachers, students, and a few of the nobility. Beyond the obvious core of readers, literacy developed as a necessity among urban residents in government or those involved with trade, law, medicine, etc. The potential purchasers of books were limited and would remain so until the technological and educational changes of the nineteenth century. This particularly is true when one distinguishes between an ability to read and habitual book reading.

If the vast majority of people were illiterate, even in the most remote community at least one person was able to read, able to communicate orally everything from stories to official documents which might be posted. The literate individual became the local storyteller, the local Homer who passed on from the printed broadside, ballad, and even book a type of popular culture which was familiar throughout Europe to anyone who would listen.

The church pulpit, too, was the source of information and inspiration for those unable to read. It is not surprising that with the advent of wider literacy and a popular press in the nineteenth century the church services lost members. Elizabeth Eisenstein suggests that the "displacement of pulpit by press is significant . . . because it points to an explanation for the weakening of local community ties,"[24] as people no longer had to come together. This may be a trifle too simplistic, as numerous other variables are also responsible, from mass transportation to urbanization.

LIBRARIES AFTER PRINTING

Reading, religion and the ownership of books were inextricably interlaced. Protestants tended to own more books—privately and in religious organizations—than Catholics. And from the sixteenth century through the early part of the twentieth century

Protestants prided themselves on owning and reading a part of the Bible each day. The Bible served in numerous cultures and countries as a reminder of the importance of being able to make out words and ideas. Repeated, intensive reading of the Bible not only increased one's reading ability, but focused on the importance of education and literacy as well as building personal libraries—if only of a few volumes.

The average, literate individual might have from six to a dozen printed books. While some may not have read the volumes, at least they had them in their homes, probably as much as status symbols as today's "coffee-table" jewel from a book club.

Montaigne (1533–92) was one of the first to describe his personal library as a place of retreat from the world in order to think, ironically enough, about the world's problems. In his *Essays* he describes the round-shaped library.[25] Montaigne is among the first Renaissance writers to celebrate the delights of having books about. Many other authors, of course, salute the joys of a library. Shakespeare's *The Tempest* (c. 1610) is, in a sense, constructed around Prospero's books; as is much of Samuel Pepys (1633–1703) and his busy world. Incidentally, Pepys often had someone read to him at bedtime. Readers (usually literate servants) were not uncommon. They read at meals—much as today one would turn on a radio.

The influence of the Reformation on the history of libraries was indirect. When the governments began to confiscate church and monastery property, the book collections came into the possession of the state, and often the old books received no gentle treatment. The situation was at its worst in England, since secularization came very soon after the triumph of the Reformation and the destructive urge was still at its height. In the first two or three decades following secession from the Church of Rome, the larger part of the 1,000 or so monastery and church libraries throughout the land were secularized, and in many instances the books fared badly.[26] Henry VIII's librarian, John Leland, made a trip around the country in 1536–42 and was able to save some of the most valuable book treasures from destruction. On the other hand, the famous library in Oxford, which went back to the fourteenth century, was plundered in 1550 by Edward VI's men, who burned some of the books and sold others. Six years later the empty shelves were also sold. Not until half a century thereafter, in 1602, was the library reestablished, through the efforts of one of Queen Elizabeth's statesmen, Thomas Bodley.

In Italy, France, Austria and South Germany, old Catholic libraries, after a brief period of disorder, continued to exist as before, and new collections were also established, especially where the Jesuits were in control. Pope Nicholas V (1447–1455) has the distinction of being the first bibliophile pope, and it is due to him that the Vatican library was revived. To a core of under 400 manuscript books, he added his own private library. Sixtus IV (1471–1484) continued the work, adding printed volumes and expanding the library to some 3,500 volumes.[27]

Division of books, by subjects, both in catalogs and in public and private libraries, became common in the sixteenth century. Not far behind were the catalogers and bibliographers. Conrad Gesner, the father of the compilers since printing, in 1545 felt satisfied he had in his pioneering bibliography "a complete catalogue of all writers in Latin, Greek and Hebrew, both surviving and perished, and old and modern to the present." His certainty about compiling a complete list was never to be heard again, although many dreamt (and dream) of a complete universal bibliography—which just may be close to possible with modern technology.[28]

One major change, due to printing and the increased number of books, was the way books were stored. The chained desk copies disappeared and in their place came a new idea—the bookshelf. As the number of books increased so did the length and height of the bookshelves which, with galleries, might go up several stories.

PRINTED BOOK ILLUSTRATION

Grandly illuminated books did not disappear with printing, and, in fact, continued to be produced by scribes and illuminators until the early sixteenth century, e.g. *Hours of Anne of Brittany* and similar Hours. Luxury manuscripts died out as much because the rich began to collect individual paintings as because the talented illuminators turned to other arts. It was not long before printed books began to have pictures printed along with the text instead of drawn in after the printing was completed.

Much has been written about the various techniques of illustration, although briefly they fall into four or five primary categories. Woodcuts came first. Examples can be traced to China, although the earliest in the West was the St. Christopher of 1423, a simple illustration of the Saint which was printed from a single block of carved wood. The technique was (and is) employed through much of the age of printing, although primarily for broadsheets, playing cards and cheap, brief illustrated block books. Prior to about 1500 it is estimated that 30 to 35 per cent of all books had one or more woodcut illustrations—primarily primitive, although charming.

While there are numerous monographs and articles on the individual schools of illumination, there are many less about early illustration until well into the seventeenth century. The wandering wood engraver makes it difficult to pinpoint particular schools. Furthermore, as experts point out: "The wood blocks themselves wandered all over Europe with the greatest rapidity, a Europe still unified in culture and still in possession of one language universally read."[29]

The first illustrated printed book was the work of Albrecht Pfister of Bamberg. In 1463 he published a second edition of popular fables by Ulrich Biner, with simple line drawings which might be individually hand colored after being printed. Others in Germany soon discovered the potential market for illustrated books and by the sixteenth century block printing had spread throughout Europe. Gunther Zainer has the claim to be the printer of the first major illustrated book. From his Augsburg presses in 1471–2 he published Voragine's *Lives of the Saints,* lavishly illustrated with dramatic woodcuts which show often the saints being tortured and killed. Possibly more important, in 1472 he printed one of the first widely circulated "encyclopedias," the seventh century *Etymologiarum* of Isidore. Drawing upon one of the thousand or so manuscripts which have survived, Zainer issued a popular work which moved from medicine to furniture in 20 books. Incidentally, it was the first work to boast a printed map of the world.

Erhard Ratdolt (1447–1537/28?) is even more renowned for pioneering illustration in the form of borders, initials, woodcuts, etc. Even today his work is considered of an unsurpassed aesthetic quality. The Venetian printer also was the first to publish an illustrated edition of Euclid's *Elements of Geometry* (1482). After Ratdolt left Italy in 1486 his influence continued to be felt; in the following years there were more and more books whose opening page, just as in Ratdolt's books, was entirely surrounded by a wide Renaissance border of imaginative and varied designs. Ratdolt earned the honor of being the first printer (if the two-colored initials in the Mainz Psalter are disregarded) to attempt the difficult feat of printing in more than one color. A few of his pictures are printed in four colors, a different cut being used for each color.

One step along the road from the earliest woodcuts to those of the Dürer period is represented by the Cologne Bible of 1478, probably the most famous of the many illustrated Bibles. Its 125 pictures were drawn by an artist of the first rank, whose name is unknown. These woodcuts were not merely outline drawings. They made extensive use of shading to give the figures a three-dimensional appearance, and the figures also seemed more alive than in earlier pictures. All the illustrations in the Cologne Bible were used by Anton Koberger of Nuremberg in 1483 and its wide distribution exerted a strong influence on Bible illustration in later times.

Antoine Verard (d. 1512) carried illustration of printed books in a logical forward step when he struck on the notion of mass-producing the highly popular Book of Hours, often with wood engravings carefully copied after illuminated manuscripts. Verard discovered one of the most profitable methods of book publishing. Before his death he published over 200 different editions of the Book of Hours, and established a French illustration style. The fine lettering, beautiful borders and miniature, and detailed figures, were copied throughout France. They were improved by such figures as Philippe Pigouchet and Thielman Kerver (Fig. 37).

Albrecht Dürer's (1471–1528) wood engravings challenged even the aesthetic excellence of the illuminated book.[30] Still, for the most part the illustrated printed books and broadsides were fairly crude affairs, depending as they did on woodcuts by often less than talented artists and engravers. Today, of course, their very simplicity exerts a charm. In 1498 Dürer's *Apocalypse* appeared in Nuremberg. Its fifteen large woodcuts represent one of the epoch-making works of graphic art, for in them the brilliant artistic effect is attained by the interplay of light and shadow alone. In these woodcuts, and in other series, Dürer depicted the life and suffering of the Virgin Mary.

me domine quoniam conturbata sunt ossa mea .
Et anima mea turbata est valde : sed tu domine vsquequo. Conuertere domine et eripe ani-

37. *Book of Hours,* published by Verard in 1498. The illustration is of
Susanna and the Elders, illustrated by Pigouchet.

Within a surprisingly short span of years the woodcut art developed to full maturity; then it became an item of fashion, and finally it declined. This art, which set its mark on several thousand German books, was centered first in Strassburg, where some of the great botanical works were produced, then in Augsburg and Basel. The last of these had early attained fame as the literary center of German Switzerland and was the place where one of the most popular books of the time was issued in 1494, Sebastian Brandt's satire, *Narrenschiff,* with its brilliant woodcuts (among them the famous "book fool" which some have considered the youthful work of Dürer). Presumably because of the great church meetings that were held there in 1431–49, Basel was one of the towns through which the Germanic world first came into contact with the Italian Renaissance.

Basel was the home of one of the greatest artists in this field, Hans Holbein the younger (1497–1543) (Fig. 38). He worked with a first rate wood-carver, Hans Lützelburger, and with the outstanding printer, Froben. Holbein and Lützelburger contributed the handsome title borders and initials cut in metal plates. In these, a host of small happy children tumble around in a framework of antique columns and arches or other Renaissance ornaments. Holbein's illustrations for the Old Testament, which first appeared in 1538 in a book issued in Lyons, and his depiction of the old Dance of Death motif, also first issued in Lyons in 1538, were among his most outstanding works. He used a clear and simple woodcut line which was suitable for either roman or italic type. It produced a pleasing harmony between the text page and the illustrations, just as in the *Hypnerotomachia,* however different the style of these books in other respects.

Printing, too, allowed the rapid production of prints, which, as Dürer and Holbein discovered, could be a lucrative source of income for artists who may or may not have illustrated books. Printing and wood engraving made possible the wide dissemination of art reproductions, crude as they may have been, as well as original work of artists from Bellini to Dürer. Later centuries would, at one time or another, allow all major artists to see reproductions of their work in books and/or in individual prints.

Dürer and Holbein aside, the general impression of illustrated sixteenth century books is poor. At least this was the opinion of

Corporis effigiem si quis non uidit Erasmi,
Hanc scite adumum picta tabella dabit.

38. Woodcut by Hans Holbein the younger, showing Erasmus of Rotterdam with his hand on a bust of Hermes—a symbol of his literary work. This woodcut, extant in only a few copies, was probably intended for an edition of Erasmus' works, but was never used. (Copper-engraving Collection, Copenhagen.)

most experts until the advent of minimalistic art and an appreciation of the cruder, yet fascinating, folk art.[31]
Illustration in printed books proved most valuable for the
natural sciences and anatomy. Human anatomical structure became widely known through the frequent reprinting of *Vesalius*
from 1543 through the sixteenth and into the seventeenth century
(Fig. 39). Herbals, with exquisite illustrations of plant species
from direct observation, began appearing in 1530 and soon
became among the most popular of the illustrated books.

The mid-sixteenth century depression and inflation hit the book
trade, and fewer and fewer books were illustrated; if pictures were
selected they normally were of a poorer quality than before.
Another change was technical. The woodcut and wood engraving
gave way to the longer-lived and more subtle copperplate engraving. By etching a copperplate, the artist (or the engraver) could
find shades of light and dark, and considerably more detail than
was possible on wood.

By the seventeenth century, copper engraving was preferable,
particularly for duplicating paintings, classical sculpture and
architectural drawings. Also, many printers and publishers issued
separate sheets of copper engravings to supplement their book
publishing, and made popular art reproductions in an affordable
form. Thus, copper engravings by the mid-1650s became the most
common form of reproduction both for books and for individual
prints.

BOOKBINDING

It was not until the introduction of printing that bookbinding
developed into a separate trade. During the first century following
the invention of printing it was quite common for printers to do
their own binding; this was especially true in the larger printing
establishments, where the books were often issued in bound form.
Usually a specially trained person executed the binding. It is
known that Ratdolt, Caxton, Koberger and others had binders
working for them, either in or outside their establishments.

Since printing had made books more plentiful and cheaper,
binding methods had to keep step; a type of binding had to be
found that was cheaper to produce than blind-stamped binding, in

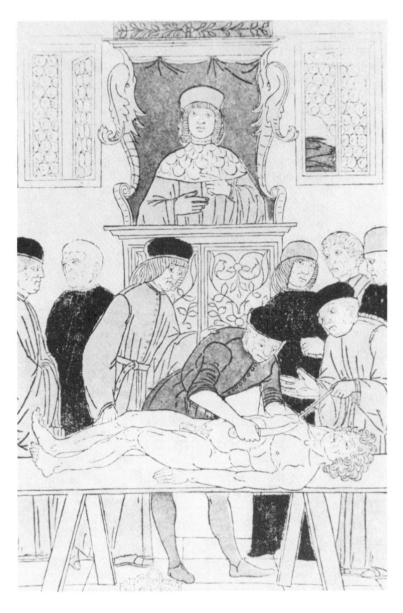

39. From a Medical Miscellany, published in Venice in 1493/4. The book includes illustrations on surgery by Johannes de Ketham.

which the decoration was made by the separate application of many small stamps. In the last third of the fifteenth century bindings began to be produced in Holland by engraving the decoration of the entire cover on a metal plate and pressing this down on the book in one operation in a screw press. This was still a blind-stamping or embossing process, the design being cut into the plate just as in the earlier small stamps. The figures represented were saints, angels, birds, flowers, grotesque animals, coats-of-arms, etc. If the binding was too large to be completely covered by the plate, the impression was repeated two or four times, and any blank spaces were filled in with small stamped borders. Since these plate-impressed or panel-stamped bindings could be produced more rapidly and cheaply than those made with the small stamps, their use spread rapidly through Holland and the Rhineland.

Panel-stamped bindings were introduced into France and England from Holland by itinerant journeyman bookbinders, many of whom, like the printers, led an unsettled life. The bindings executed for Caxton's establishment still had their decoration made with small stamps, but his followers, especially the printers in Cambridge, used panel-stamping almost exclusively. The process also made progress in England in artistic respects.

Aldus' establishment also included a bindery, and the Aldine bindings, which in large part were done in morocco leather (goatskin) from North Africa, were among the first to show definite traces of the influence of Islamic bookbinding. Their wide distribution aided in spreading the knowledge of gold tooling. At first Aldus used only blind-stamping, but later on he added gilded arabesques or flowing lines around the central panel where the title of the book was stamped in gilded roman letters, always showing a fine sense of moderation.

Aldine bindings showed Oriental influence in one respect: instead of the usual wooden core for the covers of the binding, Aldus followed the Oriental practice of using cardboard, which was much lighter and more practical, particularly for small formats. Wooden boards did not disappear from bookbinding until the eighteenth century; as late as the sixteenth century there were many bindings in which the wooden boards were only partly covered with leather, presumably to save material. Gradually cardboard came more and more into use. Often spoiled sheets, pages from discarded books and pieces of old vellum manuscripts were pasted together and used as boards; fragments of otherwise unknown texts have sometimes been found inside the covers of old books.

Of greater importance, however, than Aldus' trade bindings were the luxury bindings that he had made for rich book collectors who were not content with ordinary books but required special copies printed on vellum or large paper, and finely bound. The most famous of these collectors was Jean Grolier, who was born in Lyons in 1479. Between 1510 and 1537 he was in Italy most of the time as a French legate; thereafter he became government treasurer and lived in Paris until his death in 1565.

Extraordinary imagination, always with artistic restraint, was exhibited in the variations of Grolier designs. Only a few of the bindings were made at the Aldine press or at other places in Italy; the majority, including the most artistic, were certainly made in Paris by binders who had learned the trade in Italy. Grolier's library was sold and widely scattered in the seventeenth century; only some 400 Grolier bindings are known today. These extraordinarily beautiful calfskin and morocco bindings with their characteristic decoration and inscription are highly prized by collectors.

Some similarity to Grolier's bindings is seen in certain bindings executed for his younger contemporary, Thomas Mahieu (Maiolu), who was secretary to Catherine de Medici in 1549–60. A special feature of his bindings was the braided work, made up of rolled leaves. Mahieu also used an inscription on his bindings stating that the books belonged to him and his friends, as did Grolier. These two men were the first real bibliophiles in the modern sense, being possessed of a passion for beautiful books in beautiful bindings.

Ordinary bindings of the Renaissance were very little influenced by the fine bindings described above. They were made of calf or pigskin or vellum, and their designs were either blind or gilded panel-stampings or were made up of blind designs with roller stamps. Use of rollers became even more general in England than in France as the artisans in Cambridge gradually began using them in preference to other stamps. In fact, many of their bindings were made entirely with rollers, the central field being filled with rolled borders.

EVOLUTION AND REVOLUTION

Looking back on the first 150 years or so of printing, a definite pattern emerges. There was a revolution in the technological advancement of multiple copies. Printing helped to spread the intellectual aspects of the Renaissance as well as tear down the barriers of censorship and government control. The printer-publisher become a type of common link between Europeans. Publishers gave voice to advocates of change in everything from science and literature to religion and government.

A less obvious aspect of the spread of printing is how it served the pursuit of personal glory. The art of advertising, journalism, propaganda and aggressive self-aggrandizement was made possible by the rapid spread of publicity. Biographies and autobiographies, for the first time since the Roman Empire, became general and popular. The cult of the personality was reborn.

Scientific ideas, of course, were advanced by printing. Not only was the text readily available, but illustrations, such as detailed anatomy drawings, were given wide distribution. Images and words were fixed, and skilled artists were called upon to make actual diagrams rather than stereotypes such as those used to show rulers and cities in the *Nuremberg Chronicles.* Furthermore, the scientific illustrators by the sixteenth century went to nature to insure accuracy of phenomena. The recurrence of errors made from copying continued, but less and less as readers insisted on reality rather than fashionable generalizations. Achievements and discoveries of scientists from Copernicus to Newton were now insured rapid dissemination despite the sometime objections of the clergy.

The printed book helped not only to create the individual's own world, but a sense of privacy heretofore withheld within a tight-knitted community. While printing did not create silent reading—introduced generations before—it at least heightened the possibilities of individuals reading and learning alone. This, in turn, increased the concept/value of the individual, and the powers of contemplation—as well as action. Recognizing this added power of print, it is understandable why every government from Gutenberg's time to the present attempts control, in a varying degree, of what is published.

NOTES

[1]Actually, as in Medieval times, most of the people lived off the land, and the agrarian-urban balance would not shift towards the latter until well into the nineteenth century.

[2]The nineteenth-century introduction of destructible paper undermined the preservation benefits of printing. Still, through various copying procedures—from computers to microform—there is little danger of text loss.

[3]The impact of printing on the Reformation is demonstrated by the fact that one-quarter of all books and pamphlets published in Germany from about 1500 to 1540 consisted of Luther's writings. In addition some 430 editions of Luther's Bible in part or in whole appeared in print during his lifetime. See, too, Curt Buhler. *The Fifteenth Century Book: the scribes, the printers, the decorators* (Philadelphia: University of Pennsylvania Press, 1960).

[4]The woodblock with carved raised Chinese characters was inked. A sheet of paper was placed over the inked surface and the back of the paper rubbed with a brush. Pressure also could be exerted by a flat press surface. The printed sheet was then lifted from the block.

[5]Printing with movable types is only one aspect of the art, which must consider inks, presses, paper, binding, etc. Here it is used to indicate publishing without great attention to technology, which is abundantly discussed in countless monographs.

[6]A paper mill was drive by waterpower. The waterwheel operated a number of heavy beaters that tore up the raw material—linen and cotton rags, cordage, etc.—under water and mashed it to a thin pulp, which was then poured into a vat. A frame made of wood with brass wires stretched across it was dipped into the vat and on this frame the paper sheet was formed. The brass wires in the frame left lines in the paper that were plainly visible when it was held up to the light, and the idea soon developed of bending some of the wires to form various designs. These so-called watermarks could contain the initials or the name of the papermaker. The oldest known watermark dates from 1282.

[7]See Victor Scholderer. *Johann Gutenberg*. 2nd ed. (British Museum, 1970). See Helmut Lehman-Haupt, *Peter Schoeffer* (Rochester, N.Y.: Hart, 1950). Facts about Gutenberg and most printers and publishers are scarce until well into the nineteenth century. It would take centuries before the art of biographical involvement with the "trades" became of any importance. Conversely, the Renaissance did give emphasis to the individual artist, author, poet etc.

[8]A 1460 Bible printed by Albrecht Pfister from type cast in the Mainz

workshop of Gutenberg, and sometimes call the 36-line Bible, brought over $1.6 million in 1991 at Christie's.

[9]Probably first used in the seventeenth century, the term "incunabula" is the descriptor given to printing before 1501. Latin for "swaddling clothes" or in the "cradle," incunabula is applied, too, to the first years of printing in other places such as Mexico, the United States, etc.

[10]John Carter and Percy Muir, eds. *Printing and the Mind of Man* (London: Cassell, 1967), p. xxvii. (The quote is from Denys Hay).

[11]Their first printing in 1465, or the previous year, was a now lost grammar, the famous Donatus. The first surviving work is Cicero's *De Oratore* in the summer of 1465.

[12]See Martin Lowry, *Nicholas Jenson* (Oxford: Blackwell, 1991). Jenson is credited with the design of the first carefully thought-out roman type. As such he became a hero to William Morris and many other private press publishers of the nineteenth and early twentieth centuries. Jenson's roman still is considered to be one of the most satisfying types.

[13]Stanley Morison and Kenneth Day. *The Typographic Book 1450–1935* (University of Chicago Press), p. 21. The authors point out, however, that "the monumental beauty of gothic" is seen in the first Bible and was used for many centuries for texts of canon and civil law.

[14]Printers' devices served to give a work a distinctive advantage in that it advertised that the book was from a particular printer, usually well known for quality or a particular type of work, or both. See H.W. Davies, *Devices of the Early Printers, 1457–1560* (London, 1935).

[15]See Martin Lowry, *The World of Aldus Manutius* (Ithaca, N.Y.: Cornell University Press, 1979). Giovanni Bellini (c. 1430–1516) may have designed some of the illustrations, "but it owes still more to its printer Aldus, and its presentation is an object lesson in the enhancement of illustration by good typography, presswork and mise en page. The actual cutting of the blocks is beyond criticism and the use of white space in the pictures strikes one forcibly after the cramped and confused designs that were prevalent at the time." David Bland. *A History of Book Illustration* (Cleveland: World, 1958), p. 123.

[16]While there were over 100 Latin Bibles, based on Jerome's official Vulgate, printed before 1500, there was none in the Greek as it might be considered a challenge to the official version. Working with no more than two original Greek texts, and little comparison with other versions, Erasmus depended almost as much on his own retranslation of the Vulgate—which he noted. At any rate, it was the first in the field and remained as such for the next 250 years. Tyndale's English version (1525–26) is based on Erasmus as well as Luther's Reformation Bible of 1522. Luther turned to a number of sources, including many in Hebrew, for the Old Testament.

[17]The two French professors were Guillaume Fichet, who was also a librarian; and Jean Heynlin, German by birth. The two selected and edited all of the texts. The two left Paris in 1473 and the three printers set up a press elsewhere in Paris.

[18]There is a small library of books and articles about Caxton. Among the standard titles: Lotte Hellinga, *Caxton in Focus* (British Library, 1982); N.F. Blake, *Caxton: England's First Publisher,* 1976; and George Painter, *William Caxton,* 1976.

[19]This is the most famous version of the King Arthur story, but the author, Sir Thomas Malory (c. 1470), said he translated it from the French. Evidence indicates it was Malory who wrote the only true English epic. Nothing is known about Malory, although there is much conjecture, including that he wrote the story while in prison for rape and stealing of animals.

[20]According to Steinberg, "Before 1500, about three-quarters of all printed matter was in Latin. . . . Only in England and Spain vernacular books outnumbered Latin from the beginning. The proportion of Latin and German titles sold at the Frankfurt and Leipzig book fairs was 71:29 in 1650 . . . and 4:96 in 1800." *Five Hundred Years of Printing* (New York: Criterion Books, 1959), pp. 83–84.

[21]John Feather. *A History of British Publishing* (London: Croom Helm, 1988), p. 18. For more on this as well as aspects of importation of books, see Lotte Hellinga, "Importation of books printed on the Continent into England and Scotland before c. 1520," *in* Sandra Hindman, ed., *Printing the Written Word* (Ithaca: Cornell University Press, 1991).

[22]John Carter, *op. cit.,* p. xxviii. Latin remained the normal language for international correspondence among scholars, if not for their publications, until the early twentieth century.

[23]There are numerous works about Plantin and his publishing firm. See, for example: Colin Clair, *Christopher Plantin* (London: Cassell, 1960); Leon Voet, *The Golden Compass* (Amsterdam: Vangendt, 2 vols., 1969–72). Under the Moretus family the plant operated until 1875. It is now a museum, the Plantin-Moretus Museum and open to the public.

[24]Elizabeth Eisenstein. *The Printing Revolution in Early Modern Europe* (Cambridge University Press, 1983), p. 94. (This is an abbreviated edition of the author's two volume *The Printing Press as an Agent of Change,* 1979).

[25]*The Essays of Montaigne* (New York: The Heritage Press, 1946), Vol. 2, pp. 1122–1123. (In Montaigne's collected works this is really Volume 3, and the essay is "Of three sorts of intercourse.") "At home I

betake myself a little oftener than elsewhere to my library. . . . In shape it is round, and there is no flat wall except what is occupied by my table and my chair. . . . Miserable is the man, in my opinion, who has in his house no place [i.e. a library] where he can be alone.'' Centuries ahead of his time, as in most of his writing, he concludes that while ''books have many agreeable qualities'' they have the distinct drawback of keeping one in a chair and without exercise. ''I know of no excess more injurious for me, or more to be avoided in these declining years.''

[26]Eamon Duffy. *The Stripping of the Altars* (New Haven: Yale University Press, 1992). This traces the shift from Catholicism to the Protestant faith in England in the sixteenth century. It explains in part why so many books were lost in the transformation and the shutting down of monastic communities.

[27]Much of the credit for the Vatican Library has gone solely to Sixtus IV—an error in the opinion of the current prefect of the library (1993). See his explanation in the Library of Congress, *Rome Reborn: The Vatican Library and Renaissance Culture,* 1993. This is a catalog of the exhibition of Vatican Library treasures held at the Library of Congress in early 1993. See Phyllis Gordon, *The Renaissance Book Hunters* (Columbia University Press, 1974). The letters of Poggio Bracciolini show how the quest for significant manuscripts was conducted.

[28]Gesner's *Bibliotheca Universalis* (Zurich, 1545) was not a first effort. Prior to that St. Jerome attempted a more limited list of Christian writers, as did the Abbot of Spanheim in his 1494 work. The German-Swiss naturalist's majestic effort actually failed, in that of the 21 volumes planned, only 20 were published. The listing of natural science and medicine was started but never completed. Note, too, that Gesner was the author of an early subject encyclopedia which gained him more fame than the bibliography—*Historia Animalium* (Zurich, 5 volumes, 1551–87).

[29]E.P. Goldschmidt. *The Printed Book of the Renaissance* (Amsterdam: van Heusden, 1966), p. 41.

[30]Dürer used both wood engravings and woodcuts, although it is likely he drew the designs on the wood and let others make the engraving or cutting. Wood engraving followed and then paralleled woodcuts until the early seventeenth century, when both fell out of favor for illustration. The two processes differed in that a wood engraving allows for much finer lines and, if done properly, can hardly be differentiated from a copper engraving. An engraving employs a graver which cuts into the end grain of the wood. The flat side is used in a woodcut, and the result tends to be much more broad than a wood engraving.

[31]Writing in the late 1930s, Philip Hofer could truthfully say, ''There

has been a tradition among collectors of fine books that somehow the great period of printing and illustration was over with the year 1500.'' He added, ''fortunately, that tradition is now passing.'' Lawrence Wroth, ed., *A History of the Printed Book* (New York: Limited Editions Club, 1938), p. 398.

CHAPTER SEVEN

PUBLISHING: SEVENTEENTH AND EIGHTEENTH CENTURIES

> When I recall the memory of Diderot, [I recall] the immense
> variety of his ideas, the astonishing multifariousness of his
> knowledge, the rapid leap, the heat, the impetuous tumult of
> his imagination, all the charm and all the disorder of his
> conversation,
> —Henri Maister

Henri Maister's tribute to Denis Diderot (1713–1784) sums up the
turbulence of the seventeenth and particularly the eighteenth
century. Despite the intellectual excitement, technologically there
was a holding pattern in publishing. Little changed, although the
political and religious turmoil emphasized the importance of
education and the printed word. If publishing was relatively static,
the growth of the number of readers was more dramatic.

Introduced by the Renaissance, the seventeenth century naturally divides into two parts. The first is from 1600 to 1642 and the
outbreak of the Civil War in England. A new era opens with the
Restoration in 1660. Similar divisions are to be found in France
and Germany, as well as Holland where by 1648 the struggle with
Spain ends and the Dutch golden age of literature dawns.

The questioning attitude which shaped the seventeenth and
eighteenth centuries was reinforced by the religious and political
European battles, now called The Thirty Years' War (1619–
1648). The absolute power of Louis XIV (1638–1715) led to
conflicts later resolved by popular revolt.

The New England Confederacy was founded in 1643 to protect
the Europeans from the American Indians. The American colonies
developed throughout the seventeenth and eighteenth century to

declare their independence in 1776 and to elect George Washington in 1789.

Patterns of political and religious conflict were reflected in the published literature. Montaigne (1553–1592) asked ''What do I know''? (Que sais-je?). The late sixteenth century question echoed in the scientific findings of Galileo (1564–1642) and Francis Bacon (1561–1626). The struggle between the classics and new discoveries in science launched countless tracts and books. By the eighteenth century, the humanistic side of the scientific quest found voice in Adam Smith (1723–1790) and Immanuel Kant (1724–1804), to name only two sons of the century's Age of Reason.

Despite war, revolution, and intolerance, by the 1720s the Enlightenment dominated Western thought. From Voltaire (1694–1778) and Rousseau (1712–1778) to Benjamin Franklin (1706–1790) and Thomas Jefferson (1743–1826) there was faith in the ultimate perfectibility of people through education, reason and, in the case of the American and French revolutions, political action.

As printing greatly insured the success of the Protestant Reformation by making it possible to spread rapidly the word (or, the propaganda) of Luther throughout Europe, it had equally an effect on the eighteenth-century Enlightenment.[1] The humanitarian and scientific events were followed by the press.

Today television and rapid communication bring world events to living rooms in seconds. In the seventeenth and eighteenth centuries the printed word moved considerably slower. There was a lack of mass production of books, as well as problems of transportation, distribution and, to be sure, literacy.

INDIVIDUAL PUBLISHERS

The day-to-day business of publishing in the two centuries is documented in many places and in particular histories of individual firms. The publishers were motivated by many things, and while monetary profit was uppermost, a surprisingly impressive number of printers were concerned equally with scholarship and education of the public.

The late sixteenth and early seventeenth centuries in English publishing are remembered today for several landmark works, and particularly the printing of William Shakespeare's (1564–1616) plays. The first play to be published (1594) was *Titus Andronicus,* followed by *Romeo and Juliet* (1597). Texts were taken primarily from notes made during the play. By 1623 the collected plays appeared in the First Folio, a gigantic publishing venture of over 900 pages.[2] Typically for the seventeenth (and much of the eighteenth) century, the printing of the Folio was a near disaster. There were multiple errors, not the least of which was simply dropping two of his plays. Such was the fortune of the author throughout his life. Few of his works were printed without mistakes, and one must look to titles he may have edited, such as his poems of 1593 and 1594, for relatively free of error copies. Shakespeare and his printers have proven to be a never-ending source of books and articles for bibliographers. (Another result of the interest is that most of the printed plays are referred to not by name, but by format and date, such as Q2 for an edition of *Romeo and Juliet* published in 1599.)[3]

AGE OF ENCYCLOPEDIAS[4]

The seventeenth and eighteenth centuries, particularly the latter, are celebrated for their faith in the encyclopedia, or more precisely for the concept that the basics of science, art and the humanities could be captured in a single work. While the compilations go back to Varro (c. 116–27 B.C.) and Pliny the Elder (23–79) and before, the English philosopher Francis Bacon (1561–1626) was the first to apply scientific principles to the compilation. He introduced a classification system of knowledge which, modified, suited those who in the Age of Enlightenment dutifully collected data for various sets.

More ambitious, possibly more naive experts believed encyclopedia techniques might be used to understand not just a segment, but all of knowledge. From the close of the seventeenth century to midway in the eighteenth at least thirty to forty sets were launched by printers and publishers in Europe. They were of varying accuracy, depending as much upon the skills of the compilers as the publisher, but all indicated that progress should be expected from exploration to music and science. The Dodsworth optimism foreshadowed the public and business philosophies of the nineteenth century.

Printing, too, allowed frequent expansion upon another's work. Many, including the early *Encyclopaedia Britannica* (1768–71) drew liberally from previously published sets. Both facts and guesswork were carried from place to place, year to year, although as many students of social history have observed, the sets did establish uncontroversial dates, and certitude about facts related to events and individuals that heretofore were often more imaginative than real. Checking and double checking other works established a reliability in encyclopedias which carried over to other reference books from dictionaries to atlases.

The most famous set of the eighteenth century, or of any thereafter, was Diderot's monumental *L'Encyclopédie* (1751–66).[5] The new humanism raised the importance of the individual and helped to push forward publishing in general and the evolution of encyclopedias and related books in particular. Diderot's *Encyclopédie* was considered the embodiment of the Enlightenment. It offered a complete guide to all then-known information and knowledge. Some 2,000 subscribers insured the success of the gigantic undertaking. The close to 3,000 never to be surpassed plates, appended to the set, offered a visual enlargement—the beginning of a type of modern hypertext. With the publication of each volume, often filled with controversial ideas, the popularity and notoriety of the work increased. While, according to Voltaire, "the vast and immortal work seems to reproach mankind's brief lifespan," it was filled more with argument, brilliant or not, than facts (Fig. 40).

Other sets soon followed. By the nineteenth century encyclopedias were a common undertaking for major publishers from England and Germany to all of Europe.

State and religious censorship continued to be a problem for encyclopedias and for other publishers, although from country to country, year to year, it might be less or more important. Then, as now, censorship usually served more to celebrate what to read than what to avoid, and offered publicity for authors and publishers. Writers often hoped to be censored. The mass of free publicity usually brought about equally massive attention. Jail was a consideration; but throughout the seventeenth and eighteenth

ENCYCLOPÉDIE,

OU

DICTIONNAIRE RAISONNE

DES SCIENCES,

DES ARTS ET DES MÉTIERS,

PAR UNE SOCIETÉ DE GENS DE LETTRES.

Mis en ordre & publié par M. *DIDEROT*, de l'Académie Royale des Sciences & des Belles-Lettres de Pruſſe ; & quant à la PARTIE MATHÉMATIQUE, par M. *D'ALEMBERT*, de l'Académie Royale des Sciences de Paris, de celle de Pruſſe, & de la Société Royale de Londres.

Tantùm ſeries junɛturaque pollet,
Tantùm de medio ſumptis accedit honoris ! HORAT.

TOME PREMIER.

A PARIS,

Chez
{
BRIASSON, *rue Saint Jacques, à la Science.*
DAVID l'aîné, *rue Saint Jacques, à la Plume d'or.*
LE BRETON, Imprimeur ordinaire du Roy, *rue de la Harpe.*
DURAND, *rue Saint Jacques, à Saint Landry, & au Griffon.*
}

M. DCC. LI.

AVEC APPROBATION ET PRIVILEGE DU ROY.

40. Title page from the first volume of Diderot's *L'Encyclopédie.*

centuries, as today, it was more threatening to many authors to be overlooked.

READERS AND LITERACY

The seventeenth and eighteenth centuries witnessed a growth in literacy and the number of readers. The average number of copies of a sixteenth-century European book published was 1,500. This rose to over 2,000 in the next century. While growth was neither constant nor the same everywhere, in urban centers roughly one-third of the residents owned some, if not a great number of books; and most borrowed from time to time from the local circulating library.

The spread of printing followed or led to an extended interest in reading by the upper- and what would be called the middle classes. Education, and particularly the ability to read among women, opened the way for an increased number of publications. Then, as now, education, economics and social status seemed the best indicators of who read, who was literate, who, in fact, could afford books. The primary readers, as in the past, were theologians and their students, the nobility, officeholders, and masters of crafts and trades. The latter formed the growing bourgeoisie. Compulsory education, which began in the German dukedom, Weimar, in 1619 (later made famous by Goethe), was slow to spread, but private schools for the business and professional classes brought literacy to more and more potential readers.

While literacy did increase over the eighteenth century in England, as well as what was to become the United States, the pace was slower in Europe. The growth of the middle class (from clerks and shopkeepers to tradespeople) and the interest in literacy on the periphery of this social strata (apprentices, servants, etc.) encouraged a wider involvement in reading. By the mid-eighteenth century there were enough readers that an author could now earn a comfortable living from his/her work.[6]

The link between literacy, the greater number of books published and the development of the novel in the eighteenth century is established. Less appreciated was the rapid growth of more ephemeral reading. Almanacs and chapbooks, with limited, easy to read prose and numerous inexpensive illustrations, flourished. Prognosticating almanacs in England sold an average of 16,000 copies in two years, as compared to 1,300 copies of *Paradise Lost* for the same time frame. Ballads, broadsheets and chapbooks, as far as can be estimated, probably sold 20,000 or so each year. Probably the best known almanac is Benjamin Franklin's *Poor Richard's Almanac,* published in Philadelphia by the author and his brother from 1732 to 1764.

PERIODICAL PRESS

Although there were numerous newsletters and even versions of newspapers in the sixteenth century, it was not until 1621 that the familiar corante (or newspaper) appeared in England. Offering news from Europe, the news books were superseded in the middle of the century by the news-sheets. They published current news, as well as literary and entertainment topics. A daily paper was first issued in 1702. A proliferation of newspapers followed. Magazines also evolved. Richard Steele (1672–1729) with Joseph Addison (1672–1719) reached thousands of readers with *The Tatler* (1709–11) and *The Spectator* (1711–14). Cultivating both literary taste and gossip, the two writers established a soon to be much copied pattern. For example, the *Gentleman's Magazine* (1731–1907) gave the world the term ''magazine.'' Its popular writing and illustrations insured an impressive circulation.

An early eighteenth-century Swiss traveler to England wrote: ''All Englishmen are great newsmongers. Workmen habitually begin the day by going to coffee rooms in order to read the daily news. Nothing is more entertaining than hearing men of this class discussing politics and topics of interest concerning royalty.''[7] The rapid expansion of publishing in the periodical field encouraged scientific curiosity and knowledge. The Royal Society published its *Transactions* from the mid-seventeenth century and, in fact, claimed it to be the first journal in English. A wider audience was envisioned when the *Journal of Natural Philosophy, Chemistry, and Other Arts* was founded in 1797. Specialized journals followed in other fields throughout the eighteenth and nineteenth centuries.

PUBLISHING CHANGES

During the two centuries the book trade expanded, not only in Europe, but in North America. Distribution, no longer limited to the immediate area of the printer, covered most of Europe and was augmented by the Frankfurt book fair, which began in 1564. Distribution of books took many forms. Subscription works were favored for expensive titles. The publisher could tell from the number of subscribers how many copies to publish—or, in many cases, when to abandon the project. Pope's translation of *The Iliad* (1720) was sold by subscription, as were many classics during the eighteenth century. Reference books were sold in a similar fashion, particularly in America, until World War II. Today a rough equivalent of the system is the mail book club.

The early years of the seventeenth century marked the beginning of selling books at auction to the highest bidder. The first book auctions were held in Leiden. The seller obtained maximum financial return and the buyer was offered collections that did not have the miscellaneous composition of the ordinary bookseller's stock. Quite early, however, there were complaints that bookdealers used the auctions to get rid of the less desirable books in their stock by mixing them with those to be put up at auction. Printed catalogs were sent out in advance, usually listing the books by size: octavos, quartos and folios.

The Dutch book auctions soon attracted attention in other countries and acquired increasing international significance. An English clergyman introduced the custom into London in 1676, when he proposed that the library of a deceased parson be sold at auction. Books that were not destroyed or added to the public collections after the French Revolution were put on the auction block by the government. The auctions were held under very unfavorable circumstances, as the demand was much less than the supply. Often real rarities had to be sold at ridiculously low prices.

A peculiar twist of the seventeenth century was the recognition of payment to authors. From the early years of printing it was considered bad form to accept money for writing and Erasmus (1466–1530) denied that he had ever received anything for his work—although in fact he did rather well, if under the table. The usual method was to give the author certain rights and offices for a publication, but not a fixed sum, or as it is known today, royalties. This changed gradually until money was the primary payment.

A growing group of both writers and readers turned publishing into a profitable business and Dryden (1697) received £1,200 for his translation of Virgil. Pope's translation of the *Iliad* (1720) gave him enough money for life, about £5,230. (The average wage at the time was from £20 to £60 a year). By the middle of the eighteenth century Dr. Johnson could say, "We have done with patronage," under which authors were supported by the rich to whom they dedicated a book. The time of the author to gain from creative work, if only marginally, was at hand. English authors turned to dedicating their books to readers, not patrons, and expected in return money for copies sold. Henry Fielding (1707–1754), by far one of the most successful authors of the eighteenth or any century, made several thousand pounds from his writing, rivaled only by Pope.

THE STATIONERS' COMPANY

Among major events in English publishing, the two of most lasting importance were the death of the control of publishers by the state in 1695 and the establishment of protection for authors and publishers with the Copyright Act of 1709.

Incorporated in 1557, the Stationers' Company, a development from the fourteenth-century Scriveners' Guild company, took control of who could or could not print, publish and distribute books. Licensing by the Company proved a successful method of silencing dissent. Nonetheless, despite the right of search and seizure, not to mention jail sentences, the Company was unable to control printing completely in an age of religious turmoil.

Gradually the Company itself became a publisher, at least in the sense it controlled not only what could be printed, but who was to do the publishing. Patents to publish given titles were leased. Under Queen Elizabeth authority was tighter. By 1586 all printing was confined to London. The exception was a press each for the universities at Oxford and Cambridge.

Throughout the seventeenth century and the turbulence of Civil War, the Company lost and regained its power depending on the particular circumstance. A blow came in 1695 when Parliament refused to continue the Company's power to license publishers. This was hardly the end. The Company continued as a force to insure copyright and, in a more restrictive way, to enforce sometimes ridiculous libel laws. Only by the Industrial Revolution did the Company fade away.

The concept of copyright grew out of the Stationers' Company, which required each book to be registered at Stationers' Hall. This then gave the publisher protection in that no one else could legally print and distribute the work. From this developed the Copyright Act of 1709, which formed the basis of all copyright law to this day. The law granted protection to the owner (including author/ publisher) for a fixed period of time, after which the book became a part of the public domain, and anyone could publish it without permission of the publisher, and/or author.

PRINTING DEVELOPMENTS

By the seventeenth century ready-made type, instead of founts cast by individual printers, became the norm. Mass production of type began with Claude Garamond (1480–1561) and Robert Granjon (1513–1589). To be sure, the major printer-publishers, such as Plantin, continued to cast their own type, but small firms depended on type faces established by the large type founders.

Until well into the eighteenth century the English depended almost entirely upon type from Europe. William Caslon (1692– 1766) built his own type foundry in London in 1716. Some 16 years later he came out with probably the most famous of all types, suitably named after him. Caslon, in its many variations and sizes, was used, and continues to be used in a vast number of books and printed materials as the primary body type. After the father's death, the son, also William (1770–1778), took over the firm. And, yes, he in turn gave it to his son, William. Even today the firm continues, although under another ownership and without a William in view.[8]

There was limited advancement in technology. Willem Blaeu in 1620 introduced an improved press which would be the first introduced into North America by Stephen Daye at Cambridge in 1638. By the end of the eighteenth century America was about ready to introduce the Columbian press, one of the first metal ones in the world. The press, along with an improved Washington press, made it possible to print 250 copies an hour. Despite these gains in the ease of use of a printing press, the process itself was essentially the same as in the time of Gutenberg. Nothing greatly had changed, although at least in England the overall quality of printing had deteriorated, or at least not improved, since Caxton.

Among England's greatest printers, and unquestionably a match for any English eccentric, John Baskerville (1706–1775) gave the world an alternative to what generally was poor printing in England. He had made a fortune in the japanning trade, but by the time he was close to 50 years of age, Baskerville turned to books. He designed and cut his own type and published the classics.

With his first quarto *Virgil* (1757), Baskerville challenged the publishers to offer something more than bad type, bad binding, bad ink, bad layout, bad paper, bad illustrations and in total, bad books. Stressing the importance of what today might be termed "minimalism," Baskerville emphasized the sheer beauty of typography and a careful, simple format. He went on to publish another 49 titles, none of which at the time did well financially, but they established him as one of the world's greatest prophets of quality. Although wealthy when he published his first book, some 20 years later he had pretty well reduced himself to poverty. His insistence on small runs of expensive works proved an economic disaster (Fig. 41).

Just as a current typeface is named after Baskerville, so is Bodoni equally famous. The Bodoni typeface is named in honor of Giambattista Bodoni (1740–1813), who, influenced by Baskerville, became a type designer and, for the Duke of Parma, printed books of a quality still unsurpassed.[9]

PRIVATE PRESS

Growing out of the disgust over poor printing in the eighteenth century, the private press developed in England under the sponsorship of Horace Walpole (1717–1797). From 1757 to 1789 his Strawberry Hill Press published many noteworthy books, usually as well printed as they were decorated. Among the most famous, of course, is his own novel, *The Castle of Otranto* (1764). This was the first gothic novel.

PUBLII VIRGILII

MARONIS

BUCOLICA,

GEORGICA,

ET

AENEIS.

BIRMINGHAMIAE:

Typis JOHANNIS BASKERVILLE.

MDCCLVII.

41. Baskerville's Virgil: *Bucolics and Georgics* (1757).

William Blake (1757–1827) demonstrated that a private press could be used, too, to publish books no one else would risk. His skill as a printer and illustrator helped establish him after his death as a famous English artist. His technical skills still are the wonder of all, as are, of course, his poetry and art. Blake often avoided printers by simply engraving both the illustration and the text as a whole. This followed the procedure of early illuminated manuscripts, and in many ways the unique books are reminiscent of the best of the manuscript pages[10] (Fig. 42).

COMMERCIAL PUBLISHERS

Among the more noteworthy printers in the eighteenth century were Robert (1707–1776) and Andrew Foulis (1712–1775). The Scots became the largest publishers of the realm, particularly as printers of Greek classics (both in the original Greek and translation), philosophy and theology. The brothers have two claims to lasting fame. They again demonstrated that scholarship was important in editing.[11] They went to great expense and time to follow in the footsteps of Aldus with his attention to accuracy. Second, they offered a clean, nicely laid out title page using a consistent, usually single, typeface. Of their 700 books and pamphlets, they are remembered best today for their classics, and particularly the 1756–8 Homer.

John Bell (1745–1831) serves as a bridge figure between the eighteenth century and the industrial revolution of the nineteenth century. He turned out numerous series such as the 109 volumes of *Poets of Great Britain* (1777–92).[12] A cousin of the modern-day publishing czar, Bell saw the possibilities of mass production and distribution not only of books, but of other printed matter from magazines to newspapers. Anxious to educate the English, he published numerous inexpensive series. He hoped they would reach the common reader who was in quest of self-education.[13]

CONTINENTAL PUBLISHERS

In the seventeenth century Louis Elzevir (c. 1547–1617) became famous throughout Europe (Fig. 43). The Dutch printer and

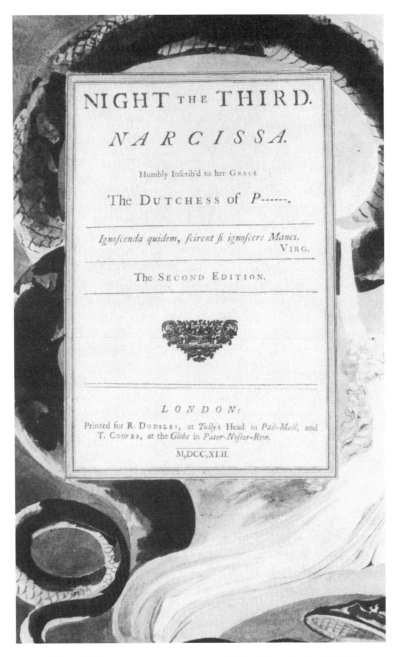

NIGHT ᴛʜᴇ **THIRD.**

N A R C I S S A.

Humbly Infcrib'd to her Gʀᴀᴄᴇ

The Dᴜᴛᴄʜᴇss of *P-------.*

Ignofcenda quidem, fcirent fi ignofcere Manes.
Vɪʀɢ.

The Sᴇᴄᴏɴᴅ Eᴅɪᴛɪᴏɴ.

L O N D O N:

Printed for R. Dᴏᴅsʟᴇʏ, at *Tully's* Head in *Pall-Mall,* and
T. Cᴏᴏᴘᴇʀ, at the *Globe* in *Pater-Nofter-Row.*

M,DCC,XLII.

42. William Blake's Night III: title page to *Night Thoughts* (c. 1796–7).

publisher learned his trade with Plantin in Antwerp, and while he retained links with Plantin he moved to Leiden. Later (c. 1600) his son opened a branch at The Hague and another in Amsterdam (c. 1640). The sons produced the famous multitude of duodecimo editions. At a time when large folios were in vogue these small books were quite unusual and, like the Aldines, considered inexpensive. They rapidly became popular because of their practical format and low price; the editions of Caesar, Pliny, Terence and Virgil were in particular demand. While they could not compare with the Aldines in philological accuracy, the general effect of their clear roman type was impressive.

43. Page from an Elzevir Edition of Virgil in duodecimo. In the octavo format the sheet is folded three times, while in the duodecimo it is folded to make 12 sheets or 24 pages. Duodecimo is abbreviated "12mo."

Plantin's printing business in Antwerp came to have even greater significance. Through the seventeenth century, the Netherlands took the lead in most aspects of book production in Europe. This was due partly to the powerful political position that the Netherlands had attained, and partly to their liberal form of government. The artist was free of the strict censorship which prevailed in other European states. In addition, the Netherlands held a position of leadership in the scientific and scholarly world. Students came from all countries to the famous University of Leiden.[14]

The Dutch monopoly, both of the literary genre and of high-quality illustration, was broken by the French. Henri Estienne produced a popular book, *The Art of Making Devises* (1645); translated into many languages, it not only obtained popularity in its own right but offered Europe a sample of high quality bookmaking and illustration. The French publishers could draw upon famous artists for illustrations; e.g. François Boucher's illustration of Molière (1734) is a sample of the high quality of work until the French Revolution.

By the mid-eighteenth century the French took the lead in major publishing projects. For example, consider the seventy-volume set of Voltaire's work (1785–9), of which Pierre Beaumarchais (1732–1799) bought the copyright. He purchased Baskerville's press from his widow and set up an elaborate scheme to secure subscribers to the Voltaire set. The collected works proved a great success, although today Beaumarchais is better known as the author of the librettos for *The Barber of Seville* and *The Marriage of Figaro*. Among his other speculations was the purchase of arms for American revolutionaries. Imprisoned during the French Revolution, he managed to escape through the aid of a former mistress.[15]

Among the most famous and earliest university presses are the two English presses, Cambridge (1583) and Oxford (1585). The history of both is impressive and confusing. Oxford did not begin to publish seriously until 1672, when John Fell's press was put into operation, and Cambridge's did not really begin until 1698. Cambridge had fits and starts at publishing, but only in the late nineteenth century did the press become a major consideration. Since then it has prospered and, along with Oxford, become a model for other university presses both in Europe and the United

States. In the period before World War II, Cambridge attempted to upgrade typography by employing the by-now masters of the art, Bruce Rogers (from America) and Stanley Morison.[16]

Official government publishers were outside the mainstream of printing and publishing and continue so today at both the local and federal level. An early example of government printing can be found in the court of Louis XIII, where in 1640 the Imprimérie Royale was established.

PRINTING IN THE AMERICAS

The Spanish set up a press in Mexico City and pulled off a small religious work in 1539. This was the first printing done in the Americas. (Argument persists that as early as 1535 there may have been a press.) Before closing in 1560, the publisher issued over thirty-seven books.[17]

Printing came to North America in 1638 when Stephen Daye (c. 1594–1668) and his two sons printed, suitably enough, the *Oath of a Free-Man* at Harvard College in Cambridge. (Despite the American sounding title, this was an oath to swear allegiance to the British government.) The printers were sponsored by Joseph Glover, who died on the voyage of the printers from England to America and left behind a widow who married the president of Harvard. The president (and/or his widow) thought it necessary to carry on the work of Glover.[18] Two years later, 1640, the first book to be published in what was to become the United States was pulled from the press. *The Whole Booke of Psalmes* (or Bay Psalm Book) was followed by other publications. By 1642 Massachusetts demanded that free citizens should master reading, writing, basic laws and, to be sure, religion. It was not until 1674 that Marmaduke Johnson moved his press to Boston to break the monopoly of Cambridge, a few miles away. Gradually printing spread to Philadelphia (1685), New York (1693) and throughout the colonies. Each had one or more printers by 1763, in time to lay the groundwork for the Revolution.

Until the late eighteenth and early nineteenth century most of the printing in America concentrated on laws, government regulations and religious works. Almanacs, popular broadsides and the inevitable newspapers and journals gave the output some balance.

The best known single work of the period is Benjamin Franklin's (1706–1790) *Poor Richard's Almanack.* In 1766 Franklin & Hall printed and sold close to 10,000 copies, which was about 9,500 more than almost any other work published by them or others during the eighteenth century (Fig. 44).

An English writer in 1789 observed that almost every large American town had a weekly paper, and several had more than one daily. Between 1694 and 1820 close to 2,000 American newspapers were published, although only about one-half lasted any length of time. Magazines were equally popular and almost as plentiful. It was a nation of magazine and newspaper readers, with much less attention given to books. Literary works were of little real importance. The primary explanation is that the educated received most of their books from England and Europe. Also, the printing equipment in the colonies was not sophisticated enough for other than slow book production—and, first and foremost, profit came from publication of religious, legal and utilitarian titles, not literature.

LIBRARIES

The seventeenth and eighteenth centuries saw two major developments in libraries. There was a renewed interest in private libraries and a move toward national libraries in most Western European countries as well as the United States. Most of the national libraries, from the Bibliothèque Nationale to the Prussian State Library, were expanded from private libraries.

Private libraries became increasingly important as a mark of class and culture. The Fuggers, for example, amassed a private library in Vienna of over 14,000 volumes. At the same time Leopold I (1658–1705) encouraged the development of the Vienna Court Library with its impressive number of priceless manuscripts. Sir Thomas Bodley (d. 1613) restored the famous library at Oxford, on November 8, 1602, with a collection of some 2,500 works from his own library.[19] In 1800 the Library of Congress was founded, 40 years after the British Museum Library (now the British Library of the British Museum) was organized in 1754.

The first lending library was established in Edinburgh in 1726, and a few years later (1731) Benjamin Franklin followed with a

M. T. CICERO's

CATO MAJOR,

OR HIS

DISCOURSE

OF

OLD-AGE:

With Explanatory NOTES.

PHILADELPHIA:
Printed and Sold by B. FRANKLIN,
MDCCXLIV.

44. Benjamin Franklin's *Cato Major* by M.T. Cicero (1744).

subscription library in Philadelphia. By the middle of the eighteenth century there were popular libraries in London and throughout centers of recreation in England. By the turn of the nineteenth century these forerunners of the public library were in every major town in Europe as well as in many American communities.

Circulating libraries encouraged novel reading, and it was not unusual that a popular work, such as Henry Fielding's *Joseph Andrews* (1742) would sell close to 7,000 copies in slightly over one year. In contrast, Johnson's *Dictionary* (1755) took more than four years to sell 2,000 copies.

Librarians in the eighteenth century faced a problem which was to plague librarians for centuries to come—too many books and not enough space. Library buildings were remodeled and rebuilt, usually in splendor. Few measured up to the Court Library at Vienna (1722–26), where interior decoration reached a new high. Mastering both the need for space and the delight of architectural design, the librarians gave birth to the by-now-familiar phrase, "books do furnish a room."

Several famous librarians and bibliographers worked during this time. Gabriel Naudé (1600–1653), in charge of the Cardinal Mazarin library in France, wrote the first modern book on how to organize a library, *Avis pour dresser une bibliothèque* (1627). It had great influence on both public and private libraries; e.g. Samuel Pepys, the English diarist, established his collection along Naudé's principles.

ILLUSTRATION

Woodcuts and wood engravings dominated illustration during this period, although copperplate was employed as well. Copperplate engravings were used first in a book issued in Florence in 1477. During the next hundred years copper engravings were employed only occasionally. In several instances books which originally had copper engravings were reissued with woodcuts. Copper engravings met with resistance from printers at first because unlike woodcuts they could not be printed in one operation with the text. The engraved frontispiece, for example, was inserted before the letterpress title page. The frontispiece contained the title of the book, often set against a background of allegorical figures which represented the contents.

In a woodcut the block is carved so that the outlines of the drawing stand out in relief, and these raised portions take the ink and make the impression. This is called relief or letterpress printing. In a copper engraving, the lines of the drawing are traced on the copperplate and cut down into it; these depressions are then filled with ink for printing, i.e. intaglio printing. In theory, copper engravings are not suited for use in books, but for some two hundred years they were the dominant method for printing fine book illustrations.

Copperplate printing was especially suited for the reproduction of paintings, since it could imitate the fine shades of color and the general artistic effect. In the fields of archeology, art history and natural history, copper engraving was an invaluable aid for accurate representation until the nineteenth century, when photographic methods came into use and made possible even greater accuracy.

SCIENTIFIC AND TECHNICAL ILLUSTRATION

The single most impressive use of illustrations was in the science and/or technology book. Thanks to sometimes detailed line drawings and etchings, the reader was able to follow precisely the line of reasoning of the author. Here it should be noted that the concept of modern science was unknown much before the mid-seventeenth century. There were few scientific centers or universities organized to teach science and there was much confusion, say, between chemistry and alchemy, between astronomy and astrology.[20] Side by side with remarkably accurate scientific illustrations one finds crude woodcuts of plants, birds, animals, etc. These tended to be for the lay public and usually were copied, and not well, from earlier illuminated manuscripts. Conversely, the carefully constructed scientific illustration was taken from nature, often by a skilled artist and engraver.

The first and earliest technical illustration was for a 1472 manual published in Verona, *On Military Matters.* The eighty-two woodcuts illustrate how engineering (from siege platforms to bridges) aids in warfare. Leonardo da Vinci is said to have owned a copy and to have found it useful when working as an engineer for Cesare Borgia.

Other technical illustrations followed, from Euclid's *Elements of Geometry* (Ratdolt, 1482) and works on architecture to the first illustrated medical book published in Venice in 1493/4. The realistic figures, and particularly a dissection scene, are drawn primarily from earlier medieval manuscripts, but it went through many editions until 1523. In 1543 the "classic" medical book was published. This was Vesalius' *The Structure of the Human Body,* with complete drawings of every part of the body, based on first-hand experience. The magnificent woodblocks set new standards for illustration.

The seventeenth and eighteenth century saw more technical illustrations drawn from life rather than earlier copies of manuscripts. For example, William Harvey's theories on the circulation of blood were illustrated in a work published in Germany in 1628. (The Frankfurt publication of one of England's most celebrated books was due to the fact it could be printed cheaper there than in London.) Other similar titles followed, e.g. a manual on dentistry in 1728 was typical of many such manuals, culminating in the 17-volume French *Encyclopedia of Sciences* (1751–65), ably edited by Denis Diderot, who had an encyclopedia of his own in mind.

By the mid-eighteenth century Benjamin Franklin published a book in which he introduced his ideas about electricity. And in the *Philosophical Transactions of the Royal Society,* Frederick Herschel (1738–1822) set down his landmark theories on astronomy in 1783. The place of illustration as a necessary corollary of scientific and technical works was established.

THE GENERAL BOOK

Representing a period of transition between the baroque and the neo-classic, seventeenth-century general book illustration hit a relatively low point. Conversely, the superior title pages, often reflecting architectural details, are now recognized as some of the best in the history of illustration.

Within the text poor engravings dominated. Illustrations were produced quickly and with a minimum of expense. The engraving of the original artwork, usually purchased from the artist by the publisher, tended to be awkward. As a result, work by such distinguished artists as Peter Paul Rubens (1577–1640) and Anthony Van Dyck (1599–1641) often was engraved so badly as to be hardly recognizable.

In international vogue, the emblem book was a popular form of illustrated work. Symbolic engravings were used to illustrate poems and sayings, establishing a symbol for life, death, fame, fortune, etc. (Today many of the symbols are often obscure.) Emblem books, made famous by Dutch printers in the sixteenth century, continued their popularity well into the next century. Many emblem books published in other countries actually were printed in Holland.

MAPS

The Netherland engravers also earned lasting fame with their maps. Plantin printed the famous Ortelius (1527–1598) *Theatrum,* which boasted 70 maps drawn from numerous authorities but engraved in a uniform style. The most popular atlas of the time, the work was used throughout the seventeenth century.

Cartography had reached a high stage of development among the seafaring Dutch. The founder of the seventeenth-century Blaeu firm, Willem Janszoon Blaeu, had acquired a basic knowledge of astronomy and cartography. In Amsterdam he issued several large editions of marine charts that surpassed all earlier ones in accuracy and attractiveness. His main work was the *Novus Atlas,* but the family attained its greatest fame from the work by the founder's son, Johann, entitled *Atlas major,* which was first published in 1662 in 11 folio volumes. Here the art of copper engraving came into its own, not only in the hand-colored maps but in the titles and ornaments. In spite of its size and cost the *Atlas major* was very much in demand.[21]

The financing of this, and of many of the other monumental publishing enterprises of that time, seems miraculous. Part of the answer undoubtedly lay in the low-paid labor that was available. But in many instances financial support must have come from patrons among royalty and the nobility, in return for dedications and eulogies in prose and verse at the beginning of the printed work. Without this support these large scholarly works would have had just as little chance of publication as they would today without grants from the government or from private foundations.

FRENCH ILLUSTRATIONS

Portrait engraving was another highlight of the seventeenth century and well into the eighteenth. France led in this, particularly as publishers could draw upon professional artists such as Nicolas Poussin (1594–1665) and Jacques Callot (1592–1635). The latter's great series of etchings, many of which found their way into books, concerned the miseries of war and were based upon the atrocities of the Thirty Years' War.

The eighteenth century was the high point for French illustration. Novels, poetry and even travel books were all embellished with some form of illustration. Vignettes were scattered liberally throughout the pages in the form of headpieces at the beginning of each chapter and tailpieces at the end. Flying cupids encircled by rose garlands were frequently used for these vignettes. The real flowering of vignette art began in 1734 with an edition of Molière containing over 200 vignettes by the famous painter Boucher. He succeeded in producing a greater three-dimensional effect than should have been thought possible in such small pictures. This effect was also achieved by other artists. Jean-Honoré Fragonard (1732–1806), strongly influenced by Boucher, illustrated a number of titles, including La Fontaine.

The French gained the reputation for offering illustrated books with a slight to magnificent air of pruriency—a reputation which held well into the twentieth century. They seemed particularly successful in illustrating books with amorous themes, such as Montesquieu's Le temple de Gnide (1772) or the sentimental verses, Les baisers (1770), of the poet Dorat, to which his slightly affected style was so well suited (Fig. 45). Pierre Clément Marillier was known for his more than 200 clever vignettes for Dorat's Fables (1775); Hubert François Gravelot used a more rigid but also more forceful style in illustrating works like Marmontel's moralizing tales (1765) and Voltaire's edition of Corneille (1764).

The glory of French book illustration ceased with the French

45. Vignette by Charles Eisen in Claude Joseph Dorat's *Les baisers* (The Hague, 1770).

Revolution. Illustration came to be seen as trivial, and not worth the effort of the citizens entrusted with reeducating the French public. Also, pictures indicated that people had the time to loll around reading when they should be working for the glory of the Revolution.

ENGLISH AND AMERICAN ILLUSTRATION

The expanding population of England (which almost doubled from the seventeenth through the eighteenth centuries), combined with a budding democracy, offered numerous opportunities for illustrators, such as popular broadsides and the rapidly developing child's book. Popular black and white illustration ruled, on cheap engravings and often worn and damaged woodcuts. The rough woodcuts and engravings were vital and crude. They were found in chapbooks and broadsides seen by many more people than the elaborately illustrated books across the English Channel.

In 1770 Thomas Bewick perfected the woodcut relief technique. Here the cross-section of a wood block, rather than the long grain, was used for the wood engraving. Individual artists again dominated in England with, as noted, William Blake as well as William Hogarth (1697–1764), whose work satirized the British social institutions. England had less costly illustrated books and ephemera than any other part of Europe. The growth of the popular novel meant important work for illustrators, and *Robinson Crusoe* (1719), *Gulliver's Travels* (1726) and the *Vicar of Wakefield* (1766) were provided plates.[22]

Outside the main-stream of books, John Boydell (1719–1804) became synonymous with oversized illustrations for Shakespeare plays. He commissioned paintings from the then leading artists and used the plates both as individual prints (for sale in his Boydell Shakespeare Gallery in London) and for the nine folio volumes, *The Dramatic Works of Shakespeare*, published in 1802. Today the individual plates and books are valued as much for the artists as for the fine engravings, which often are more striking than the original paintings.

Eighteenth-century America had some illustrated books, particularly those featuring portraits and maps. Still, the vast majority were copies of English and/or European work. The first American print was by John Foster in 1670, of Richard Mather, the Puritan theologian who translated the psalms for the *Bay Psalm Book*. Following a crude map and broadside, the first book illustration was in a 1684 almanac printed by Samuel Green in Cambridge. The woodcut of a man playing a harp more closely resembles a sinister criminal than King David. Finally, in 1717–19, four illustrated books were published in Boston, with an engraving possibly by Ben Franklin's brother. The rather inauspicious beginnings set the course for countless illustrated almanacs and crudely illustrated religious books. Alex Anderson was the most skilled of American engravers. He worked well into the next century, and his pupils set the stage for the artists and craftsmen who first appeared in the 1840s.

BOOKBINDINGS

The architectural magnificence of the seventeenth century was reflected in elegant bookbinding. Most books were in ordinary bindings. There are still many French calf and sheepskin bindings of that period, marbled to give a tortoise-shell appearance or simply stained black, with no decoration except on the spine. A still more Spartan effect was presented by the English bindings in brown sheepskin. Their plain appearance was further emphasized by the fact that the insides of the covers did not even have paper pasted over their gray cardboard.

The wealthy collectors were not satisfied with the plainer types of binding, and the art of fine bookbinding continued to be cultivated in France. At the beginning of the seventeenth century the fanfare style with its conventional laurel branches was still dominant, but in the later years of Louis XIII's reign a new style of decoration appeared. Stamps with dotted lines (fer pointillés) began to be used; the fine curved or spiral lines were broken up into a series of small dots and arranged to form a web or network over the entire cover or around the central panel containing the owner's coat-of-arms.

Lacework bindings soon became prominent in the French collector's rococo bookcase. As a rule, the decoration consisted of a wide laced edge with projections extending in toward the middle of the cover, where space was left for the owner's mark, or super ex libris. This type of decoration was used in many variations on a great number of bindings. The spine of the book was also decorated, often with a conventional flower in each of the panels and small ornaments in the corners of each panel. The designs were gilded but not often tooled, as on seventeenth century bindings. The lace pattern was treated with special grace and virtuosity on the bindings made by Jacques Antoine Derôme and his son Nicolas Denis Derôme; some of these had the special feature of a small bird with outspread wings set in the corners of the decoration.

EX LIBRIS

The ex libris book mark custom to indicate ownership appeared in the fifteenth and sixteenth centuries. The bookmarks of that time were printed from woodcuts, but in the seventeenth and eighteenth centuries the use of ex libris spread with the increasing fashion of book collecting, and they were printed from copper engravings.

The ex libris was a label of varying size pasted on the inner side of the cover, stating the owner of the book by initials, by full name, or by his coat-of-arms framed in a cartouche. Heraldic emblems were quite common, even when the ex libris was in the form of a small picture. These pictures might be symbolic, might represent the interior of the owner's own library, or might be small landscape vignettes. These bookplates were so named because they often contained the words ex libris (or ex museo or ex bibliotheca) before the name of the owner. At the beginning of the nineteenth century the ex libris art showed signs of decadence, but at the middle of the century it blossomed anew. Currently it has lost popularity among book collectors.

In the previous centuries ex libris was not only the sign of a collector, but a source of delight to those who took collecting to mean bookshelves and hundreds of volumes in a small personal library. Samuel Pepys (1633–1703) claims to have designed the first domestic bookshelves. The twelve bookcases are now the proud possession of Cambridge's Magdelen College.[23]

Shelving could be a danger. The English minister Richard Baxter (1615–1691) recalls: "As I sat in my study, the weight of my greatest folio books broke down three or four of the highest shelves, when I sat close under them, and they fell down on every side of me, and not one of them hit me save one upon the arm . . . it was a wonder they had not beaten out my brains, one of the shelves right over my head having the six volumes of Dr. Walton's Oriental Bible all of Austion's Works . . . etc."[24]

NOTES

[1]The Enlightenment (or Age of Reason) is a loaded word (phrase) which indicates more than it produced. Still its group of ideas fostered a new appreciation of humanism, and if Kant asked (in 1784, the year of Denis Diderot's death), "What is enlightenment?" today most historians accept the descriptor, if only in a general way.

[2]Many of the 230 extant complete First Folios will be found in the Folger Shakespeare Library in Washington, D.C. Despite the interest in the work it is only relatively rare.

[3]There are countless articles and books about Shakespeare, his compatriots and printers of the period. The best: Charles Hinman, *The printing and proof reading of the first folio of Shakespeare* (Oxford University Press, 1963). Hinman developed a reader for comparing side

by side the various editions. It is, suitably, known as the Hinman Collator.

[4]The basic history of encyclopedias will be found in Robert Collison's *Encyclopaedias: Their History Throughout The Ages,* 1964. For an updated, brief version, see the latest edition of the *Encyclopaedia Britannica;* or, for that matter, any encyclopedia.

[5]Much has been written about Denis Diderot. The "latest," and in many ways the best: P.N. Furbank, *Diderot: A Critical Biography* (London: Secker, 1992).

[6]For detailed studies of European and particularly French literacy from about 1580 to the nineteenth century, see Roger Chartier, ed., *The Culture of Print* (Princeton University Press, 1989). For a broader view, see Harvey J. Graff, *The Legacies of Literacy* (Indiana University Press, 1988). See, too: H.S. Bennett, *English Books and Readers* (Cambridge: Cambridge University Press, 3 vols., 1969–1970). The first volume, in a new edition in 1969, covers 1475–1557; the second, 1558–1603; and the third, 1603–1640. See also H.J. Graff, ed., *Literacy and Social Development in the West: A Reader* (Cambridge: Cambridge University Press, 1981). Other useful works on literacy: Jack Goody, ed., *Literacy in Traditional Societies* (Cambridge University Press, 1968). *Perspectives on Literacy* (a collection of essays) (Cardondale: Southern Illinois University Press, 1988).

[7]J.H. Plumb. *England in the Eighteenth Century* (London: Penguin Books, 1974), p. 30. "All" is somewhat misleading in that only a minority were literate and, at best, the most popular magazine of the time, *The Spectator,* had no more than 3,000 subscribers. *The Gentleman's Magazine*'s maximum circulation, some 30 years later, was no more than 15,000. At the same time the number of individual English magazines (some estimate well over 800) indicates the potential market.

[8]Talbot Reed. *A History of The Old English Letter Foundries* (London: Faber & Faber, 1942). This has a chapter on Caslon as well as Baskerville and traces the development of type to the beginning of the twentieth century.

[9]See F.E. Pardo, *John Baskerville* (London: Muller, 1975). All but forgotten in the nineteenth century, Bodoni was brought back to prominence in the twentieth century by the Italian publishing firm, Officina Bodoni, where his typefaces are much in use.

[10]As poet, artist, political figure and the greatest genius of the period, Blake is the object of an ongoing cottage industry of publications. For a good overview, limited to his books, see G.E. Bentley's *Blake's Books,* 1977. His major works are found in many museums, and particularly in The Tate in London.

[11]S.H. Steinberg points out that they gained famed for the "care

devoted to proof reading; every sheet was scrutinized six times, thrice in
the office and thrice by the two university professors whom the brothers
employed as editors." *Five Hundred Years of Printing* (New York:
Criterion Books), p. 146.

[12]The pocket-sized 18 volumes were illustrated, and Bell's words
about such works was applicable: "We have earnestly consulted correct-
ness, neatness, ornament, utility and cheapness of price." See Stanley
Morison, *John Bell, 1745–1831,* (London 1930).

[13]Bell, too, was responsible for a major change in the letter "s." Up to
c. 1749 the long s (an f without the crossbar) was used, but Bell changed
over to today's familiar "s." The reason, of course, is that the old long s
was easily confused with "f." Also the "s" helped to make a cleaner
page, particularly in newspapers which Bell published.

[14]Plantin represented interests of the southern Roman Catholics, while
the Elzevirs dominated Protestant interests in the north. Between them
they were the major Netherland, and for that matter European, publishers. The grandchildren carried on the firms, but by the end of the
seventeenth century the Elzevirs had more or less passed into history.
See D.W. Davies, *The World of the Elzeviers 1580–1712* (London,
1954).

[15]Because of, or despite his wild life, the Voltaire set remains a
masterpiece of editorial skill and is a major typographical accomplishment. Beaumarchais gave up publishing with this one adventure.

[16]There are several histories, official and otherwise, of the two English
university presses, e.g. *Cambridge University Press 1584–1984,* 1984;
and *A History of the Oxford University Press,* in progress.

[17]Esteban Martin apparently was at work in Mexico City from 1535 to
1540, and records show he was a printer who was given official resident
status in 1539. Other records indicate that he printed several items, but
none is extant for the period 1535–1539. In 1539 one Juan Pablos, an
Italian from Spain, published the first book in Mexico City.

[18]Daye press became the forerunner of Harvard University Press,
considered the oldest press in the United States and certainly the first
university press. See Helmut Lehmann-Haupt, *The Book in America.* 2nd
ed. (New York: R.R. Bowker, 1951). Related works: Lawrence Wroth,
The Colonial Printer, 2nd ed. 1938; Douglas McMurtrie, *A History of
Printing in the United States,* vol. 2 (never completed), 1936; William
Joyce, ed., *Printing and Society in Early America,* 1983; William
Charvat, *Literary Publishing in America, 1790–1850,* 1959; John
Oswald, *Printing in the Americas,* 1937; Rollo Silver, *The American
Printer 1787–1825,* 1967; John T. Winterich, *Early American Books &
Printing,* 1935.

[19]Bodley's name, of course, was given to the library at Oxford. An

agreement with the Stationers' Company in 1610 made the library an official depository and it received at least one free copy of all books printed in England. With the founding of the British Museum Library in the nineteenth century the depository was shifted to London, but by then the holdings were close to 800,000 volumes. (Today the collection is around 3 million.) Much has been written on the Bodleian; e.g. Ian G. Philip, *The Bodleian Library in the Seventeenth and Eighteenth Centuries*, 1983. See, too: J.C. Dana and Henry W. Kent, *Literature of Libraries in the Seventeenth and Eighteenth Centuries* (Metuchen, NJ: Scarecrow, 1967).

[20]Elizabeth L. Eisenstein. *The Printing Revolution* (Cambridge University Press, 1983). One of her best sections covers the impact of printing on science, and not simply illustration. The two, to be sure, cannot be separated. See the section, ''The book of nature transformed; printing and the rise of modern science.''

[21]J.B. Harley, ed. *The History of Cartography* (University of Chicago Press, 1988—in progress). A multivolume work which is the standard reference work of its kind. The first printed map was found in an edition of Isidore's *Etymologiarum*, 1472, and the first edition of *Ptolemy* with maps was issued in Bologna in 1477. Woodcuts rarely were used; instead the printer looked to copper engravers.

[22]Hans Hammelmann and T.S.R. Boase. *Book Illustration in Eighteenth-Century England* (New Haven, CT: Yale University Press, 1975). This has 1780 entries, under the names of the illustrators, as well as an excellent introduction.

[23]Along with the bookcases, the famous diarist bequeathed his books to Cambridge. These are frequently studied not so much for content as for an example of what a well-educated seventeenth-century Englishman would have collected. Some of it was pornography.

[24]*The Autobiography of Richard Baxter* (London: Dent [Everyman Library], 1931), p. 77. See, too, p. 198+ where Baxter gives an account of the Great London Fire of 1665 and how libraries and bookdealers' stocks were lost.

CHAPTER EIGHT

THE GREAT LEAP FORWARD: PRINTING AND PUBLISHING FROM 1800 TO 1920

Poets sang of a golden age returned,
and they hymned industrialism in
exquisite language
—John Seeley, 1869

The nineteenth-century Industrial Revolution spurred the greatest leap forward in publishing since the invention of printing. Technology and wider education explain most of the impressive forward movement. Power transportation made it possible to bring books to markets heretofore untouched. The rapid dissemination of print went hand in hand with equally impressive developments in science—developments which revolutionized the world.[1]

There was a literate, economically secure middle class clamoring for the latest book. Publishers expanded as rapidly as the number of readers. Education advanced to a point where literacy was the rule rather than the exception, at least among the urban middle classes, although not often among the poor. The standard of living, at least for the middle classes, rose. With the fall of Napoleon (1815), England realized a long period of peace, as did much of Europe. All of this explains, if only in part, the increase in book production and the renewed interest in reading.

From the humanism of Johann Goethe (1749–1832) to the English romantics, from Percy Shelley (1792–1822) and Lord Byron (1788–1824) to Sir Walter Scott (1771–1832), the century got off to a grand start in the development of the novel and poetry. Between Jane Austen (1775–1817) and Charles Dickens (1812–1870) and William Thackeray (1811–1863), the middle classes were presented with the social novel, which moved into the realistic works of Leo Tolstoy (1828–1910) and Gustave Flaubert (1821–80), as well as pre-World War realists from Henry James (1843–1916) to Henrik Ibsen (1828–1906). The roll call of authors explains the popularity of the novel which, in turn, helped to make possible mass publishing.[2]

The spread of industrialism to Europe from England not only brought about the middle classes but a liberal and nationalistic front which culminated in the revolts of 1848. Failure of the popular uprisings brought countless numbers of intellectuals to the United States to help in the expansion of education and, to a lesser degree, the industrial growth of the country. After the Civil War America grew in the East and in the West, and by 1900 had reached a place where it was able to challenge Britain for industrial leadership. Improvements in publishing followed and a new modernized system of distribution as well as the beginnings of advertising made the popular magazine a major consideration.

World War I dominated the first quarter of the twentieth century. Europe suffered tremendous losses in economic strength and manpower while the United States prospered. The location of economic power was no longer solely in Europe. The impetus for industrial and scientific advances shifted and new forms of self-expression found voice in equally new as well as larger publishing houses. The World War ended in 1918 with America on the edge of an explosion in literary talent and a Europe prepared to recognize the genius of such as W. B. Yeats (1965–1939) and James Joyce (1882–1941).

TECHNOLOGICAL ADVANCES

The major technological advances in printing included: (1) The Fourdrinier brothers established the first manufacturing of paper in England by 1803. Replacing the laborious hand-made process, the machines could turn out from ten to twenty times as much paper in a day. By the turn of the century all the paper needed was available for publishers, and at much less cost than before. One drawback to the mechanization of papermaking was the substitution of wood pulp for rags, c. 1840–1850. This proved disastrous when sulphur and other chemicals were introduced into the process to break down the wood. Today paper produced 50 to 100 years ago literally disintegrates. Much research has gone into both preserving the older works and replacing the chemical ridden paper with other processes.

(2) Essentially the same press used by Gutenberg, the nineteenth century press was automated first with the use of steam power, c. 1814. The real breakthrough came in 1847 when R. Hoe & Company in America introduced the rotary press. This allowed the publishing of newspapers, magazines and books at speeds heretofore impossible. At best a hand press could produce 300 to 350 sheets a day. A power rotary could print from 12,000 to 16,000 sections, not simply sheets, in the same period of time.

(3) Introduced in 1885, the linotype proved to be the other revolutionary advancement. The invention of Ottmar Mergenthaler (1854–1899), it allowed the automatic composition of type and replaced hand work for routine type setting of all kinds. Until the advent of the computer it was the standard composing method throughout the world. Like the various other composing machines developed later (monotype, intertype, etc.), the linotype casts the type ready for printing. The actual composing is done by striking keys similar to those of a typewriter.

Machine composition can be done much faster than hand composition, and the combination of the composing machine and the high-speed press revolutionized the printing trade. The final break between the publisher and the printer was made, and the two became separate businesses. Gradually, too, publishers of magazines separated from book publishers. The combined process by the end of the first World War was more the exception than the rule.

MASS MEDIA IS BORN

With the nineteenth century, technological advances made the mass media possible. Books could now be printed and distributed at relatively low cost. More important for the general public, the widely distributed magazine and newspaper became common.

Newspapers, as well as the numerous popular weekly papers, magazines, etc., benefited by the rapid rate at which they could be produced and distributed by railroad. By the end of the 1830s cheap newspapers were found everywhere. The development of magazines encouraged a wider reading public for books. In America, for example, one might deplore the overall literary quality of *Godey's Lady Book,* and later *The Century, Scribner's* and the like, but they did publish, if only from time to time, the work of leading writers from Herman Melville to Mark Twain and Henry James.

Similar periodicals were available in England. Both countries had much in common, including low prices. And by the turn of the century prices went even lower as publishers tried to deliver up to advertisers, increasingly important in both magazines and newspapers, a large audience.

PUBLISHERS

By the nineteenth century, publishers offered additional services, not given by early printers. A written manuscript might be altered and edited so that the finished book was as much the work of the publisher/editor as the author. Publishers now sought out authors and developed plans for the mass distribution and sale of their books. The role has remained much the same, although today the publisher may employ a variety of formats, and not simply the printed book. The nineteenth century English copyright law, which stipulated that a book was in the public domain seven years after the death of the author or 40 years after publication, boosted the profits and sales of numerous reprint houses and fostered the series concept of republishing classics.

Publishing as a profession was firmly accepted by the mid-nineteenth century. Many of the firms, in Europe and the United States, which were established then are now in operation, although often as parts of larger conglomerates.

The most famous and above all the best known popular English publisher of the first half of the century was Charles Knight (1791–1853). Determined to educate and inform the lower middle classes, Knight published a series of books and journals. *The Penny Magazine* achieved the then remarkable circulation of over 200,000 copies. The numerous wood engravings drew people into easy-to-read, easy-to-understand articles on a vast number of subjects. William Chambers (1800–1883) founded a similar firm. He, too, gained fame because of his effort to bring information and entertainment to the mass public. He achieved this in numerous ways, including the publication of *Chambers's Journal* and *Chambers's Encyclopaedia* as well as a group of equally respected reference works. Unlike Knight's *Penny Magazine,* the *Journal* had no illustrations, but it did feature fiction and numerous pages of how-to-do-it material. As a landmark in the development of the mass media, the *Journal* served as a model for countless penny and halfpenny publications sold from one end of the British Isles to the other.

George Routledge (1812–1888) was another of the giants of the popular press, particularly famous for his firm's Railway Library, which he began in 1848. The inexpensive reprints of classics and current authors could be purchased at every train stop as well as in bookstores. He followed this with the Universal Library. Thus was born the notion of the book which could be bought and read and disposed of, much as a newspaper or a magazine.

GROWTH OF THE READING PUBLIC

The American Revolution, the French Revolution, political changes of a less violent type in England—all conspired to favor free and often compulsory education. By the mid-nineteenth century public schools of various quality were common in most of Europe and the United States. Literacy became the goal of government and business. Paralleling these social developments, publishers brought out cheaper and widely distributed books, available from Newcastle railway bookstalls to San Francisco libraries.

The drive to educate, motivated by dozens of reasons, from producing better workers to insuring upright citizens, was carried on through the twentieth century. If only the middle classes are considered, the majority could read and write, at least in England, the United States and much of Europe.[3] Fewer read books, although many did turn to newspapers and popular magazines. As the gross number of readers dramatically improved publishers discovered a new, promising market. In England, for example, the number of titles published in the 1850s was between 2,500 and 3,000. By the end of the first World War, the number was closer to 13,000 annually.

While reading of magazines and newspapers by some 80 per cent of the American public is accepted today, it was not until just before or after the first World War that the majority of people joined the ranks of readers.[4] Even now one may argue that illiteracy, which is estimated at a low of three per cent to a high of close to 50 per cent, depending how illiteracy is defined, may make the 80 per cent an optimistic figure.

Reading aloud in the home continued through most of the nineteenth century, but with the increase in literacy, and the availability of more reading matter, this type of leisure activity declined. And with the shattering of the rigid class systems, both in England and Europe, the habit of the master reading pious works to the servants decreased. On the American frontier, where both literacy and books were scarce, reading to one another was common.

Although a difficult topic to analyze, particularly when dealing with more than one national situation, the type of books read did follow general patterns. A reader's social background, education, economic status, etc., continued to influence what was read. There was general acceptance of the popular novel—much to the annoyance of many educators. This was universal. If James Fenimore Cooper was popular in America, so were Scott and Victor Hugo. According to one amazed French critic, even "prostitutes spent hours reading love novels."[5] Contemporary novels and light works of nonfiction made a steady inroad into the territory heretofore occupied primarily by the classics.

The serialization of novels was a natural result of the mass production of newspapers and magazines. The paperbacks were distributed and accepted as a type of magazine. *Pickwick Papers* (1836–37) not only introduced Dickens to the world but was among the first books to be issued in parts. The serial form of publication appealed greatly to publishers and to readers, who could share the cost of a novel over a long period of time. The equivalent of what are now inexpensive paperbacks, these books issued chapter by chapter took on a life of their own with the "penny dreadfuls," which caught the fancy of the reading public for the next half-century and beyond. Although there were versions of today's familiar paperback, a German firm in 1841 originated the actual form, in the Tauchnitz series. These were inexpensive reprints of British authors purchased by English-speaking travelers in Europe.

Possibly the single advantage of the first World War (1914–1918) was that it encouraged reading. Both at the front and at home, whether in England, France, Germany or the United States, the severe cutback on entertainment possibilities, coupled with massive amounts of idle time, filled the publishers' pocketbooks. A similar situation occurred with the second World War and, for that matter, is often a side effect of economic depression, individual or national, when it is less expensive to buy (or borrow from the library) a book than to seek other forms of distraction.

ILLUSTRATION

The technological and cultural breakthroughs in illustration began with a new use of an old process. On April 7, 1804, *The Times* of London printed a wood engraving of a murdered man's house. This was one of the earliest newspaper illustrations, and indicative of the type of material which would fascinate readers to this day. By the end of the century, popular reading matter was identified by masses of similar illustrations. In keeping with the sensational pictures in broadsides and chapbooks of earlier centuries, illustrations differed now only because they could be mass produced.

Fairly well replaced by the copper engraving, the wood engraving was out of favor until Thomas Bewick (1753–1828) revived wood engravings for book illustration near the close of the eighteenth century.[6] Bewick and his many pupils and followers developed new woodcut techniques. In the old woodcuts the black lines had been the most outstanding feature; Bewick made the white line the dominant element in the picture, accentuated by a background in which the varying density of the lines created the effect of light and shadow. The effectiveness of these shaded woodcuts was also due to the fact that they were cut in very hard boxwood, and the carving was not done with a knife as formerly, but with a burin like that used by engravers.

Bewick was an excellent draughtsman, especially skilled in

animal subjects. His major works were two large books on mammals and birds, with copious illustrations distinguished not only by an accurate representation of each animal's outward appearance, but also by a definite feeling for its individuality. Bewick's art reached its highest point in the numerous small vignettes with which he decorated his books, and in which, often with true Dickensian humor, he depicted life in the country as lived by men as well as animals. The woodcut art of the Bewick school was not only influential in England but was brought to the Continent and also to America by English xylographers (Fig. 46).

The majority of book illustrations, depending as they did upon crude woodcuts and more often copper engravings, were poor to terrible. Remedy came from several firms, including the Dalziels (George, 1815–1902; Edward, 1817–1905), who saw that the problem was the sloppy work done by the engraver from often good illustrations. One might take a fine painting, say by Reynolds, and by using a badly trained engraver to "place" the painting on a woodcut or an engraving plate, simply destroy the impact of the painting. The Dalziels encouraged accurate engraving. The result was a vast improvement in both book and periodical art by the 1850s. The later illustrated papers, from the

46. Vignette by Thomas Bewick in his *History of the British Birds, 1797–1804.*

Illustrated Times and the *Graphic* in England to *Harper's Illustrated Weekly* in the United States, generally offered good to even superior illustrations.

Steel engraving (invented in Philadelphia by Jacob Perkins in 1806) competed by the mid-1830s with wood and copper. Engraved entirely in line, the plates showed little wear after much use. Also, the artists could use finer lines—almost to the point where some are difficult to tell apart from photographs. Steel engravings reached their height in the vignettes which were used in annuals and poetry volumes. (Vignettes were preferable because steel is hard to work, and primarily suitable for small illustrations.) Particularly noteworthy were the Turner engravings employed in Samuel Rogers' *Italy* (1830) and *Poems* (1834). (Fig. 47) Turner also used steel for the mezzotints in the 1824–30 series, *Rivers of England,* and for the line engravings in *Rivers of France* (1833–5).

Steel engravings have a sleek and unnatural quality about them that tends to destroy their artistic effect. They were used quite extensively in England but the results attained were seldom of any great significance. When a process was developed later for coating copper engravings with an electrolytic deposit of steel to give them a hard surface, the day of steel engravings was practically over.

Another forward leap in illustration was made possible with the invention of lithography by Aloysius Senefelder (1771–1834). This served as an inexpensive way to reproduce illustrations. Drawing on stone allowed countless impressions, particularly of music and posters. Rudolf Ackermann opened a famous press in 1817 which developed a process for color lithographs used extensively in book illustration. Prang, a Boston firm, gained fame with the same art in America by the middle of the nineteenth century. Polychromatic illustrations, which ranged from the ghastly to the superior, were the invention of George Baxter (1804–1867). From his 21st to his 30th birthday Baxter struggled with the process, which he finally developed in 1832. The process, although involved, served to make colored prints popular, and did much to insure the ultimate use of color in book illustrations, along with the earlier chromo-lithography process.

Photography, which by the end of the century dominated book illustration, was first introduced by William Henry Fox Talbot

COMO.

I LOVE to sail along the LARIAN Lake
Under the shore—though not to visit PLINY,
To catch him musing in his plane-tree walk,
Or angling from his window : * and, in truth,
Could I recall the ages past, and play
The fool with Time, I should perhaps reserve
My leisure for CATULLUS on *his* Lake,

* Epist. I. 3. ix. 7.

47. A steel engraving by Turner for Samuel Rogers' *Italy,* 1830.

(1800–1877), who published his own photographs in *The Pencil of Nature* (1844). By the turn of the century the photographic line block and the half-tone had almost entirely replaced hand-engraved wood blocks. A refined approach allowed superior detail for art books. This was called photogravure.[7]

ILLUSTRATORS

The nineteenth-century book, magazine and newspaper work reflected some of the period's worse and, yes, best art work. Victorian illustration styles varied from country to country, decade to decade, artist to artist. There were numerous superior English illustrators, many of whom were professional artists. A leading example would be George Cruikshank (1792–1878). The best known of his works include the illustrations for *Oliver Twist* which appeared in *Bentley's Magazine* (Fig. 48). The 24 plates were as famous as the novel, and Cruikshank became a much sought after illustrator, from further work on Dickens (*Sketches of Boz*) to Scott's Waverly novels.[8]

Another landmark illustrated book was Lewis Carroll's *Alice in Wonderland*, 1865. The illustrator, John Tenniel (1820–1914), caught the exact spirit of the book, although Carroll found the illustrations less than satisfactory. Tenniel by then was a well-known artist and continued to be popular in England until his death.

The final years of the nineteenth century saw an almost total focus on realism and explicit representation of figure and land-scape. This gradually changed with the rise of the impressionists, among others, in France, but realism dominated book illustration well into the twentieth century, and remains still a strong force.[9]

French woodcut art reached a high level in the work of artists like the great satirist Honoré Daumier (1808–1879), and later in the century, Gustave Doré (1833–1883), whose enormous produc-tion extended from Rabelais to the Bible, from Dante to Edgar Allan Poe. Doré equally was outstanding in depicting mob scenes and individual human features. With Doré the nineteenth-century flowering of woodcut art in France came to an end.

Prominent French artists took an interest in illustration; e.g. Delacroix's *Faust* (1828) and Manet's illustrated *The Raven*

48. An etching by George Cruikshank for Dickens' *Oliver Twist*, 1838.

(1875), followed by Lautrec's illustration for Clemenceau's *Au pied du Sinai* (1898). Series of books illustrated by famous artists have become a French tradition. Ambroise Vollard (1867–1939) was the father of the publishing adventure, and he began a group (today often referred to simply as ''Vollards'') with the work of Pierre Bonnard (1867–1947) in 1900. This was the first of twenty-seven titles underwritten by Vollard. Today most are found in museums and include the illustrations of such as Marc Chagall (1887–1985), Georges Roualt (1871–1958) and Pablo Picasso (1881–1973).

AMERICAN ILLUSTRATION

One of the most famous, and certainly the most widely circulated illustrated American book was the family Bible published by Harper Brothers in 1842. It had both wood engravings by Joseph Adams (1803–1870) and electrotypes which were made from the engravings and could withstand many press runs. While Nathaniel Currier (1813–1888), later joined by James Ives (1824–1895), began his series of famous prints in 1835, he was not primarily a book illustrator. The majority of the some 7,000 different subjects (and an estimated 10 to 12 million copies sold) did prepare Americans for illustration of a journalistic type with a stress on the sensational and the sentimental.

The wider use of newspaper and magazine illustrations began in 1855 with *Frank Leslie's Illustrated Newspaper,* America's first news magazine.[10] Two years later the by-now-more-famous *Harper's Weekly* was established. By the close of the Civil War, which both publications had covered carefully, circulation for each often was above 100,000. During the War such artists as Alfred Waud made over 750 drawings of war-related subjects. The most famous artist, though, was Winslow Homer (1836–1910), who painted and sketched numerous war scenes at Harper's in 1862 and beyond. He went on to become America's most famous painter of New England and Maine coastal scenes of the nineteenth century (Fig. 49).

One of America's most popular illustrators, Howard Pyle (1852–1911) first gained recognition for his work in children's

49. Winslow Homer's "Thanksgiving in Camp," *Harper's Weekly*, November 29, 1862, p. 724.

books in 1888. His colorful action paintings arrived in parallel with color photography used to reproduce art work for books.[11]

PRIVATE PRESS

The appearance of the printed page deteriorated during the nineteenth and early twentieth century, primarily because of mass production and the effort to publish a book at as little real cost as possible. Esthetics in publishing never had been high, although here and there in every country and in every period there was a publisher who set standards, often assisted by a private fortune (Horace Walpole, John Baskerville) or by a patron such as the Duke of Parma, who underwrote the work of Bodoni.

Working for quality rather than simply quantity was an exception, but throughout the nineteenth century there were examples of dedication to craftsmanship. Two printers, Charles Whittingham (1795–1876) and William Pickering (1796–1854), met in 1829, and by 1840 had established the Chiswick Press as one of the finest commercial publishers in England.[12] Unlike many other firms, the emphasis was on both quality printing and quality of content. Imaginative decorations were tastefully added to the text, and the borders and initials gave the press an instantaneous recognition. In the 1840s the press broke ground with a series of small books with wood engravings for children. Both format and style were copied by publishers. By the mid-nineteenth century, the two partners had died or retired and the press declined.

The "ideal" Victorian publisher may be John Cassell (1817–1865), who championed temperance although his father operated a pub, and came to publishing through printing temperance pamphlets. He did much to spread popular education with his books and magazines. His name was carried into the twentieth century by the firm that issued many distinguished books.

Using photoengraved line blocks, Aubrey Beardsley (1872–98) was brought to the attention of the world by the Chiswick Press when it published his black-and-white illustrated Pope's *Rape of the Lock* in 1896[13] (Fig.50). The most fascinating of all the illustrators and artists, Beardsley died at age 26 after a stormy career. Today he is considered a major figure, and closely linked to Oscar Wilde whose *Salome* he illustrated in 1894, bringing down the howl of the censors—as did most of his work. The Japanese-like prints still discourage some critics; e.g. the otherwise less than excitable historian of book illustration, David Bland, remarks about Salome: "Yet when due allowance has been made for their technical skill these pictures are as repellant as most of Beardsley's work."

In the 1880s and 1890s a reaction set in against poor illustrations and typography. A small group of English artists of the Pre-Raphaelite brotherhood was led by the painters Edward Burne-Jones (1833–1898) and D. G. Rossetti (1828–1882). One of the most active members was William Morris (1834–1896), who was a painter, architect, poet and socialistic agitator. His versatility and unflagging energy made him the spiritual and practical leader of the Pre-Raphaelites' counterattack against technology. It was their aim to revive original methods and to recreate the purity of style that characterized the best craftsmanship of earlier periods. Another manifestation of Romanticism,

50. Title page by Audrey Beardsley for his unfinished novel, *Under the Hill*, 1896.

the preference was for art of the Middle Ages and the Renaissance. Morris and his co-workers made furniture, wall coverings, woven material, glass paintings and other things for the home, using the methods of the old hand-craftsmen.

Morris pioneered what came to be known as the private press movement. He founded his famous Kelmscott Press in 1890, and employing a hand press his employees printed fifty-three books in small editions of no more than 500 copies from 1890 to 1898.

Motivation and explanation of intent were explained by Morris in a lecture at the Arts and Crafts Exhibition in London in the closing months of 1888. He called for overall attention to the book from good printing (including, it later happened, type drawn by Morris himself), to considered design of the pages, illustrations, designs, binding, and everything else which constituted an ideally printed book. In his printing as in his other work he went back to the models of the past; the types that he designed and had cut in collaboration with Emery Walker included a roman (Golden type) in the style of Nicolas Jenson, and two black-letter gothic types (Chaucer and Troy) based on those of the earliest printers. The ornamentation with which he so lavishly decorated his pages was derived from the same sources. The woodcut initials and borders of vine branches that he designed for his roman-type books were clearly inspired by Venetian woodcut art of the Ratdolt and Aldus period. One of Morris's chief works was a large Chaucer edition with illustrations by Edward Burne-Jones (Fig. 51). Another illustrator who worked with Morris was Walter Crane, who also took Italian Renaissance woodcuts as his models. Morris's books produced a powerful effect with their heavy type and profuse ornamentation. In spite of the close relationship of his work to that of earlier periods, it was not purely imitative.

The major problem with all of this, at least by today's standards, is that the books are difficult to read. And despite his efforts at universality, the titles are locked into Victorian notions of beauty. Morris's emphasis on pseudo-gothic type, black ink, heavy hand-made paper and crowded illustrations reflected more the romantic period than a breakaway from the mass production of books.[14] Granted, even today not everyone accepts this notion; and Kelmscott books are collected and praised as much for their "beauty" as for their place in the history of printing.

The influence of Morris was felt throughout the Western world, and shortly after the Kelmscott Press closed one could find evidence of improved book production commercially. Everyman's Library, the inexpensive reprints of classics, is a case in point. Launched in 1906, and still being issued, the books are identifiable immediately by the Kelmscott-like title page, which has been modified but remains a reminder of Morris.

The movement inaugurated by Morris soon spread to the Continent. Its influence can be traced in Belgium and France and especially in Germany, where it was introduced by the Belgian architect Henry van de Velde. He was one of the most enthusiastic exponents of the Jugend style, so-called from the periodical *Jugend*. The effect was produced by line designs in geometric patterns combined with animal figures and flowers. At the close of the nineteenth century the Jugend style had considerable influence in Germany.

Two associates of The Kelmscott Press, Thomas Cobden-

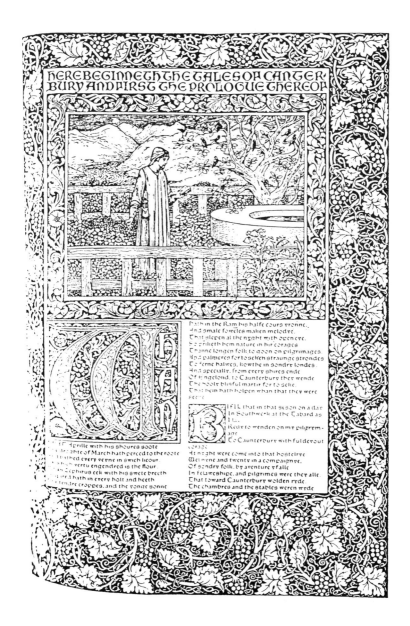

51. Page from William Morris' edition of Chaucer (1893) illustration by Burne-Jones.

Sanderson (1840–1922) and Emery Walker (1851–1933), designed their type for the Doves Press and between 1903 and 1905 printed the five volume *Doves Bible*—considered by many to be the finest product of any private press at any time. Free of all ornament except for a colored initial discreetly placed, the Bible, and subsequent works, differed wildly from Morris and others in that it relied entirely upon simplicity and freedom from ornament. After fifty more works the founders closed the press by sending the type to the bottom of the Thames in 1916.

Among other famous private presses of the period, the Ashendene Press, founded by C. H. St. John Hornby (1863–1946), existed for close to half a century and its books are identifiable by the beauty of the type and the red or blue initials. The Golden Cockerel Press, founded in 1920, was taken over by Robert Gibbings in 1924 and gained fame for publishing the illustrations of Gibbons as well as many other famous artists, from Eric Gill and John Nash to David Jones.

Theodore L. De Vinne (1829–1914) proved to be the commercial William Morris of America. He led the movement back to simplicity and pride of design, particularly in his association with *The Century* magazine, and books from his own press. Today he is best remembered for his thoughtful writing about typography, illustration and design and as a founder of the Grolier Club (1884), the New York bastion of collectors and those interested in high standards of printing and publishing.

The outstanding American typographer, Daniel Berkeley Updike (1860–1941), was active at one of these private presses, The Riverside Press, in the 1880s, and in 1893 he set up his own press, The Merrymount Press. He was well versed in the history of the craft, and his book *Printing Types* (1922), is an authoritative work on the history of this subject.[15] Updike was a printer, but two of the other great men in modern American typography, Bruce Rogers (1870–1957) and Frederic W. Goudy (1865–1947), were primarily type designers. Rogers, like William Morris, started with Jenson's roman type and from it designed a new series of types.

Stanley Morison (1889–1967) became the century's most important arbiter of taste in typography and book design. The Englishman was hired by the Monotype Corporation in 1922, and with them helped to develop type faces as well as bring back more classic designs. As consultant to the Monotype Corporation, Morison brought out Garamond, Baskerville and Caslon type in forms suitable for machine composition; for the London *Times* he also created the first really good newspaper type, the very readable "Times Roman," which has also been adapted for use in book printing. Among the best-printed English books of the present day are those issued by the two university presses, Oxford and Cambridge, which date back to the sixteenth century; the clear, quiet effect of their books is typically English.

The Nonesuch Press, founded in 1923 by Francis Meynell (1891–1975), broke ground after World War I by offering relatively inexpensive books to the public which were designed with the care and love of those issued from private presses. All of the work was done by machinery and sold through bookstores. Actually Meynell designed the books, but did not print them. Instead he chose a private publisher for the work. Today their best known publications include the seven-volume Shakespeare and a five volume Bible. They are collectors' items.

PUBLISHING IN AMERICA[16]

From the 1890s through the first World War, compulsory primary education, an increase in high school attendance and the spread of public libraries contributed to a literate American public. Between 1825 and 1860 elementary schools and libraries tripled. At the same time commentators noted with alarm the watering down of the literary culture as evidenced by the quality of material in popular books, magazines and newspapers. They had less to say about the lack of copyright laws which allowed American publishers until near the turn of the century to pirate the work of English writers such as Charles Dickens. American authors made the point that copyright laws did them a disservice too. Publishers would pay, say, James Fenimore Cooper (1759–1851) no more than a minimum as long as they could get the work of English authors free.

The value of books manufactured between 1820 and 1860 went from $2.5 million to over $13 million. The number of individual titles grew from about 2,500 in 1870 to close to 12,000 by 1925. Incidentally, that number, give or take one or two thousand, remained much the same until well after World War II. Today it is closer to 45,000 to 55,000.

Publishing houses began to assume importance in America, and among the earliest (and still in existence) was Harper & Brothers.[17] Founded in 1817, the publisher became equally famous for books as for magazines, i.e. *Harper's Magazine* and *Harper's Illustrated Weekly.* Appleton-Century-Crofts (1825), which later became the Century Company (1870), produced the *Century* magazine and numerous popular books. Many publishers took advantage of the need for inexpensive, quality books. Thomas Nelson (1780–1861) founded the British publishing firm which opened American offices late in the nineteenth century. Nelson issued works of reference from Bibles to atlases, as well as standard sets such as the New Century Library (1900).

The center of the book trade was New York, and to a lesser extent Boston and Philadelphia. This remained the case until after World War II and the gradual increased importance of the West Coast; but even today the primary publishing centers are in the East.

A printer/publisher, Isaiah Thomas (1749–1831), gained lasting fame in America by writing and printing *The History of Printing in America* in 1810. It remains a valued source of information on early printing, particularly as Thomas was an active participant in publishing from 1750 to his retirement in 1802.

LIBRARIES

Organizational skills marked the development of the library in the nineteenth century. What for the most part had been haphazard growth and acquisitions took a turn towards planning and, often as not, a national program for public and academic institutions. The primary leader in this movement was Anthony Panizzi (1797–1879), an Italian political refugee who became principal librarian in the British Museum in 1856. He understood the necessity for order and, for example, a detailed catalog, a reading room, rules for acquisitions and administration. His ideas then and now dominate the scholarly national and academic scene.

Panizzi made the British people see the Museum as a monument to their good taste and intellectual capacities, and, most important, deserving of their financial support. A similar professional impetus was given to the Bibliothèque Nationale by Léopold Delisle (1826–1910). Other national libraries followed, from the Library of Congress to the Leningrad library. Today all western countries and many others have their own large national library.[18]

The English loved bibliography, and one of the earliest eighteenth-century advocates was Joseph Ames (1689–1759), who in 1739–40 printed a preliminary bibliography of English printers from Caxton to 1700. The ship's chandler, ten years before he died, issued a bibliography which became the basis for the *Short Title Catalogue* of 1926. A less commendable hobby was the collection of individual title pages, a notion followed by many, e.g. John Bagford (1650–1716) took apart thousands of books to paste down title pages and illustrations, a common enough thing among book collectors of the seventeenth century and even into the twentieth.[19]

Jacques Charles Brunet's (1780–1867) great bibliographical work, *Manuel du libraire* appeared first in 1810 and later in several enlarged editions. It gave a detailed description of the literature that was worth collecting. He gave special attention to Latin and French books and included the particularly valuable and rare titles from incunabula to the eighteenth century. Historical information was provided for each entry; also a list of the prices that had been paid for it at auction. The influence of Brunet's handbook was very great; collectors paid more attention to early books and became interested in the history of the various books as they had passed from one owner to another. They also developed an appreciation for first editions of classical literary works, including those of the great English and German authors.

PUBLIC LIBRARIES

The notion of a library open to all and supported by taxes was not a new one, although by the nineteenth century it became an accepted idea. In England and the United States the development began around the middle of the nineteenth century when laws were adopted giving governmental units the right to assess a special tax for the establishment of public libraries. In England the beginning was made at Manchester, and the free public library of this great manufacturing town is still one of the largest and most active in England. Peterborough, New Hampshire was the first to found a public library in 1833. Many followed, including libraries in Boston, New York and much of the Northeast.

The single "mover" in financing library buildings from one end of the United States to the other was Andrew Carnegie. The steel industrialist constructed close to 1,700 libraries from 1900 to 1917. His insistence that the local community first guarantee tax support of the library encouraged public libraries. Today there are close to 10,000 in the United States, although probably no more than 150 to 200 are large enough to support research size collections. An example is the New York Public Library, which came into being in 1848 when John Jacob Astor presented the city with a book collection to form the nation's first large public library.

COLLECTORS

Many of the national and academic libraries profited, particularly in the early twentieth century, from gifts of whole collections by wealthy collectors. England could boast an imposing array of collectors in the nineteenth century. Sir Thomas Phillipps (1792–1872), in the course of his travels on the continent, collected about 60,000 manuscripts and became the greatest private manuscript collector the world has ever known. His famous collection was broken up later at prolonged auction sales. One of the buyers was German-born Bernard Quaritch, who in the latter decades of the nineteenth century became the "Napoleon of the antiquarian book trade," and controlled the European book market in this field for many years. Many other large and valuable collections were scattered by auction. However, Lord Spencer's (1758–1834) collection, which had reached 40,000 volumes, was purchased in 1892 by the widow of the wealthy Manchester manufacturer, John Rylands. She had already made her husband's library public, and by the purchase of Spencer's books and later the manuscripts and fine bindings of the Earl of Crawford, the John Rylands Library was expanded to become one of England's wealthiest book museums.

Lord Spencer's librarian was a village curate by the name of Thomas Frognall Dibdin (1776–1847). Dibdin left handsomely printed accounts of Althorp Castle, where Spencer's books were housed, and also of his own travels in Spencer's service. These, like his book on bibliomania, are a hodge-podge of more or less reliable bibliographical and historical information, written in a rather affected style and interlarded with ''learned'' footnotes. Dibdin was probably guilty of vanity and snobbishness, but he must be given credit for an almost religious devotion to old and rare books. He was instrumental in forming the Roxburghe Club in 1812, the first of many English book clubs.[20]

One of the greatest American collectors was John Pierpont Morgan (1837–1913), who, with some justification, has been compared to the Medici in Florence. At his death in 1913 his New York City private library was valued at around ten million dollars. Today the sum would be in the billions. Still greater in size and value is the collection that the railroad magnate Henry E. Huntington (1850–1927) brought together in a palatial library building on his estate in San Marino, near Los Angeles, and which is now owned by the State of California. Huntington did not begin collecting until he was along in years, but he had a good knowledge of books and often bought entire private libraries in order to pick out the best items; his fantastic purchases contributed in a considerable degree to raising the prices of rare books. The Huntington Library is among the world's finest research libraries, particularly in literature and history.

The American bibliophile Richard Hoe (1812–1886), who owned the world's leading factory for the manufacture of rotary presses, established a library in the true collector's tradition; he was also a founder of the famous association of bibliophiles, the Grolier Club, in New York. Henry Clay Folger's (1857–1930) unique library of Shakespeare editions and material from the Shakespearean period is housed in a monumental building in Washington, D.C., alongside the Library of Congress. Many collectors in the United States naturally gave preference to early American printed books, as well as to books about the colonization of America, the Indians, and the later history of the country.

Among the older collectors of Americana were James Lenox, whose collection is now in the New York Public Library, and John Carter Brown, who presented his books to Brown University in Rhode Island. The Newberry Library in Chicago contains a large portion of the books collected by Edward E. Ayer; besides ornithology his field was literature on the Indians and about Mexico and Central America.[21]

BINDING

The Romantic movement, with its interest in the Middle Ages, characterized the intellectual life of this period and provided the background for the historical interests of bibliophiles. In the Napoleonic period neo-classicism was still predominant and it found expression in a predilection for decorative features of the art of the Roman Empire. This is shown in the bindings that were produced. With the fall of Napoleon the Empire style declined and the gothic of the Middle Ages became the style to imitate. Architects built ''gothic'' castles and villas, craftsmen made gothic furniture, and bookbinders used gothic motifs for their decoration, sometimes to such a degree that the entire cover of the book was filled with adaptations of pointed arches and other elements from the church architecture of the Middle Ages. This style has quite properly been called ''à la cathédrale.''

The Empire style continued to be used alongside the cathedral style, and the growing appreciation of earlier bindings led to imitations of the Grolier, fanfare, Gascon and other styles, often executed with considerable artistry. For a time this historical interest involved a high regard for the rococo style; a ''neo-rococo'' appeared in the 1840s on many books in France as well as elsewhere. Large rococo ornaments were displayed on the covers of books and on the smooth, loose spines that had gradually become common because they were easier to decorate than the rigid spines, and because they made the books easier to open.

Bookbinding of the nineteenth century was largely character-ized by imitation and by a mixture of styles, and only in exceptional instances was there a personal contribution by the binder. This concern for the styles of earlier periods led bookbinders back to mosaic and plastic work in leather; these methods came into fashion increasingly after the 1870s and were used to produce picturesque effects on book covers. A special variation within this style was the so-called "narrative binding" which made its appearance in France toward 1880; the intention—often rather forced in its execution—was to have the picture on the cover tell something about the contents of the book. This style was imitated in other countries but quite often the results were poor. England's most outstanding bookbinders in the second half of the nineteenth century were Joseph Zaehnsdorf and his son Joseph William.

In step with the mass production of books, popular bindings changed radically. Until the 1820s, the average individual bought the book in sections and then had these bound. Some publishers as early as Aldus offered inexpensive bindings, but this was unusual. Only books for the relatively poor were bound. The breakthrough came with the "Diamond Classics" published by William Pickering (soon to be of Chiswick Press fame) in 1821. Set in diamond size type, about the same as used in today's classified advertising, the classics were bound in the publisher's own cloth. This became common throughout the century, and by the 1890s machine binding had taken over completely from the hand-binders. As a result, bookbinding by hand today is limited to a few experts who may be working for rare book libraries, dealers or collectors.

NOTES

[1]The scientific impact of print in the nineteenth and early twentieth centuries may be illustrated quickly with a simple glance at only a few of the nonliterary titles published during those years: Michael Faraday, *Experimental Researchers in Electricity,* 1831–1838; Florence Nightingale, *Notes on Matters Affecting the Health . . . 1858;* John Stuart Mill, *On Liberty,* 1859; Charles Darwin, *On the Tendency of Species to Form Varieties,* 1859; Karl Marx, *Das Kapital,* 1867; Sigmund Freud, *Die Traumdeutung,* 1900; Wilbur and Orville Wright, *The Experiments of the Brothers Wright,* 1941; Albert Einstein, *Die Grundlage der Allgemeinen Relativitatstheorie,* 1916; Le Corbusier, *Vers un Architecture,* 1923.

[2]Scholarship and the science of the nineteenth and early twentieth centuries were far from determined by English speaking publishers and

readers. And while Britain and the United States are stressed here, it is well to remember "cultural primacy was shared by Germany and France . . . and [they] set their seal on advanced teaching elsewhere in Europe and in North America." John Carter and Percy Muir. *Printing and the Mind of Man* (London: Cassell, 1967), p. xxxii. See, too, Richard Brown, *Knowledge in Power* (New York: Oxford University Press, 1989), subtitled: "The diffusion of information in early America 1700–1865."

[3]Women played a major role in the spread of literacy. "Female literacy improved rapidly in the nineteenth century, and many mothers taught their children to read. Women were avid readers of serialized fiction." *A History of Private Life* (Harvard University Press, 1990), vol. 4, p. 194. Again, though, the women were primarily from the middle classes. The frequent omission of women in the history of nineteenth-century books is an oversight of some proportions. Women actively were engaged, often in relatives' print shops and in the trade, particularly in America of frontier days. There are, fortunately, articles covering women in printing. A favorite English personality, with a marvelous and suitable name, is Emily Faithful (1835–1895), who opened a feminist printshop in England.

[4]One estimate is that a literacy growth rate in America indicates "39 per cent of Americans were literate in 1840, but almost 50 per cent could read by 1860." *Book Research Quarterly,* Winter, 1985–86, p. 18. See: Richard Altick, *The English Common Reader: A Social History of the Mass Reading Public 1800–1900* (Chicago, University of Chicago Press, 1957). There are many related titles. Peter Burke, *Popular Culture in Early Modern Europe* (New York University Press, 1978); David Vincent, *Literacy and Popular Culture: England 1750–1914* (New York: Cambridge University Press, 1989).

[5]*A History of Private Life, op. cit.,* p. 536.

[6]John Jackson. *A Treatise on Wood Engraving* (London: Charles Knight, 1839). With over 300 illustrations "engraved on wood by John Jackson," this offers 700+ pages of background and history on the art. A trifle erratic, and not totally reliable, it serves, nevertheless, as a foundation for countless other books on the subject.

[7]Another avenue of illustration, often overlooked in printing history, is the simple postcard. On October 1, 1869 "postcards were introduced by the Austrian Government. . . . The early postcards gave work to the jobbing printers, for they were much used for advertising purposes." Photochromy, developed in 1887, allowed the wider use of illustrated postcards. See W. Turner Berry, *Annals of Printing* (University of Toronto Press, 1966), v.p. Postcards may be termed "ephemera," which in the history of printing refers to almost any printed matter other than books and serials, e.g. advertisements, train tickets, film posters, etc. For

a history of ephemera, including notes on postcards, see John Lews, *Collecting Ephemera* (London, 1976).

[8]The bicentenary of Cruikshank's birth resulted in numerous articles and books. Certainly the most exhaustive, and still in process, is Robert L. Patten's *George Cruikshank's Life, Times and Art* (Cambridge: Butterworth, 1992). Vol. 1 (1792–1835). The first volume offers an excellent account of the artist's beginnings as an illustrator.

[9]Gordon Ray. *The Illustrator and the Book in England from 1790 to 1914* (New York: Pierpont Morgan Library, 1976). In 330 pages, and with even more illustrations, this catalog of a show at the Morgan Library is one of the best single overviews of the subject. Extensive notes for each artist and examples of books illustrated. Ray only hints at the relationship between Victorian novels and their illustrations—a subject of several studies. At one extreme there is a notion that illustration reflects the true meaning of the novel, and at the other is the more prevalent idea that the illustration is just that, and no more. For a sometimes difficult argument for the first point of view, see J. Hillis Miller, *Illustration* (Harvard University Press, 1992).

[10]Budd Gambee. *Frank Leslie . . .* (Ann Arbor: University of Michigan, 1964). This is a basic study which throws much light, too, on the illustrated press of the day and particularly from 1855 to 1860.

[11]In the latter half of the nineteenth century, and through most of the present century, illustrators of children's books by and large were more impressive than those working with adult titles. Among the noteworthy illustrators of books for children, and each deserves much attention: Walter Crane, Kate Greenaway, Randolph Caldecott—to name but three. See Janet Smith, *Children's Illustrated Books* (London, 1948); Percy Muir, *English Children's Books, 1600–1900* (London, 1954); Barbara Bader, *American Picturebooks* (New York, 1976); F.J. Darton, *Children's Books in England: Five Centuries of Social Life*. 3rd ed. (New York, 1982). There are numerous other studies.

[12]In 1828 Pickering first used the device of the dolphin and anchor originated by Aldus. "Whittingham in 1844 revised the old face type of Caslon on the Chiswick Press . . . but theirs were voices crying in the wilderness." S.H. Steinberg. *Five Hundred Years of Printing* (New York: Criterion Books, 1959), p. 224. Still, it was at the Chiswick Press where Morris had his first books printed.

[13]*A History of Book Illustration* (Cleveland: World Publishing, 1958), p. 272. For a study of the artist, see B. Brophy's *Beardsley and His World* (London: Thames & Hudson, 1976).

[14]"It is generally regrettable that his medievalism led him, as far as he could go, to belittle the roman letter. . . . He might have done much more for our present needs had he been less under the spell of the fifteenth

century Venetian style in use before the advent of Aldus.'' Stanley Morison and Kenneth Day. *The Typographic Book 1450–1935* (University of Chicago Press, 1963), p. 50. At the same time, the authors quickly add that Morris, ''by focusing interest in the craft . . . made possible the variety and excellence which characterized present day typography.'' See William Peterson, *The Kelmscott Press* (Berkeley: University of California Press, 1991); Susan Thompson, *American Book Design and William Morris* (New York: R.R. Bowker, 1977).

[15]Daniel B. Updike. *Printing Types, Their History Form and Use.* 3rd ed. (Cambridge: Harvard University Press, 2 vols. 1962). (Dover paperback, 1978) A basic study of the history of typography and typographers, Updike's work now suffers from some glowing biases as well as less than an imaginative approach to time and people. A brief approach, yet sound, is offered by Johnson in *Type Designs: Their History and Development.* 3rd ed. (London: Deutsch, 1966); Harry Carter, *A View of Early Typography Up to About 1600* (Oxford: Oxford University Press, 1969). See also Morison.

[16]The American Antiquarian Society has a program in progress on the History of the Book in American Culture, which is to complement such works as the six-volume series, *The History of the Book in Britain.* Progress on the American program is reported periodically in the newsletter, *The Book,* from the Society at 185 Salisbury St., Worcester, MA 01609.

[17]Eugene Exman. *The Brothers Harper* (New York: Harper & Row, 1965). There are scores of good to excellent histories of publishing firms in America. This, while not necessarily the best, is typical. The first volume covers the founders and cultural needs of Americans from 1817 to 1853. A second volume published in 1967, *The House of Harper,* moves the story from 1817 to 1967.

[18]For a brief history of the Library of Congress, ''which begins with the history of the United States,'' see Michael Harris, *History of Libraries in the Western World* (Metuchen, NJ: Scarecrow Press, 1984), p. 183+. See, too, Donald G. Davis Jr. and John Tucker, *American Library History: A Comprehensive Guide to the Literature* (Santa Barbara: ABC Clio, 1989); and Wayne Wiegand's updates on the literature of American history about every two years in *Libraries and Culture* (formerly: *The Journal of Library History*); and Denis Keeling, *British Library History: A Bibliography* (London: LA, 1962–to date, irregular).

[19]The collection and preservation of books (and, for that matter periodicals and other printed materials) in whole is a relatively new idea. Until well into the nineteenth century it was common to cut up books for illustrations, title pages, etc. The otherwise reserved John Feather

describes one John Bagford (1650–1716) as "book collector and destroyer of books." *A Dictionary of Book History* (London: Croom Helm, 1986), p. 17. Much the same might be said of other collectors, from Thomas Dibdin (1776–1847) to Thomas J. Wise (1859–1937).

[20]E.J. O'Dwyer. *Thomas Frognall Dibdin* (Middlesex: Private Libraries Assn., 1967). A brief history and bibliography of the greater "lover of books in merry England." Even today Dibdin's three-volume *Bibliographical Decameron* (1817) offers much information—and not a little amusement.

[21]One of the most charming and still useful guides to the fine art of book collecting for the person with less than a million dollars is John Carter's *ABC for Book Collectors*. 6th ed., rev. (London: Granada, 1980). (Revised by Nicolas Barker.) The information presupposes the reader has little or no background in collecting, bibliography or the history of the book. The guide, literally, is an ABC to what must be known for intelligent, enjoyable collecting. Related titles include: William Rees-Mogg's *How to Buy Rare Books,* 1985; Gordon Ray's *The Rare Book World Today,* 1982.

CHAPTER NINE

THE TWENTIETH CENTURY AND BEYOND

We're not just a publisher anymore, but a creator and exploiter of copyrights. We sell information in any form, in any way you want it.
—Richard Snyder, Simon and Schuster Chairman

The period from World War I until the close of the twentieth century sometimes is called the birth of modern times. Despite two disastrous European wars and a number of minor conflicts the stronger industrial powers survived. Nations took their place in the newly formed United Nations. The strength of the UN, while still in question after the collapse of the USSR, at least offered hope for a truly modern, peaceful world . . . if not a literate one. While Western countries boast of a high education level and a relatively equally high rate of literacy, this is not the case with many developing nations. The general growth in prosperity is not matched in all countries, but the scale of scientific and technological research suggests that the next century might be more kind to less prosperous nations.

The right to communicate, an international United Nations hope, is aided tremendously by the computer and electronic messages which can penetrate any border, any group of censors. The opportunities for communication provided by the diverse electronic media have yet to be explored consequences. A determined government can block signals, but, more to the point, the vast number of languages undermines any real communication unless there is a universal language (which English has become, at least among the better educated) or one is dealing almost entirely in scientific jargon.

The rise of a reading public is matched by a corresponding development in printing technology which allows the greater production of books. In worldwide book production, the United States, Germany, the United Kingdom, Japan and France lead in number of different titles and overall press runs. Fiction generally comes first in popularity, followed by science and sociology. Textbooks, reference works, and juvenile titles are close behind. The question is what constitutes the boundaries of each subject. The indicators are only general.[1]

The ubiquitous paperback is one explanation for a larger reading public. Whether a popular novel found in a supermarket or airport, or a reprint of a classic sold only in university bookstores, the paperback is by and large the most common format for books read by the general public. The paperback as known today by most Americans and Europeans originated in 1935 when Allen Lane introduced the world to the by now well known Penguins and established the notion that quality books could be distributed in large quantities at low prices. Carefully designed and printed, often with the help of such international figures as Jan Tschichold, the paperbacks carried on the tradition of reprints [and later, original work], for a mass audience with many interests and probably limited budgets.

ENTER THE COMPUTER

From the second quarter to near the end of the twentieth century, the Industrial Revolution continued at levels which caused upheaval and a new focus on services and scientific advancements. The greatest single change in printing was the introduction of the computer, followed by ever more sophisticated methods of storing more and more data in smaller and smaller spaces. This brought about dramatic change—today the publication of ideas and information is more important than the publication of a book *per se*. The essential development was the shift to information organization and distribution. If New York, London, Paris and Rome were the centers of publishing in the twentieth century, anywhere a computer is located is now a potential publishing point. Desk-top publishing makes it possible for an amateur to publish a book by using little more than imagination and the page layouts, type faces, illustrations, etc. at his or her fingertips.

Between 1940 and 1950 the world marked 500 years of printing, and with that turned full speed to automation of many of the practices employed from Gutenberg to shortly after World War II. The first computer in the United States was in operation by 1946. It weighed 30 tons and filled the equivalent of a small house. In the mid-1990s any desk-top computer could outperform the original ENIAC, and at a minimum cost. By the 1960s computer-assisted typesetting had replaced the linotype machine and, combined with film setting, almost all of hand-set type. The technological revolution began with faster presses and moved then to photoreproduction and storage of words and pictures in mainframe computers. The widespread implication of these technological developments is known to everyone and has changed society in general and printing-publishing in particular.

Until the late twentieth century, type designers followed and imitated Aldus, Jenson and others. This began to change when photography, in the late nineteenth century, made it possible to create new type faces by photo manipulation of type forms. Today computers facilitate the modification of existing types to create different faces, i.e. bits from one face can be tacked onto another or others. The computer can bend, twist and reduce and enlarge so that type no longer need to follow set sizes. Abode Inc., of Mountain View, California, for example, offers a program which allows the user to create an infinite number of various sized type fonts. The user can use the Multiple Master software to make fonts to meet a particular level of esthetics or need.

AUTHOR/PUBLISHER

Today many publishers rely upon authors to use word processors as a preliminary publishing step. The author sends the copy-perfect manuscript to the publisher on a disk, or possibly via modem to the publisher's computer. The text is then printed and, voilà, the book is ready. (Another version of this is to supply the publisher with camera-ready copy which is turned into data for the press without typesetting.) The problem with automation is possible loss of control by both author and publisher over any final editing. Often, too, the finished book is in an unappealing format in an unappetizing typeface. The new technology may be an economic dream for publishers, but it can end up as a nightmare for the purchaser of the book, particularly if virtually unedited from author to reader.

Many publishers of reference works, as well as those in specialized areas, may turn exclusively to electronic databases and away from the printed book. Readers and users are now able to determine what format to purchase or to tap via computer.

The future of printing in the United States, and in most developed countries, is complex. It is certain, though, that change will follow a general route or pattern. Letterpress, as practiced from the time of Gutenberg, is virtually obsolete except for small, private presses, and even here the computer has replaced type and the press. Offset, lithography, gravure are themselves in danger. They, too, will be replaced by electronic composition and printing. Binderies are automated, as are almost all aspects of printing.

Not everyone, within or without the new technology, is pleased. Many suggest it offers problems: (1) True, increased amounts of information are available from all parts of the world, but this increases nervous anxiety. What in the growing information heap is of worth and what is of no value? Some argue convincingly that this makes the publisher even more valuable, the book even more necessary. The publisher filters out what is relevant. (2) The information explosion creates more elites. It costs money to isolate data (whether online or in some other electronic form) and only those with funds can reclaim what is needed. Many public and academic libraries, for example, are unable to afford the sophisticated new databases; as are, of course, numerous individuals. (3) If the book has been bypassed, if only in part by the computer, it is alarming to realize that in America at the beginning of the 1990s, only about ten per cent of the population have a home computer.

PUBLISHING CHANGES[2]

This side of the new technologies, the three major publishing events since the 1920s would include: (1) The takeover of independent publishers by conglomerates. (2) The resulting attitude that the book is a mass commodity to be marketed, like soap or shoes. (3) The rise of the small desk-top publisher to meet needs of authors and readers ignored by the larger publishers.

There is now a sharp division between publishing as developed in the nineteenth and twentieth centuries and what is likely to happen in the next century. Independent publishers, often headed by wealthy individuals who could afford loss with profit, have virtually disappeared. Between 1925 and 1930, 20 of the largest book publishers in the United States accounted for about 50 per cent of all books published. Today the figures are closer to 80 per cent, or even higher if the figure is limited to mass circulation books (82%), technical (78%) and textbooks (85%). Today's large publishers differ from those of a few decades ago in important respects. The larger ones are multinational, from Bertelsmann in Germany to McGraw-Hill, which operates in two dozen countries. And the conglomerates account for the greatest number of titles published not only in the United States, but throughout the Western world. What is true in New York is equally true in London, Paris or Madrid.

In many cases books are only an incidental aspect of the conglomerates' interests. For example, Gulf Western is among the largest of the conglomerates and controls publishers from Prentice-Hall and Pocket Books to Harlequin romances and Monarch notes. Its most famous publisher is Simon & Schuster, which moved from being primarily a trade publisher to becoming the country's largest school and college publisher with sales of more than $1.3 billion in 1991. The other giants include: (1) Time-Warner, with Little Brown, Warner Book, Book of the Month, Home Box Office, and, of course, the film studio and the Time magazines. (2) A.G. Bertelsmann, a German firm, which operates Bantam Books, Doubleday, Dell, the Literary Guild, RCA records, plus scores of book clubs and publishing firms in Europe. (3) Reed-Elsevier, an Anglo-Dutch company with interests in R.R. Bowker, the Reed Reference Group, Cahner's Publishing (*Library Journal, School Library Journal, Publishers Weekly*) and Elsevier, the world's largest scientific publisher, as well as Pergamon Press. These are the largest, although close behind are Rupert Murdoch's News Corporation (HarperCollins, among others); Matsushita, the Japanese firm, with interests in Putnam and Berkeley books.

The formation of conglomerates is predicated on several suppositions: (1) A larger financial base assures the capital necessary for expansion of publishing. (2) Diversification of a company—which includes television, films and recordings as well as books—assures success. (3) Electronic methods of communication necessitate alliances for the technological future. (4) The increasing internationalization of the world requires that publishers offer global coverage; hence the foreign investments in American publishing houses. (5) Recognized by some in the mid-twentieth century as consumer products rather than cultural artifacts for gentle people, books assumed a new financial importance.

Two changes took place because of the new focus: (a) There is aggressive advertising and distribution of books, particularly by large chains such as Barnes & Noble and Waldenbooks, as well, of course, as by the publishers who see themselves as merchants. Marketing is the key word in publishing today, at least among conglomerates. Books are commodities to be shipped in and out of stores without much thought of back lists. Still, there are exceptions. From time to time a small press work may, without marketing but with word of mouth, become a success; and (b) partly as a consequence, the majority of smaller publishers are now paying more attention to sales while trying to retain their independence. This group is divided into several subgroups from institutional and university publishers to the independent small press.

CONGLOMERATE PROBLEMS

There are standard questions about the conglomerate phenomenon. A publishing firm, as part of a larger organization, will hesitate to bring out books which are financially risky. Most poetry, first novels and controversial subject matter fall into the risk category. Librarians note, too, the difficulty of acquiring many important, although not fast selling older titles. Conglomerates, no matter how famous the author or title, tend to let them go out of print if they don't sell X number of copies per year. Understandably, the publishers disagree.

Through advertising, or promises to withhold it, the conglomerates dominate the popular book reviews and many of the literary outposts, from *The New York Review of Books* to *The Times Literary Supplement*. The large publishers command space in bookstores, and they can market their books through television, magazines and newspapers which they own.

It is a common error to presuppose that all conglomerates operate in the same fashion, and in many of them the individual publisher is free to make major decisions about what is or is not published—as long as it is profitable.

Today's few independent publishers, from Farrar Straus to Norton must, of course, make money. The difference is both the amount and the willingness of an independent to publish a book which might not be profitable but which furthers literature, science etc.

With the roaring 1980s behind them, the conglomerates have had to reconsider their goals. Aside from best-sellers, book publishing has proven less than profitable in relation to other holdings such as film and television studios. The more successful conglomerates in the 1990s turned back to the rules of publishers for the past 400 to 500 years; i.e. develop back lists of quality which will keep the company in profit from year to year, and gradually build on the success of certain subject areas and authors. Those who fail to do this are likely to sell off the publishing firms or merge them with other components so they lose their identity as publishers.

SMALL PRESS AND DESK-TOP PUBLISHING

The preoccupation with books as a commodity, with the best-seller and the mass-audience paperback has driven many authors to smaller independent publishers. In rebellion against the poor quality of most of the media, including conglomerate best-sellers, many Americans are demanding and supporting good writing. They are enthusiastic about what is genuinely good and look to the specialized, small presses and university presses to meet their needs. This in turn offers hope to authors who are more than formula writers.

Desk-top publishing, an imprecise term for the ability to generate and combine text and graphics from a personal computer, revolutionized the small press in the latter half of this century.

Being able to set a page on a computer screen and then print it on a laser printer made it possible to: a) either simply bind together the printouts as a magazine or a book; or, more likely b) use the laser printouts for camera-ready copy which often follows the normal process of being printed and run off on a press. At any rate, the home computer eliminates typesetting and layout. It considerably cuts costs, thus making it possible to publish a book for much less than the investment in standard publishing methods. Given this ability, the publishers of little magazines, i.e. magazines often produced by one or two people at home, skyrocketed from a few thousand in the early part of the 1980s to well over 5,000 in the United States alone. Many of these presses, too, publish books from time to time. Desk-top publishing is a revival of the old cottage industry where one or two printers did everything but write the book. Today, of course, the writer may be printer and publisher as well.

The small press has been in existence since Walpole and Morris, but only in the past two decades has it had such an influence, both in numbers and in types of books published. The large publishers who long ago dropped first novels, poetry or anything which might be objectionable in terms of politics, religion, etc. might have destroyed creative writers. They did not because the small presses stepped in, and often flourished, by publishing precisely what the large publisher would not touch. As a result there are more poetry, esoteric fiction, and ideas being brought into print today than ever before. Whether or not this cultural phenomenon is due to the computer, managerial reorganization of publishing conglomerates, or a new renaissance in creative thought is worthy of consideration.

PHOTOCOPYING

Photocopying emerged as an important scholarly tool after World War II. In fact, many believe the process influenced scholarship even more than the computer. The photocopy allowed rapid transmission of texts from library to library, from student to student, and eliminated the necessity for laborious hand-copying of needed material. Another major step forward was the ubiquitous electronic network, such as Bitnet or Internet. They offer a new form of communication which, while primarily confined to electronic mail and gossip as well as standard databases, suggest a potential replacement or substitute for the periodical, newspaper or even the book.

Another aspect of electronic publishing is that the user may pay only for what is used. This is when the user is charged per minute, for example, online and in contact with information stored in a main frame computer. Conversely, the publisher may continue to charge so much per unit, by a single payment or a subscription. An example is CD-ROMs, much of video, etc.

Photocopying, networks, computers and other advances established what many see as the real publishing battleground. Each suggests an endless maze of the future concern about who owns what, or copyright. How does the publisher compensate the writer when a story or article is available electronically to hundreds of thousands of potential readers? How does the online vendor or the CD-ROM distributor compensate the publisher? How does the individual user, in or out of a library, pay or not pay for what originated with the author? Publishing is now a mass of partnerships without any clear direction of ownership. In 1991 Simon and Schuster Chairman Richard Snyder summed it up: "We're not just a publisher anymore, but a creator and exploiter of copyrights. We sell information in any form, in any way you want it."[3]

COPYRIGHT

Although the present United States copyright law is a lawyer's dream, there are certain basics which are understood—subject, to be sure, to future interpretation and legislative alteration. Most of these provisions are protected, too, under the international Berne Copyright Convention. (1) The law protects the right of the author(s) to his/her property; as well as the right of the publisher. (2) A certain amount of sharing of the property is allowed, from copying parts of a book or an article for personal use, to using quotations. The fair use section of the law allows a teacher to duplicate material for classroom use. Here, however, interpretation of how much can be copied or quoted and for what purpose is up for legal grabs.[4]

The explosion in the media formats creates a legal entanglement which, unless resolved by what promises to be intricate patterns of costs and payments, may delay progress. The problem is not confined to the United States; the reality of global publishing—with books from England or France freely moving to Japan or Canada or vice versa—suggests various methods of avoiding copyright, reproducing specific titles and pirating them to anyone, anywhere who will buy. On a more controversial, legitimate stage the Third World countries argue, much as the Americans did in the nineteenth century, that their obligation is to furnish their people with information. Their obligation to the copyright holder is secondary. Ideological lines are more difficult to combat than outright theft.

READING PUBLIC[5]

Despite television technology and computers there are many more readers than in past times. Numerous reasons are given for the increase, although the baby boom of the 1950s and 1960s and the resulting increase in population is the basic explanation. Couple this with 70 per cent of the population now graduating from high school (as compared with about one-half that number in the 1940s) and another 20 per cent with academic degrees, and the increased production of books is understandable.

According to the U.S. Bureau of Economic Analysis, Americans spend approximately one-third of one per cent of their personal consumption (or about $100 per head per year) on books, and another six-plus per cent on sports, television and records. The figure seems to be pretty much a constant. The proportion of the population reading books (i.e. at least one book a month), depending on how the survey is taken, is about 33 to 40 per cent. Newspapers and magazines are read by close to 80 per cent of the population. While price is a factor in how many books are purchased and/or read, it is a minor one for most categories. Books remained relatively inexpensive, particularly when published as paperbacks. The real yardstick of readership is another constant. The more education, the better the income, the better the job, the more likely an individual is to be a reader. Obviously, there are exceptions to all of this, but in a general way the yardstick holds from year to year.

Comparatively, the British Publishers Association Trade Year Book for 1992 reports a ten-year survey showing that 55 per cent of the British read at least one book a month, as compared with 32 per cent in France. Only Germany is higher, with 67 per cent of the population reading at least one book a month. In terms of sales, the British spend an average of $80 for books as compared with $100 for Americans.[6]

The basic skills of reading and writing are relatively widespread throughout Western countries, but there is a serious question as to the depth of literacy, and particularly the ability of people to read more than simple material.

Periodically authors and publishers complain about the current decline in readership. Many reasons are given, but whether it is a matter of television, mass culture or shifts in the way people work and live, Philip Roth believes: ''There is a change in the mental landscape having to do with concentration,'' and the novelist believes that explains in part the lack of serious readers. At the same time, he concluded his interview with what most librarians think: ''Some people believe in God, and I believe in the reader. But I don't want my faith tested too strongly.''[7]

LIBRARIES

The period from the 1930s to the 1990s has been one of the saddest in the history of libraries. While public libraries achieved a stronger position than ever before and experienced an extraordinary growth in both their internal and external functions, this period witnessed the greatest destruction of books, particularly during the second World War when European libraries lost from a quarter to almost all of their holdings. Fortunately many of the more important books were buried in mines during the war. The most important library treasures at Monte Cassino, for example, were saved. At the same time the holdings of the British Library suffered a severe loss.

As Francis Bacon might have put it, the two national libraries of France and England are now ''arks to save learning from deluge.'' Their experiences in constructing new buildings for their ever-expanding holdings are instructive. With 18 million books in the old library, together with 13 million miscellaneous periodicals, maps, manuscripts, etc., the 160 miles of shelving in the new building are filled before they are ready. The culprit is not only a greater production of information, but the laws of deposit which, at least in England, require not one, but six copies. This brings in untold numbers of books, from pulp fiction to classics. In 1990, for example, the number of books deposited in the British Library alone rose by 50 per cent.

Many countries continue to construct new libraries. Others do not; e.g. at the Lenin Library in Moscow—considered to be the largest in the world—economic conditions have made it impossible to keep up with acquisitions, and parts of the library actually are falling apart. In Leningrad, in the late 1980s, four large libraries were destroyed by fire or flooding.

The national libraries are in crisis, including the Library of Congress. Every plan to meet the challenge goes aground upon the rock of poor budgets, and even poorer recognition of the problem by those in charge of the budgets. At the same time these libraries must keep up with the flood of electronic works and other new formats. One possible partial solution is to call on private funding; e.g. The New York Public Library has traditionally welcomed private donors.

Although they began modestly, public libraries by the middle and end of the twentieth century are found in most western countries. Supplemented by networks, county library systems, interlibrary loan and the like, today's public library can bring the whole world of printed matter (as well as other forms of communication) to the lay person.

One generalization may be made about the 9,000 public and 5,000 American academic libraries, applicable as well to most school libraries. They are chronically underfunded. There is never enough money for books, periodicals or, in the past decade or so, electronic and multi-media resources. Given this fact, coupled with inflation, a shortage of both staff and space, the library has been in a critical state for decades. It is likely to continue to be short of funds until such time as Americans put more emphasis on the importance of education and brain power.

The basic question is: what will people of the next century expect from libraries? The answer is much the same as before, although with specific technological aids. First and foremost, no matter what the format or how information is obtained, the library exists to offer a comprehensive collection of data. This may be broad, as in the case of our national libraries; or popular, as with public libraries; or specialized; or a combination of all. And combination is the key to the future. Libraries will collect material, but also will give the users various combinations to unlock information, whether it be on the same floor or six thousand miles away stored in a computer. This, in turn, presupposes cooperative libraries throughout the nation and world that collect in given areas and make their work available to all.

A more important function for the librarian will be acting as a mediator bits of random information, piles of garbage and gems required by the anxious reader. The role will be not so much to collect and to provide as to select—to sort out items which have true value for the library and for its types of users.

In order to collect, select and sort, the library will call upon the new technologies from online computer searches to CD-ROMs to Internet and whatever other forms will come in the years ahead. To be sure, the book, the printed periodical and newspaper still are likely to be an important part of the library. The library has been and will continue to be an institution always in the middle of change; and if the Alexandria Library contained papyrus rolls and a zoo as well, there is no reason why the library of the twenty-first century should not contain books and Hal, the ''living'' computer from the film ''2001.''

BOOKSTORES

In a 1990–1991 study by the Book Industry Group, it was found that about 40 per cent of the American population buys books. Of all adult trade books sold, the vast majority (63 per cent) were titles found in drugstores and mall book chains; and of these, 91 per cent were popular fiction. Depending on attitude, one may say this demonstrates either that the conglomerates offer no better or that the problem is not the quality of books but the quality of readers. Even the best known successful literary novelists—from John Updike to Anne Tyler—rarely sell more than one hundred thousand copies, as compared to a million plus for popular supermarket types.[8]

From the time Gutenberg pulled his first book from his press, the problem of how to distribute and sell books has been an intractable one. In the fifteenth century there were only a few titles available. Today, in the United States alone, over 1.2 million separate books are available. The question is, how can these be brought to the individual who needs them? The nineteenth century offered hope of fast, cheap transportation of books, and the twentieth offered outlets from standard book stores and supermarkets to bookclubs and television promotions.

There are many responses to the inability of most Americans to find books. The latest is the super bookstore offered by Waldenbooks and Dalton, to name only two, where at least 50,000 to 150,000 separate titles are available to the person who walks in off the street. Still, these are limited to urban centers and suburbs; and they are no answer to readers living in thinly populated areas. There are from 20,000 to 25,000 bookstores in the United States, depending on the definition, but close to 90 per cent are little more than card shops with books added. One future response may be the electronic book, sent at will to every home in America that wishes it.

Confined to individually owned stores until the mid century, bookselling by the early 1990s took on some of the same features as the publishing conglomerates. Four groups control most of the stores in shopping centers and in urban communities. The names are familiar. First is Waldenbooks, which combined with Borders as part of the Kmart Corporation. They have 1,400 stores, of which two dozen are superstores. Others of their outlets are called Brentano's and Basset. Next, Barnes & Noble, under names from Scribners and Bookshop to B. Dalton and Doubleday, have about 900 stores. Third, Crown Books is part of a discount chain with 200 outlets, of which 40 stock some 100,000 titles. And fourth, with 76 record stores, Tower sells books and has 15 super outlets affiliated with its music stores.

There are numerous facets to distribution of books. These may be put in questions, each of which would require a lengthy study to answer, but which at least indicate the sectors involved. First, how can books be moved from the publisher, to the wholesaler, to the bookstores or library, more efficiently? Second, why do books often go out-of-print rapidly, even though there remains a demand, no matter how small? One reason may be due to poor distribution at both the publisher and the jobber level. Third, why are there no more points of distribution than relatively small outlets (from department stores and drugstores to supermarkets) where selection is limited? Why is there not more control over remainders, i.e. unsold books, returns and titles simply reprinted over and over again by the wholesaler and called "remainders?"

ILLUSTRATION

Book illustration in the twentieth century follows several distinctive roads and byways. Artists, as in the past, continue to employ familiar techniques, from woodcuts to engravings; although with the advent of the computer the possibilities of using electronic means for projections and various dimensional drawings, particularly for technical and scientific works, were grasped immediately.

The French continue to develop the deluxe editions of a few copies illustrated by some of the world's leading artists (Fig. 52). Prices, astronomical at the time, now command auction bids which are in the same league as the artist's original drawings, if not paintings. Following the lead of Vollard, the French publishers continue to offer limited editions of works by current artists. Unfortunately, the content is not always equal to the illustrations (Fig. 53).

In America and England some attention is given to deluxe works, but much less than in France. Typical, for example, was an offering of The Yolla Press of California in early 1993. D.H. Lawrence's last novel was illustrated with woodcuts by Leonard Baskin. "Two versions are offered," according to the advertisement. "Vellum version: Thirty copies bound by hand . . . accompanied by an extra suite of signed prints, the whole in a handmade box . . . $3,850 each. Cloth version: Sixty copies . . . $875." Although a celebrated American printmaker, Baskin hardly commands the prices of even better known artists. Still, it indicates the current direction and type of expensive illustrated book offered the public—usually by small presses.

Some help comes from book clubs such as the Folio Society in England and the Heritage Society in the United States which, sticking with reprints, stress design and illustration as the primary selling point. Unfortunately, much of the work is neutral to indifferent.

National styles remain for both illustration and typography, but they are much less pronounced than in the past. "The homogenizing forces of our times have broken many barriers of national style, and sometimes it is difficult to tell at a glance the origin of a book"[9] (Fig. 54).

Art Spiegelman, and his Pulitzer prize winning illustrated-cartoon-narrative *Maus,* 1991, suggests a continuation of another type of illustrated book. The inventor of the book in pictures, usually without text, or with only a limited number of words, was Frans Maesereel (1889–1972), a Belgian Expressionist who created a series of 12 woodcut novels shortly after World War I. Lynd Ward and Milton Gross, among others, continued the tradition with picture sequences during the 1930s. Many of these were acts of social protest. In late 1992, Eric Drooker's *Flood* was published, indicating that the idiom is as powerful, as assured as always.

The most interesting illustrators of the period are confined generally to the splendid children's books—which are beyond this brief study. Reference works more and more rely upon photographs and computer drawings, and less and less on imaginative, individual illustrators.

BINDING

Even though modern artistic bindings are usually done entirely in leather, half-leather bindings are far more numerous. In these only the spine and the corners are of leather, the rest being covered with paper, cloth or other material. There are many kinds of paper available to bookbinders and very attractive bindings can be made entirely of paper. This is done to some extent in current publishers' bindings, but aside from these and the sturdy English cloth bindings that usually have no decoration other than the title on the spine, publishers' bindings are frequently in half-leather. There has been a clearly detectable improvement in trade bindings.

The fine bindings produced in France present the same variegated appearance that we see in modern French illustrative art, which is generally inclined toward the picturesque. Bookbinding

Ne fronce plus ces sourcils-ci,
Casta, ni cette bouche-ci,
Laisse-moi puiser tous tes baumes,
Piana, sucrés, salés, poivrés,
Et laisse-moi boire, poivrés,
Salés, sucrés, tes sacrés baumes.

52. Typical of modern book illustration, although published in 1900, is Bonnard's lithograph for poetry by Verlaine.

53. Picasso's drawing for an edition (1934) of Aristophanes' *Lysistrata*.

54. Woodcut by Aristide Maillol for Longus' *Les Pastorales, ou Daphnis et Chloe,* 1937.

in the southern European countries follows the historical tradition more closely. There is no common or uniform style for all countries and for all aspects of book art, as there was in the baroque and the rococo periods and even during the Empire. It is questionable whether any such uniformity, in spite of the greater communication among nations, could develop today, when artistic considerations must often give way to demands for speed, and life itself is seldom distinguished by any balance or harmony.

Today the standard cardboard case binding has all but replaced fine leather and cloth bindings. The change took place about 200 years ago, and gradually cloth became the preferred substitute as, by the early twentieth century, did the simple colored board of heavy paper.

Hand binding has been superseded by machines which do little more than glue the covers to the signatures. The simple case binding has reduced the cost, and can be quite pleasing in appearance, although the majority are more functional than beautiful.

The book jacket, or dustcover, was a recent development. The first example was from England in 1833, but by the turn of the century it was relatively common. The jacket now commands the attention of typographers and artists as the leather binding did in previous centuries. And, of course, it is the primary place where the famous "blurb" about the qualities of the particular book and the author are found.[10]

THE DEATH OF THE BOOK?

"Some years ago, a friend and I co-managed a used and rare book shop in Ann Arbor. . . . One day we took a call from a professor of English . . . I'm selling everything, he said . . . I'm getting out of books . . . I don't want to see any of them again."[11] The change was due to the fact the professor had switched from books to a computer. He and many others believe the book culture is over and the electronic culture is here. Networks which link home/university/public library/government offices/data sources (both public and private) and countless other points in the United States, Canada and the world are not only here, but are likely to replace printing for ephemeral, instant communications. Prodigy, CompuServe and Genie are three large national computer networks which with minor cousins offer about four million Americans access to bulletin board discussions about everything and everyone from popular television programs to opera and Proust. Add to this the 4.5 million-plus noncommercial users of Usenet (used by universities, libraries, research groups, etc.) and an impressive number are enjoying a form of publishing peculiar to the last decade or so. Publishers, in fact, such as Bantam Books offer sample chapters of new books on a network.

In an age of ubiquitous electronic entertainment, it's easy to find undertakers who foresee the death of books and libraries. According to a computer sage, "the big research libraries and the great national libraries . . . will go the way of the railroad stations and the movie palaces. . . . Libraries will be nothing more than museums of the printed word."[12] Few technocrats stop to consider how much better we are with railroads, giant movie screens and, yes, books and libraries.

Others, usually more numerous and definitely more literate, observe that in America alone $17 billion is spent on publishing. The number of bookstores and books increases each year. At its most pragmatic, "reading remains the cheapest form of sustained entertainment, and millions of Americans still like it."[13] If anything, computers help sustain more publishers, more books and more bookstores.

The differences between print and electronic orientations are challenged by others as being more theoretical than real, i.e. most computers still rely on printouts and/or the user reading material from the screen. The format changes, but not the human who depends on print, no matter how it is presented or organized. The fundamental relationship between the writer and the reader will remain a constant—as it has since the first Sumerian put stylus to clay to form a pictogram.[14]

The librarian will continue to serve as a mediator between the user and the vastly increased amount of information. The librarian not only will quickly locate what is needed, but will evaluate its worth for a specific type of user. Beyond that no one can really say, and certainly no one in the mid 1990s can be certain when and if the printed book will be a museum piece. So, for now at least, the book as known since Gutenberg is likely to be about until the next chapter is written in the twenty first century.

NOTES

[1]For a dated, although useful study, see Peter Curwen, *The World Book Industry* (New York: Facts on File, 1986). The annual roundup of American publishing in *Publishers Weekly* is useful, too.

[2]In this section and following sections the changes are illustrated primarily with American examples, but, for the most part, the same

situation exists throughout Europe. In fact, the largest European publishers are part of the international conglomerates which own American firms. For details, see John Tebbel, *History of Book Publishing in the United States* (New York, 1972–1981); and for England, see John Feather, *A History of British Publishing* (London, 1988); Robin Myers, *The British Book Trade from Caxton to the Present Day: A Bibliographical Guide* (London: Deutsch, 1973); Ruari McLean, *Modern Book Design, From William Morris to the Present Day* (London: Faber & Faber, 1958). There are numerous other national histories, some of which are found in both Tebbel and Feather.

[3]"Publishing Books," *Media Studies Journal,* Summer 1992, p. 41.

[4]The United States Copyright Law of 1978, amended in the 1980s, was an effort to solve at least some of the problems of multimedia presentation of a message, but in the interpretation of "fair use" the law proved less than satisfactory and litigation continues to determine what can or can't be copied or reprinted.

[5]Richard Hoggart. *The Uses of Literacy* (London: Chatto and Windus, 1957). This is a "classic" of the study of readers and popular literature in England after World War II. The subtitle explains it all: "Aspects of working class life, with special references to publications and entertainment." See, too, the equally famous *The Long Revolution* by Raymond Williams, (Penguin Books, 1961).

[6]*Times Literary Supplement,* October 2, 1992, p. 14. This is a summary of the Publisher's report.

[7]"Roth says Roth and Roth are Real," *The New York Times,* March 9, 1993, p. C18.

[8]Diana Laurenson, ed. *The Sociology of Literature* (London: Paladin, 1972). Contributors consider the economic position of authors, past and present, as well as the rise of the reading public. Emphasis is on English publishing. See, too, Louis Dudek, *Literature and the Press* (Toronto: Ryerson Press, 1960). Subtitle: "A history of printing, printed media and their relationship to literature."

[9]Norma Levarie. *The Art & History of Books* (New York: Heinemann, 1968), p. 303. Almost 30 years later, the problem of origin is even more pronounced.

[10]For a dated discussion on the history of the book jacket, see Charles Rosner, *The Growth of the Book Jacket* (1954). Many studies cover bookbinding from manuals on how-to-do-it to histories. Among the latter, the still outstanding work is Edith Deihl, *Bookbinding: Its Background and Technique* (New York, 1946), 2 vols. See, too, Helmut Lehmann-Haupt, *Bookbinding in America* (Portland: Southworth-Anthoensen Press, 1941); Ruari McLean, *Victorian Publisher's Book Bindings . . .* (London: Fraser, 1983). M.T. Roberts and Don Ethering-

ton, *Bookbinding and the Conservation of Books: A Dictionary of Descriptive Terminology* (Washington: Library of Congress, 1982).

[11]Sven Birkerts. "Into the electronic millennium," *Boston Review,* October 1991, p. 14.

[12]Birkerts, *op. cit.,* p. 18.

[13]Roger Cohen. "Publishing," *The New York Times,* September 2, 1991, p. 29.

[14]The real danger to the book may not be CD-ROMs, according to one eccentric and amusing view, but theft. "Books are being stolen in record numbers. In 1990 a thief . . . stole from 327 libraries around the country." Police found 11,000 rare titles in his Iowa home. He took them "because he just wanted to be near them." Michael Olmert. *The Smithsonian Book of Books* (Washington: Smithsonian Books, 1992), p. 286. There are thousands of other examples through history, but it is questionable that theft, headache that it is, will do in libraries before CD-ROMs. (See any issue of *Library and Archival Security,* or *AB Bookman's Weekly* for more on theft.)

ADDED READING

This is an annotated listing of selected basic titles. The purpose is to offer in-depth readings for areas surveyed in this text. Some of these, and other books, will be found in the notes after each chapter. The readings are limited to books, most of which were published after 1970 and for the most part are still in print. There are thousands of articles—many of which will be found in the bibliographies listed here.

A. GENERAL HISTORIES AND BIBLIOGRAPHIES

Bibliographies

The Annual Bibliography of the History of the Printed Book and Libraries. Martinus Nijhoff for International Federation of Library Associations and Institutions, 1973 to date, annual.

National committees report bibliographical scholarship for their countries and this is compiled in the annual. There are numerous shortcomings, including lack of subject indexes, but at least the bibliography is a springboard, and a useful one at that. (A somewhat similar approach, by a single editor and more limited in scope: *Bibliographie de Buch- und Bibliothekgeschichte,* 1980 to date). There are excellent bibliographies in most of the general and specific titles listed here. See, for example, the well organized and current listing of titles in Leila Avrin's *Scribes, Script and Books* (Chicago: American Library Association, 1991).

Brenni, Vito. *The Art and History of Book Printing.* Westport, CT: Greenwood Press, 1984.

An exhaustive bibliography (1,060 citations) on major aspects of printing. Logically organized under 14 subject headings, with author, subject indexes and checklists. See, too, the same author's *Book Illustration and Decoration: A guide to research* (Greenwood Press, 1980) and *Bookbinding: a guide to the literature* (Greenwood Press, 1982).

Tanselle, G.T. *Introduction to Bibliography.* Seminar Syllabus. New York: Columbia University, Dept. of English Literature, Fall, 1990. (Distributed by Books Arts Press, Columbia University, 516 Butler Library, New York, NY 10027.)

A 100-page mimeographed bibliography, the 12th revision was issued in 1990. Its aim is to provide background for "the analysis and description of books," primarily as physical objects. The one-page "textbooks" section gives eight basic titles, followed by an "Introduction" which concentrates on bibliography. Books, periodicals, articles, etc., are included in the subsequent 12 parts.

Now considerably dated, but useful in that the titles listed remain standard, and unlike Tanselle, are annotated: Helmut Lehmann-Haupt, *One Hundred Books About Bookmaking* (New York: Columbia University Press, 1949). A more current, scholarly approach, with annotations for about 180 basic items will be found in Paul Winckler's *History of Books and Printing: A Guide to Information Sources* (Detroit, Gale, 1979); See also Alice Schreyer, *The History of Books: A Guide to Selected Resources in the Library of Congress,* 1987.

General Histories

Aries, Philippe and George Duby, eds. *A History of Private Life.* 5 vols. Cambridge, MA: Belknap Press of Harvard University Press, 1990–92.

The five-volume translation of a work edited by two famous French cultural historians is useful in that it gives a brief but accurate running account of how "ordinary" people viewed and used the written and printed word. The difficulty is that too much emphasis is on France and not enough on Europe. In the tradition of work by Fernand Braudel (e.g. *The Structure of Everyday Life,* 1979, etc.) and in England, Raymond Williams (e.g. *The Long Revolution,* 1961, etc.) and Richard Hoggart (e.g. *The Uses of Literacy,* 1957).

Avrin, Leila. *Scribes, Script and Books.* Chicago: American Library Association, 1991.

The latest in a general history of the book, this is the first of a two-volume work. It is noteworthy for the massive number of excellent illustrations and the clear text. There is too much detail for the beginner, particularly about the Middle East, but the first volume presents an excellent overview up to the time of printing. The second book will move from Gutenberg to the present.

Bland, David. *A History of Book Illustration.* Cleveland: World Publishing Company, 1958. rev. ed., 1969.

The basic general history of the subject, at least from the advent of printing through the mid twentieth century. Early illustration and medieval manuscripts are considered in only 40 of the 424 pages of this well illustrated guide. There are scores, literally, of general and specialized books on illustration. For an annotated bibliography see:

Encyclopedia of Library and Information Science. New York: M. Dekker, 1968 to date.

Here one finds numerous articles concerning the history of the book, publishing, libraries, etc. They vary in length from a few paragraphs to many pages. Most are well written, equally well researched and relatively current. See, too, the readings for many of the subjects covered.

Harris, Michael and Elmer Johnson. *History of Libraries in the Western World.* 3rd rev. ed. Metuchen, NJ: Scarecrow Press, 1984.

Elmer Johnson's *History of Libraries* was published by Scarecrow in 1965, and Harris updated. There are three well-written and documented sections: Libraries in the ancient world; Medieval libraries; and Modern library development in the West, i.e. from 1500 to the mid-1980s. See, too, Harris' *Reader in American Library History,* 1978; *A Guide to Research in American Library History,* 2nd ed., 1974; and *American Library History: A Bibliography,* 1978.

Related works: George Bobinski, *Carnegie Libraries* (American Library Assoc., 1969); Paul Dickson, *The Library in America* (New York: Facts on File, 1986); Elizabeth Stone, *American Library Development, 1600–1899,* 1977.

Hunter, Dard. *Papermaking, The History and Technique of an Ancient Craft.* 2nd ed. New York: Alfred Knopf, 1947. (Dover Paperback, 1978).

Although dated, this remains the basic history of papermaking. It is by now a classic of its kind and the first place to turn to trace the development of paper. Related works: Hunter's *Papermaking in Pioneer America,* 1952; David Smith, *History of Papermaking in the United States, 1691–1969,* 1970; *Papermaking: Art and Craft* (Library of Congress, 1968).

Jackson, Sidney L. *Libraries and Librarianship in the West.* New York: McGraw-Hill, 1974.

This remains one of the best surveys of library history. The scope is wide, the writing style good and the historical research excellent. Jackson covers all major points. See, too, Elmer Johnson, ''Ancient Libraries as Seen in the Greek and Roman Classics,'' *The Radford Review,* Spring 1969, pp. 73–92. A delightful survey of libraries from c.

500 B.C. to c. 500 A.D. by a professor of history. The quotations are supportive of the view that private and, later, public libraries were found in Greece and the Roman Empire. See, too, almost any issue of the *Journal of Library History* for material on libraries. An excellent example from that journal: Lorne Bruce, "Palace and Villa Libraries from Augustus to Hadrian," Summer 1986, pp. 510–552. The exhaustive bibliography will serve the needs of most looking for additional information.

Miner, Dorothy. *The History of Bookbinding.* Baltimore: Baltimore Museum of Art, 1957.

This illustrated catalog of an exhibition covers basic binding styles from 525 to 1950 A.D. and is an ideal introduction for lay persons. A more detailed museum catalog will be found in Paul Needham's *Twelve Centuries of Bookbinding, 400–1600* (New York: Morgan Library, 1979). See, too, the much cited Edith Diehl's two volume *Bookbinding: Its Background and Technique* (New York, 1946).

Olmert, Michael. *The Smithsonian Book of Books.* Washington: Smithsonian Books, 1992.

A professor of English offers a coffee table book about the history of books. It is three quarters photographs and the remainder anecdotes in loose chronological order from *The Book of the Dead* to computers. Thanks to a lively writing style and a healthy respect for scholarship, this is an exceptional overview which can be recommended. What it may lack in detail it makes up in the illustrations and the historical background.

Schottenloher, Karl. *Books and the Western World, a Cultural History.* Jefferson, NC: McFarland & Company, 1989.

A translation of the two-volume, 1968 German work, this covers the history of books from antiquity through the years after World War II. As the title suggests, the focus is as much on cultural history and the process of education as it is on the finer points of writing and printing. The primary focus is on Germany and Europe.

Whitrow, G.J. *Time in History.* Oxford: Oxford University Press, 1989.

This basic historical analysis of how people are aware of time begins with the earliest records and has two excellent chapters on the Near East and Classical Antiquity. Aspects of time in the Middle Ages introduce the other half, which is concerned with ideas about time since the discovery of the clock. Valuable for the major topic, as well as the cultural slant it gives on ordinary people throughout the ages.

B. SCRIBES TO PRINTERS

Middle East

Ceram, C.W. *Hands on the Past.* New York: Knopf, 1966.
The author of *Gods, Graves and Scholars* (1951) here offers a compilation of stories, by the archaeologists themselves, on digging up the past. Most of the focus is on the Near East, although there are sections on the Americas. The writing is for the lay person and much of it reads like a grand detective story. See, too, Seton Lloyd, *The Archaeology of Mesopotamia* (London: Thames and Hudson, 1978). An illustrated guide from the time of neolithic man and settlements in the Near East to the late Assyrians and the fall of Babylon. While it is detailed and scholarly, the style is at a more popular level. Wilbur Jones, *Venus and Sothis* (Chicago Nelson Hall, 1982): a history professor offers a satisfactory, short review of archaeology and cultural discoveries made in the Near East. This tends to update both Ceram and Sothis.

Gaur, Albertine. *A History of Writing.* London: The British Library, 1984. 224p.
There are scores of books on writing and its history (see, for example, Gaur's ''select bibliography''). This is one of the best because it closely ties social developments with writing, and the author's style is as clear as her facts are accurately presented. Two chapters cover the history, a third discusses decipherment, a fourth examines ''social attitudes to writing and literacy,'' and the last looks to the future, and includes a useful section on printing. Among other histories, see: C.B.F. Walker, ed., *Reading the Past; Ancient Writing from Cuneiform to the Alphabet* (London: British Museum, 1991). A collection of six pamphlets issued by the British Museum in 1987, this moves from cuneiform to Etruscan inscriptions. Its purpose is to give the general public an understanding of script as found often in museums. It is of limited aid to the expert. Robert K. Logan, *The Alphabet Effect* (New York: William Morrow, 1986), which considers à la Marshall McLuhan et al, ''the impact of the phonetic alphabet on the development of Western civilization.'' Roy Harris, *The Origin of Writing* (London: Duckworth, 1986). Head to head with Logan, the Oxford professor challenges the notion that the alphabet is the most advanced writing system. Florian Coulma, *The Writing Systems of the World* (Oxford: Blackwell, 1989). A good, general survey of the subject. Another popular, easy to read classic is Silvestro Fiore, *Voices from the Clay* (Norman: University of Oklahoma Press, 1965). Diringer, David, *The Alphabet, A Key to the History of Mankind.* (2 vols. 3rd ed. New York: Funk and Wagnalls, 1968). A massive amount of

detail and a lugubrious writing style make this more of a reference work than one to be read. Still, it is a useful overview, although several of the opinions are debatable. Michelle Brown, *A Guide to Historical Scripts from Antiquity to 1660* (London: The British Library, 1990). A popular history of writing and the development of various type faces. Other similar titles: Donald Anderson, *The Art of Written Forms,* 1969; Nicolete Grey, *A History of Lettering.* 1986; Jan Tschichold, *An Illustrated History of Writing and Lettering,* 1946. Alexander and Nicholas Humex, *Alpha to Omega* (Boston: David Godine, 1981). Both a cultural and intellectually adroit view of the alphabet, this is a popular guide divided into twenty-four sections, i.e. one for each letter of the Greek alphabet. Actually, most of the focus is on Greek history and its contribution to modern English; but it is an entertaining, instructive guide for anyone involved with the history of the book.

Grant, Michael and Rachel Kitzinger, (eds). *Civilization of the Ancient Mediterranean.* New York: Charles Scribner's Sons, 1988. 3 vols.
   A subject approach to the history of Greece and Rome by 88 scholars in classics, this is an ideal point of departure and reference for anyone interested in particular aspects of early civilizations. The writing is free of jargon, and the three volumes are as much for the interested scholar as the involved lay person. Each topic, from book production to Greek marriage, is given its own section. After each article one finds a working bibliography, and an index ties the set together. Highly recommended for the half-dozen pieces related to the history of books and publishing.

Harris, William. *Ancient Literacy.* Cambridge: Harvard University Press, 1990.
   This statistical and historical study of Greek and Latin readers and writers makes the point about the limited number of people able to read in Greece, or throughout the Roman Empire and later areas won over by Christianity. The uses of literacy between the eighth century B.C. and the fifth century A.D. are well documented. His central thesis: literates were always a minority.

Lichtheim, Miriam, ed. *Ancient Egyptian Literature.* Berkeley: University of California Press, 1976–1980. 3 vols.
   A "book of readings," this moves from the Old and Middle Kingdoms to the New Kingdom in the second volume and "the late period" in the third volume. The translations are preceded by numerous, well-written background explanations. Marvels of literacy discovery, particularly for the lay person. A related work: James Pritchard, *The Ancient Near East* (Princeton, NJ: Princeton University Press, 1958,

1975, 2 vols.) opens with Egyptian myths and tales, but most of the concentration is on Mesopotamian materials, from S.N. Kramer's decipherment of "The Deluge" to South-Arabian inscriptions. Numerous illustrations but much briefer notes than in Lichtheim.

Montagu, Ashley. *Man: His First Million Years.* Cleveland: World Publishing Co., 1957.
A prominent English anthropologist offers a popular history of the beginning years from "Man's nearest relations" to an explanation of cave arts. He touches briefly on writing and forms of communication, but the narrative is of benefit primarily for its easy-to-follow overview. Some material is debatable and now outdated, but it remains a grand introduction. See, too, Stuart Piggot, *Ancient Europe* (Chicago: Aldine, 1965). A standard work by a University of Edinburgh professor, this opens with a background chapter of material covered in more depth by Montagu, and then moves to the settlement of Europe from the seventh millennium B.C. to the Roman Empire. Well illustrated. T.G.E. Powell, *Prehistoric Art* (New York: Oxford University Press, 1966). A paperback in the "World of Art" series, this covers all aspects of early art and writing. Black and white illustrations on every page. A good lay person's introduction. Another useful work: Paul Bahn and Jean Vertut, *Images of the Ice Age* (Leicester, England: Windward, 1989). This covers the Paleolithic art of the later Ice Age in the caves in Western Europe. The book has the advantage of being as up to date as it is accurate and fascinating.

Moscati, Sabatino. *The Face of the Ancient Orient,* London: Routledge & Kegan Paul, 1960.
A classic of its type, here one finds a survey of Near Eastern history (including the Egyptians) from 3,000 B.C. to Alexander the Great. Extremely well written and easy to follow, this moves along like a fascinating novel. It's in the tradition of the more famous James Henry Breasted's *Ancient Times* (2nd ed., New York: Ginn, 1944). Written by the University of Chicago professor in 1916, this was updated, but it is still somewhat out of phase with current findings. Nevertheless, both as a textbook and as a guide it is a marvel of precision and style. See, too, Jack Finegan, *Archaeological History of the Ancient East* (New York: Dorset, 1986), first published in 1979. A bit dry, but useful for chronological approach, with about two-thirds of the book given over to the Egyptian dynasties. George Roux, *Ancient Iraq* (2nd ed., London: George Allen, 1980). A good overview of Mesopotamian history, with particular focus on the economic and cultural aspects. A modern guide, but extremely useful for the background it provides as well as the

numerous diagrams, tomb plans, etc., is William Murnane, *The Penguin Guide to Ancient Egypt* (London: Penguin Books, 1988).

The Oxford Companion to Classical Literature. 2nd ed. Oxford: Oxford University Press, 1989.

A basic work which covers in various length entries and articles not only the literature of classical antiquity, but related matters from Athenian democracy to Roman law. Thanks to numerous cross references, a useful alphabetical listing and clear writing, this guide will answer most questions of a general nature about the period and its people. An excellent overview of the cultures which supported or destroyed the book. About 200 pages longer (882 p.), *The Oxford History of the Classical World* (Oxford: Oxford University Press, 1986) is equally useful as a general introduction to the politics and social history of the Graeco-Roman world. There are three main sections: Greece, (700–200 B.C.); Greece and Rome from Alexander the Great to Augustus; and the Roman Empire through to the adoption of Christianity. Numerous illustrations and maps.

Pettinato, Giovanni. *Elba: A New Look at History.* Baltimore: The Johns Hopkins University Press, 1991. 290 p.

A translation of an Italian's current view of the findings at the 3rd millennium site of Elba, this offers a well-written, current picture of the development of early writing and libraries in the Near East. See, too, Paul-Alain Beaulieu, *The Reign of Nabonidus King of Babylon 556–539 B.C.* (New Haven: Yale University Press, 1989) for developments some 2,000 years later in the same general area. See, too, Sabatino Moscati, ed., *The Phoenicians* (New York: Abbeville, 1989). An oversized volume with text and a massive number of illustrations in color which, for the first time, gives a scholarly overview of Phoenician civilization.

Middle Ages

Alexander, Jonathan. *Medieval Illuminators and Their Methods of Work.* New Haven: Yale University Press, 1992.

From the fourth to the sixteenth century, the author traces the development of the illuminated manuscript. The book is well illustrated and the text is written for the lay person. See, too, the books by de Hamel. There are numerous illustrated titles which cover various aspects and periods of the illuminated manuscript. A good example: Walter Cahn, *Romanesque Bible Illumination* (Ithaca: Cornell University Press, 1982). From ancient beginnings to the beginning of printing, the author considers various aspects of biblical illustration under chapter headings such as "themes and variations." Other basic titles (published after 1970) might include: Alexander's *The Decorated Letter* (New York: Bariziller, 1978); Giulia Bologna, *Illuminated Manuscripts* (London: Weidenfeld, 1987); Otto Pacht, *Book Illumination of the Middle Ages* (Oxford University Press, 1986).

de Hamel, Christopher. *A History of Illuminated Manuscripts.* Oxford: Phaidon, 1986.

By and large the best general history of books during the Middle Ages. It is a refreshing departure from both the over-popular rendition of illuminated manuscripts to the scholarly nit-picking monographs. A combination of wit, knowledge and unique observations, the guide is divided by type of book and by type of publication. Another report is offered by the same author in his *Scribes and Illuminators* (University of Toronto Press, 1992). Here the focus is on the artisan who produced the illuminated manuscript in Europe before the invention of printing. While this is of some help to the lay person, the author's previous work is far better as an introduction.

See also Israel Shenker, "The Greatest Sport," *The New Yorker,* May 29, 1989, pp. 48–68. In this profile of the author of *A History of Illuminated Manuscripts* (Christopher de Hamel), Shenker offers much entertaining and informative lore on the human side of both the production and the collection of manuscripts.

Diringer, David. *The Book Before Printing.* New York: Dover, 1982.

The Cambridge lecturer offers a massive amount of material, in 11 chapters, with illustrations, about the development of the book. Much of the focus is on the technology of production, and Diringer includes "outlying regions" beyond Europe and the Mediterranean. The basic problem is one of style. This, as with many of Diringer's contributions, tends to read more as a catalog of data than a narrative—and some of the data are controversial, although this rarely is indicated in the text. (Originally published in 1953 as *The Hand-Produced Book.*)

McKitterick, Rosamond, ed. *The Uses of Literacy in Early Medieval Europe.* New York: Cambridge University Press, 1990.

Eleven separate papers by as many authors covering the uses of literacy from Ireland and Merovingian Gaul to late Anglo-Saxon England. The significance of literacy from c. 400 to c. 1000 is measured by each of the contributors. All papers are documented. A valuable work.

Putnam, George. *Books and Their Makers During the Middle Ages.* New York, G.P. Putnam's Sons, 1896–97. 2 vols.

Dated and a trifle romantic, the text does offer a relatively good description of scriptoria and working conditions during the Middle Ages. The overview is worthwhile for beginners, but of little value to anyone who has more than gone over the surface of the history of publishing.

Reynolds, L.D. and N.G. Wilson. *Scribes & Scholars: A Guide to the Transmission of Greek & Latin Literature.* 2nd rev. ed. Oxford: Clarendon Press, 1974.

"This book is designed as a simple introduction for beginners to a field of classical studies . . . which outlines the processes by which Greek and Latin literature have been preserved." Ancient books and their transmission are considered in the first chapter and five others move through to the Renaissance. A final chapter on textual criticism point out the basic principles of evaluating texts. See, too, R.R. Bolgar, *The Classical Heritage and its Beneficiaries* (Cambridge: Cambridge University Press, 1954). This is a classic which covers much of the same material as Reynolds but in more detail. Throughout both works, as in numerous titles listed in their respective bibliographies, one will find information on publishing, libraries, readers, literacy, etc. For a specific analysis of a single work, see the popular Richard Elliott Friedman, *Who Wrote the Bible* (New York: Harper & Row, 1987). The author offers, in easy-to-understand language, research on the authorship and the transmission of texts of the Old Testament, and to a lesser extent the New Testament.

Related works: Jesse M. Gellrich, *The Idea of the Book in the Middle Ages* (Ithaca: Cornell University Press, 1985); George Calkins, *Illuminated Books of the Middle Ages* (Cornell University Press, 1983).

Strayer, Joseph. ed. *Dictionary of the Middle Ages.* 13 vols. New York: Charles Scribner's Sons, 1982–1989.

An exhaustive encyclopedia/dictionary with numerous articles about manuscripts, individual monastic communities, reading, education, etc. The final volume is a detailed index.

Thompson, James. *The Medieval Library.* rev. ed. New York: Hafner Publishing Co. 1957.

A basic history of the medieval library and one much used in library schools and by lay persons until well toward the end of the twentieth century. By now it has been found to be filled with errors and hasty generalizations. Be that as it may, the work remains one of the most readable of its type and the major aspects of the medieval library are covered quite well. It remains a useful departure point for lay persons.

C. GUTENBERG TO THE TWENTY FIRST CENTURY

Berry, W.T. and H.E. Poole. *Annals of Printing, a Chronological Encyclopedia.* Toronto: University of Toronto Press, 1966.

The first date is 105, "the date usually given for the invention of printing," and in chronological order and some 283 pages later, the last is 1949. For each year the basic events are noted, usually with a 100- to 250-word description. Particularly useful for the period from 1450 to 1900. A similar work: Colin Clair's *A Chronology of Printing,* 1969, but not as detailed.

Blumenthal, Joseph. *Art of the Printed Book, 1455–1955.* Boston: Godine, 1973.

Primary emphasis is on illustration. Key books, in an exhibition at the Morgan Library, are briefly annotated with illustrations. See, also, the same author's *The Printed Book in America,* 1977.

The Book. American Antiquarian Society, 185 Salisbury St., Worcester, MA 01609.

This four- to six-page newsletter, which is free, gives information on "the program in the history of the book in American culture." A useful way of keeping up with research in the area. (For background on the program, see David Hall's "A history of the book in American culture," *The Book,* No. 16, November 1988).

Buhler, Curt F. *The Fifteenth Century Book; the Scribes, the Printers; the Decorators.* Philadelphia: University of Pennsylvania Press, 1960.

A scholarly, highly imaginative approach to why the book, in transition from manuscript to print, remained for the average reader simply another form of the book. He asserts that much too much is made of the great gulf between the manuscript and the printed form—at least for the vast majority of Europeans at the time. He offers a superior exploration of format and production, as well.

Carpenter, Kenneth, ed. *Books and Society in History.* New York: R.R. Bowker, 1983.

The ten papers on various aspects of the book as offered at the 1980 Association of College and Research Libraries Rare Books and Manuscripts preconference are gathered; but sadly, there is no index. Robert Darnton opens with a general paper on "What Is the History of the Book?" which is more rhetorical than practical for anyone who teaches the course. Elizabeth L. Eisenstein sets matters right with her "From Scriptoria to Printing Shops," an extension of her two volume study. The remainder are more specialized, moving from studies of publishing in the Ancien Regime to censorship, book production etc. Focus primarily is on France (three articles), with a nod to England and the United States. The papers are much too narrow, the first two excepted, for lay persons, but of obvious value to the expert.

Cave, Roderick. *The Private Press.* London: 2nd ed. New York: R.R. Bowker, 1983.

The standard general history of the private press with a primary emphasis on England and a nod to Europe and the United States. For a descriptive, non-evaluative current listing of American private and small presses see the annual *International Directory of Little Magazines and Small Presses* (Paradise, CA: Dustbooks).

Chappel, Warren. *A Short History of the Printed Word.* New York: Dorset Press, 1989. (Copyright 1970, Alfred A. Knopf).

A working typographer, Chappel offers a lay person's version of D.B. Updike's *Printing Types* (1922). The primary focus is on the history of type, title pages, and makeup. The first three chapters are background on type and type casting and cutting. Chapters four through ten cover progress from the 15th through the mid-20th century, with about one chapter to one century. Along the way major trends and printers and publishers are touched upon, but never in any great depth. There are useful black and white illustrations on almost every page. The overview is well written and draws upon practical experience. A good beginning for the average reader.

Chartier, Roger. *The Cultural Uses of Print in Early Modern France.* Princeton, NJ: Princeton University Press, 1987.

Although, as the title suggests, this is concerned only with printing and the spread of literacy and culture in France, it is a model for cultural studies of the subjects elsewhere. Equally, it is more detailed and scholarly than the much-used pioneer study by Lucien Febre and Henri-Jean Martin, *The Coming of the Book* (London: Verso Editions, 1984/first published 1958). Chartier begins with "Ritual and print" and eight chapters later ends with "The literature of roguery." See, too, his related *The Culture of Print* (Princeton University Press, 1989) which is a compilation of articles by others on much the same topic. See, also, his broader *Cultural History: Between Practices and Representations* (New York: Oxford University Press, 1989) which includes a chapter on peasant reading during the enlightenment. See, too, Allen, James, *In the*

Public Eye, A History of Reading in Modern France, 1800–1940 (Princeton: Princeton University Press, 1992.) In the tradition of Roger Chartier et al., this is a model for a major topic which has not been all that well covered in the history of books. Allen asks basic questions, from who reads, when and where, to what is to be learned from the study of book sales. See, too, Cressy, David, *Literacy and the Social Order: Reading and Writing in Tudor and Stuart England* (Cambridge University Press, 1980). In this close study of sixteenth-seventeenth century literacy in England, the author believes that male literacy throughout the country was from 20 to 40 per cent; and no higher than ten per cent for women. The statistics are based on slippery definitions and methods, although they are all used to explain the rise in Elizabethan literacy, particularly among the middle and higher levels of the social ladder.

Eisenstein, Elizabeth. *The Printing Revolution in Early Modern Europe.* New York: Cambridge University Press, 1983.

An abridgement of her two-volume *The Printing Press as an Agent of Change (1979),* this is more for the lay reader than the expert. There are added illustrations and a superior bibliography, but the footnotes are deleted. Unlike many histories before, here the emphasis is on the cultural-intellectual aspects of a communications revolution brought about by printing. Numerous original insights and conclusions make this must reading for anyone who would understand the European world between the beginning of printing and its development in the sixteenth and early seventeenth centuries. Note: This is background for the perhaps better known, and, of course, earlier Marshall McLuhan's *The Gutenberg Galaxy* (Toronto, 1962). The Canadian literary scholar became a media "expert" with notions concerning the evolution of print which are valuable today not so much for his ideas (debatable) as for his bringing attention to the importance of printing to a psychological and social understanding of our times.

Feather, John. *A History of British Publishing.* London: Croom Helm, 1988.

In four chapters the author covers the history of books in England from Caxton to the mid-twentieth century. The 19 chapters are written for the lay person and cover related aspects from the novel to periodicals. One of the best of its kind, although limited to Great Britain.

Febvre, Lucien and Henri-Jean Martin. *The Coming of The Book; The Impact of Printing 1450–1800.* London: NLB, 1976.

A translation and edited version of the French 1958 edition, this is both a social history and a history of printing and publishing. The book is almost entirely the work of Martin and the translation of the original 1958 title has been faulted. Nevertheless, it remains a classic and is in the same general class as Eisenstein's efforts.

Gaskell, Philip. *A New Introduction to Bibliography.* rev. ed. Oxford: Clarendon Press, 1978.

Originally published in 1972, this is the most current and by and large the best introduction to descriptive bibliography and the development of printing techniques which influenced the physical makeup of the book. Related works: Fredson Bowers, *Principles of Bibliographical Description,* 1949; Ronald McKerrow, *An Introduction to Bibliography for Literary Students,* 1927.

Goldschmidt, Ernst P. *Medieval Texts and Their First Appearance in Print.* Oxford: University Press, 1943.

An imaginative, well-written explanation of the transition from the medieval manuscript to the printed book. See also the author's *The Printed Book of the Renaissance: Three Lectures of Type, Illustration, Ornament,* 1950.

Mumby, Frank A. and Ian Norrie. *Publishing and Bookselling: History from the Earliest Times to the Twentieth Century.* 4th ed. London: Cape. 1956.

A basic, relatively popular history with particular emphasis on the booktrade after the advent of printing. Most of the interest is in English and European concerns. Another more scholarly effort will be found in Marjorie Plant's *The English Book Trade* 3rd ed. (London: Allen & Unwin, 1974).

Steinberg, S.H. *Five Hundred Years of Printing.* New York: Criterion Books, 1959.

The best relatively current overall history of printing, this is as well-written as it is organized. There may be too much emphasis on English interests (as it was published in England) and not enough on twentieth century publishing, but for what it does, it does better than anyone. Arrangement is chronological, with a focus on both technology and on publishing and reading.

Related titles by English authors: Sean Jeannett, *Pioneers in Printing* (London, 1958), with colorful profiles of major printers and publishers. See, too, the same author's *The Making of Books* (4th ed. New York, 1967). Colin Clair, *A History of European Printing* (London, 1976) and the same author's *History of Printing in Britain,* 1965; and his *Chronology of Printing,* 1969.

Stanley Morison, *Four Centuries of Fine Printing,* 4th ed., 1960; and the same author's *The Typographic Book, 1450–1935,* 1963 (a revision of the first title). John Carter and Percy Muir, *Printing and the Mind of Man,* 1967.

Tebbel, John. *History of Book Publishing in the United States.* 4 vols. New York: R.R. Bowker, 1972–1981.

An exhaustive study of the subject by an experienced writer, this is a basic source of information—at least about further readings. Unfortunately, as critics pointed out, Tebbel tends to accept the facts and conclusions of others without too much double checking of facts. So while it may not be totally reliable, at least it is totally readable—in parts—and one of the first places to turn.

Wroth, Lawrence, ed. *A History of the Printed Book.* New York: Limited Editions Club, 1938 (Issue No. 3/The Dolphin).

Numerous illustrations and a good text makes this among the better overall histories. Edited by a well-known librarian, the work is a classic of its kind. Of particular interest is the emphasis on the book as an art form; e.g. see Chapter 13 on *The Illustration of Books* by Philip Hofer.

INDEX

A

abbey and cathedral schools   107, 108

abbreviations   91

academic libraries.   *See* libraries, university and academic

Ackermann, Rudolf   224

acquisitions.   *See under* collection building

Adams, Joseph   228

Adobe Inc.   248

advertising and marketing   165, 179, 250, 251–52, 259
   periodicals   42, 217, 219

Age of Reason (the Enlightenment)   186, 212n.1

Akkadians and Akkadian alphabet   4, 11, 33n.9

Alcuin   96, 100, 101, 104n.17, 111

Aldus
   bookbindings by   153, 177, 178, 241
   italic type by   153, 154
   legacy of   159, 160, 197, 232, 248
   as printer-publisher   30, 153–55, 160, 199
   of *Hypnerotomachia Polophili,* 153, 155, 173, 181n.15
   of Virgil   148, 153, 154
   printer's mark   150, 153

Alexander the Great   19, 50, 62

Alexandria Library and Museum   xiv, 21, 50–53, 54, 62, 258
   and book trade   46
   catalog of   38, 50, 51–52
   transmission of texts at   29, 36n.30, 52, 56

alphabets   7–10.   *See also under* Greek (language)

altar bindings   121

American Antiquarian Society   244n.16

American Revolution   186, 200, 201, 220

Americana   239–40

Ames, Joseph   237

Amman, Jost   143

Anderson, Alex   210

Anglo Saxon Chronicle, 98

Anthony, Saint   86–87

Appleton-Century-Crofts   236

Arab and Islamic worlds   86, 99–100
   bookbinding   177
   libraries   100, 104n.15
   papermaking   139, 141

Aristarchus of Samothrace   52, 56

Aristotle
   availability of, in Middle Ages   107–8
   on education   45, 46, 59n.8
   library of   54–55

art reproductions   173, 175, 205, 210, 224, 229

Ashendene Press   234

Ashurbanipal   22–23, 26

Assyria   4
   libraries and archives   19–20, 22, 34n.18
   literature   22–23

Astor, John Jacob   238

Athens, University at   55, 85

atlases.   *See* maps

auctions, book   192, 238
   of Bibles   142, 145, 180n.8

ABOUT THE AUTHOR

BILL KATZ (Ph.D., Chicago) is Professor, School of Information Science and Policy, at the State University of New York in Albany. He is the author of the standard text on reference services, *Introduction to Reference Services,* now in its sixth edition. Currently he edits *The Reference Librarian* and *The Acquisitions Librarian* and is a former editor of *RQ* and the *Journal of Education for Librarianship.* For Scarecrow Press, he has edited *Reference and Information Services: A Reader for Today* (1982); *Reference and Information Services: A New Reader* (1986); *Reference and Information Services: A Reader for the Nineties* (1991); and from 1971 to 1988, the annual *Library Lit.—the Best of* ... covering the years 1970 to 1987. His most recent Scarecrow Press publication is *A History of Book Illustration: 29 Points of View,* published in 1994, which he edited.